NANCY PARROTT HICKERSON
Texas Tech University

Linguistic Anthropology

HOLT, RINEHART AND WINSTON, INC.
New York   Chicago   San Francisco   Dallas
Montreal   Toronto   London   Sydney

To my teachers, my colleagues, and my students—with thanks.

Library of Congress Cataloging
in Publication Data

Hickerson, Nancy Parrott.
Linguistic anthropology.

(Basic anthropology units)
Bibliography: p. 163
1. Anthropological linguistics.   2.   Linguistics.
                                        I.   Title.
P35.H5   401'.9   79-28328
                  ISBN 0–03–006956–4

Requests for permission to make copies of any part of
the work should be mailed to: Permissions, Holt,
Rinehart and Winston, Inc., 111 Fifth Avenue,
New York, New York 10003
Printed in the United States of America

8   9   016   14   13   12   11   10

Foreword

THE BASIC ANTHROPOLOGY UNITS

Basic Anthropology Units are designed to introduce students to essential topics in the contemporary study of man. In combination they have greater depth and scope than any single textbook. They may also be assigned selectively to cover topics relevant to the particular profile of a given course, or they may be utilized separately as authoritative guides to significant aspects of anthropology.

This series was planned over a period of several years by a number of anthropologists, some of whom are authors of the separate Basic Units. The completed series will include units representing all the basic sectors of contemporary anthropology, including archeology, biological anthropology, and linguistics, as well as the various subfields of social and cultural anthropology.

THE AUTHOR

Nancy Parrott Hickerson is associate professor of anthropology at Texas Tech University in Lubbock, Texas. She majored in anthropology for her bachelor's degree at Barnard College, and received the Ph.D. in anthropology from Indiana University, where she also developed a special interest in linguistics. Hickerson has done fieldwork in both linguistic and cultural anthropology in the Caribbean area. Her current research interests are in ethnolinguistics and cognition, focusing on such topics as color terminology and environment, and in the evolution of language, society, and world-view. She has been on the faculty of Texas Tech University since 1972, and teaches courses in linguistic anthropology, ethnology, and anthropological theory.

THIS UNIT

Cultural anthropology is as much a study of language as it is the study of nonlinguistic behavior, artifacts, or habitats. For many anthropologists, the study of language and speech is the essential focus of their work and thinking. Humans sort and classify the phenomena of the world about them with words. They think about and interrelate these phenomena with words. They communicate mainly with words. The major distinction between humans and animals is language. The present complex form of our brains is, to a large extent, a result of their evolving as language evolved.

And yet, many students leave the first course in anthropology with an inadequate understanding of the relationship between language and culture, of the structure of language and its role in human evolution, and of its many-faceted appearances in different human groups in different places and times. And for many students in the more advanced levels of study, linguistics is endowed with a sinister and forbidding quality, like statistics is for others.

This is at least partly due to the fact that most writings on linguistics, including textbooks, are not for beginners or for those who simply want to know what anthropological linguistics is about. This Basic Anthropology Unit is written for such people. It describes and explains linguistic anthropology. It can be read and understood by any normally bright and modestly motivated reader. It contains knowledge that every educated person ought to have and furnishes students with a beginning that can lead them on to more advanced understandings and skills.

This unit should be widely used as a supplement to other texts in beginning social and behavioral science courses. It will also serve well as a core text for beginning courses in language and culture and the introduction to anthropological linguistics. The author has written this Basic Anthropology Unit with the beginning student in mind. It is clear, extremely well-organized, and it moves precisely and logically through each progression of linguistic concepts and their application. To help instructors and students formulate useful follow-ups in the study of this text, the author has supplied a list of suggested topics, in the form of questions, at the end of each chapter.

George and Louise Spindler
General Editors
CALISTOGA, CALIFORNIA

Preface and Acknowledgments

This module is an introduction to the study of language and an overview of the importance of linguistics for general anthropology. The coverage is not highly technical, but it is broad. Separate chapters treat historical linguistics, the classification of languages, descriptive linguistics, psycholinguistics, sociolinguistics, language and culture, and the origin and evolution of language.

It is intended that this book be used as the text for the linguistics component in a general introductory or survey course in anthropology. It is appropriate, too, as assigned reading in general anthropology courses in which little actual class time is devoted to linguistics. The chapters which deal with linguistics in connection with historical approaches (archeology, social and cultural anthropology, and biological evolution) should help the student see the relevance of the subject to the content of anthropology courses, even when these are not heavily linguistic in content.

Although this book is brief and nontechnical, it can be used as the core text for an undergraduate course in anthropological linguistics, if supplemented by extra illustrative readings. The bibliography at the end of the book can serve as a guide for this purpose; most of the readings listed are drawn from recent collections which are easily available.

Finally, instructors who emphasize analytic methods in their teaching of linguistics may find *Linguistic Anthropology* helpful as a supplement because it surveys, in a concise form, a range of topics which are outside the scope of most textbooks in descriptive linguistics.

This book is a product of several years of attempts, by trial and error, to put together a one-semester course on language for undergraduate anthropology students. During this time, I have shifted away from a format which dealt almost exclusively with descriptive linguistics, to increasing the emphasis on the interaction between language and culture, and, finally, to a bias in the direction of sociolinguistics. At the same time, I have increasingly tried to steer clear of specialized vocabulary and, when possible, to introduce linguistic concepts in a way which relates them to a general anthropological framework. I am grateful to several groups of students, graduate and undergraduate, who have read and criticized sections of this book; as I prepared the final version, Penny Gregorie, Helen Clements, and Fern Cuddeback were especially helpful in contributing to the discussion materials which appear at the end of each chapter.

I want to thank Linda Austin, Department of Anthropology, Texas Tech University, for her help in preparing the manuscript; and Robin Gross of Holt, Rinehart and Winston for assistance, especially in securing and preparing the illustrations.

Like many other anthropologist-authors, I am especially grateful to David Boynton of Holt, Rinehart and Winston for friendly editorial advice and persuasion; and to George and Louise Spindler, General Editors of the Basic Anthropology Units series, who have always been patient and positively reinforcing.

N. P. H.

Contents

1

Anthropology and the Study of Language

THE PLACE OF LANGUAGE IN ANTHROPOLOGY

A newcomer to anthropology—a beginning student, or an amateur who has become interested in anthropology through reading about primitive or prehistoric peoples, by participating in archeological "digs," or by visiting museums and historical sites—often has only a vague or partially accurate idea of the total scope of this field. Students in introductory anthropology courses are usually told that there are four subfields: *biological anthropology, archeology, cultural anthropology* (or *ethnology*), and *linguistic anthropology* (or *linguistics*). These four subfields are seldom given equal treatment in a general or introductory course; linguistic anthropology is sometimes slighted, and can appear to be highly specialized and marginal to other areas of anthropological interest. However, it should be noted that contemporary approaches in anthropology give an increasingly important place to the study of language.

Anthropology is a comprehensive field of study which deals with the human species in its biological aspects, and with the entire range of human social behavior. It deals as well with the products of human behavior, material and nonmaterial, and with the plans and concepts which underlie and organize behavior. If anthropologists were asked where, in all of this, language is involved, the answer would have to be that it is everywhere.

Humans talk, and in this we see ourselves as unique. Animals, including the other primates, *communicate,* but we usually reserve the word *language* for our own human brand of communication. Special physical characteristics, both in gross anatomy and in neurology, shows us that adaptation for the use of language is a part of the evolutionary endowment of our species. Our human penchant for language makes possible most of the other behavior which we think of as uniquely human: cooperating in hunting, farming, or sports; counting kin or arranging marriages; conducting religious rituals or organizing military expeditions—all of these depend on the use of language.

Language, then, meets a universal human need for an infinitely subtle and precise system of communications, a system which can convey a great deal of information of a sort not needed by other species of animals. That information is, roughly, what is called *culture*. Like language, culture is a distinctively human phenomenon. Human beings categorize and classify the features of their environments, and they

1

invest their daily activities with an enormous variety of meanings and motivations. They people the universe with unseen beings—gods and spirits—and come to understand the forces of nature in a diversity of ways. Each human society has its literature, philosophy, and theology. All of this would be impossible without the medium of language.

Surely, then, anthropologists must take language into account and must study languages in order to analyze and describe human populations and their social behavior. The study of language is, as we have seen, one of the major subfields of modern anthropology. Like other areas of specialization, linguistic anthropology has its special methods, analytic procedures, technical terms, and concepts. Proficiency in linguistic study requires special courses, field training, and practice in methods and techniques. Linguistic anthropologists must beware of becoming too specialized to maintain contact with other subfields of anthropology, while at the same time, other anthropologists tend to lose sight of the bearing which language has on their own special domains.

For students, especially, there is a need to maintain the integration of anthropology, to show the relevance of linguistics, and to synthesize information in such a way that biology, prehistory, ethnology, and linguistics all contribute to a whole study of human life. This book is an attempt to stimulate interest in and to answer questions about linguistic anthropology, and to demonstrate that this is not a marginal subfield, but one which is essential to the anthropological perspective. Language, as communication, is the basis for human society; it is also the medium which binds together and integrates the diverse interests and specialized knowledge of anthropologists.

ASPECTS OF THE STUDY OF LANGUAGE

As a universal human attribute, language is an integral part of human biology. The study of the human physical adaptation for language falls within the scope of biological anthropology. Recent contributions to this study have come from medical and natural scientists, such as neurologists and anatomists, as well as from specialists in speech and hearing. The important parts of the body (for language) are the vocal tract (which produces the sounds of speech); the auditory canals (which receive and transmit sound waves to the brain); and, most especially, the brain itself, within which are special localized areas for the encoding and decoding of language, as well as motor areas which control the musculature used in speech. There have been many recent advances in the biological approach to language. Researchers have learned a great deal about the anatomical and neurological endowments, and the interworkings of these, which enable human beings to formulate messages of greater complexity, transmit them more rapidly, and utilize them in a greater diversity of ways than do membrs of any other species.

Anthropologists have an interest in the biology of language because of its place in the larger context of evolution, an area in which new discoveries continue to be made with great frequency. Two approaches to an understanding of the evolution of our species are human paleontology (the study of fossil humans in comparison to other evolving primate species) and primatology, which deals with both the biology and behavior of living primates. Both of these fields can help us to appreciate the origin and nature of language as a special product of primate evolution. (The evolution and biological aspects of language will be discussed in Chapter 2).

While language is a universal occurrence in human life, human languages are many and diverse. They are systems of learned behavior, transmitted from generation to generation. Like all cultural systems, languages change over time and can be adapted to particular needs and circumstances. Most linguists—those who have a broader interest in anthropology as well as many who do not—devote at least part of their energies to studying, analyzing, and describing the structure and content of particular languages. This approach, *descriptive* or *structural linguistics,* takes a view of language as distinct and separable from other systems of behavior, and available to description without any particular reference to the social context or environment in which speaking takes place. Languages, then, can be viewed simply as systems of sounds (phonetic and phonemic units) selected and combined in particular ways, and as systems of larger units (morphemes, words, and sentences) which make up the totality of language. The writing of grammars, or of more specialized studies of particular aspects of grammatical structures, is the objective of this type of study (see Chapter 4 for a discussion of approaches in descriptive linguistics).

Beyond the circumscribed and self-contained approach of descriptive grammars, the study of languages as systems overlaps, and has the potential to contribute to, many other fields of interest. Philosophers have long discussed the attributes of language which underlie logic and reason, world view, and ideology. Poetry, song, and other verbal arts build or elaborate on the grammatical or semantic patterns of the spoken language; structural linguistics provides an objective approach to the analysis of such special uses of language. In this regard, linguistic studies are often undertaken by students of literature and language arts, and they have also contributed methodologically to the teaching of languages.

In contrast to the static perspective of the descriptive approach, languages can be studied over time as systems in flux. The differences which can be seen in any language viewed at different periods in its history (Chaucer's English compared with today's, for example) reveal the fact of regular, systematic change. Many linguists are interested specifically in the history and development of certain languages or groups of languages. Language history is fascinating in itself, and also contributes to the study of the history of peoples and civilizations. (This is discussed in Chapter 4; Chapter 8 presents a resumé of languages and language families of the world.)

Language, as a part of human behavior, can contribute to all of the behavioral sciences. Compounded terms identify the special fields of study which emerge from the overlapping interests of linguists and members of other disciplines. *Psycholinguistics* treats the relationship between language and mind. Of special concern is the study of the stages and processes in the child's acquisition of language (this is discussed in Chapter 3). Another type of study which has been quite revealing deals with the effects of various disabilities, such as aphasia, on language. Contributions to psycholinguistics come from psychologists and educators, as well as linguists, and have had an equal impact on linguistic theory and on applied areas such as education and speech pathology.

Sociolinguistics deals with the variations in language within a community which are directly related to the sociological makeup of the community. Speech variations may be regional, and explanations for the differences between rural and urban speech may also be found in the distribution of ethnic groups, the occurrences of migrations, and other historical and sociological factors. Sociolinguistics may be of interest to historians, sociologists, social anthropologists, political scientists, and others (Chapter 6 deals with a variety of topics in sociolinguistics).

Finally, *ethnolinguistics* (or "language and culture") treats the close connections between the cultural systems of people and the grammatical and lexical systems of their languages. This type of study, more than any other, has been the focal interest of linguistic anthropology for many years. Cultural anthropologists have looked to language as both a practical tool for fieldwork and as a source of insight and inspiration in cultural study. In turn, the study of language in its cultural setting has contributed depth and variety to general linguistics, especially in determining universal features of language and the study of meaning (Chapter 7 deals with the field of ethnolinguistics).

LINGUISTICS AND THE STUDY OF CULTURE

Today anthropologists who are setting out to do fieldwork in a remote area of the world usually try to prepare themselves with some knowledge of the language or languages with which they will be in contact. With luck, there may already be grammars, dictionaries, and other material (perhaps even tape recordings) available from previous researchers; at least, there may be studies of related languages. It helps, at the beginning of one's residence in a strange community, to have at least a rudimentary vocabulary, to know some useful questions, greetings, and other common expressions, and to be familiar with the grammatical structure of the language, even if one plans on doing most of the real language-learning on the spot.

There are, of course, simpler ways to make contact with other people. Ethnologists may do fieldwork with people whose language they already speak. Even in out-of-the-way locations, it is not unusual to find a few bilingual individuals who have learned some English or French or Spanish in school or while working away from home. If the anthropologist speaks one or more of these European languages, he or she may be able to do research with the assistance of a bilingual translator. However, even when there are number of bilinguals at hand, there is still a great advantage in learning to use the native language of the community; it is, many anthropologists would say, the best way to get to know and understand, and to be accepted by, the people.

An interested amateur can hardly be expected to appreciate the pervasive, yet variable, role that language plays in human life. When we read books or view films that portray the life and customs of exotic and physically remote people, we still get very little insight into their use of language. We may be left wondering:

How do these people communicate with one another? What are their rules of etiquette? How do they greet, advise, encourage, praise, or insult one another? What are their prayers, orations, jokes, and poetry really like?

It may seem just as frustrating to approach the principles of a language by studying its grammar or vocabulary. Lists of words and statements about the grammatical rules of a language appear to be far removed from an ethnologist's description of the culture and society of its speakers. What can speech sounds and grammatical forms, nouns and verbs and syntax, have to do with anthropology? But the raw materials of linguistic and cultural study are very nearly the same materials, and many anthropologists have contributed to both subfields. A linguistic study can give unique insights into cultural "world view" and values, and cultural anthropologists would be unable to study and describe the life of any community of people without somehow dealing with language (whether they study it themselves or rely on the knowledge of others).

One of the early advocates of linguistic study in anthropology was Franz Boas, who set an example for later ethnologists in his own field research and teaching. Boas (1858–1942) was a German scholar who is often considered to be the founder of modern anthropology, and especially of American anthropology. He came to North America as a young man to study the Eskimo of Canada and, later, the Indians of Western Canada and the United States, and was affiliated with American universities and museums for most of his professional career. To American anthropology, Boas contributed a vision of an integrated "study of man," drawing evidence from laboratory, field, and documentary research, and synthesizing the separate historical strands of race, language, and culture. As a teacher at Columbia University, he developed a curriculum in anthropology along these lines, with linguistics as an important component—as it still is, in the 1970s at many American universities.

Boas's greatest research contributions were in the description of American Indian languages and culture. He collected volumes of data on the Kwakiutl, a native people of the northwestern coast of North America, and also transcribed and translated many Kwakiutl tales, orations, life histories, and other texts. Based on this research of the Kwakiutl language, he wrote a grammatical study which is published, along with the work of other researchers (many of them his students and associates), in a famous series called *The Handbook of American Indian Languages*.

Franz Boas's "Introduction" in *The Handbook of American Indian Languages* (1911) is an important statement of the relevance of linguistic study to anthropology. In it, Boas included a discussion of linguistic methods and concepts which foreshadowed much that has developed since. The usefulness of linguistic study to the study of culture is twofold:

(1) It serves a practical need, because the anthropologist who knows a native language is not dependent on interpreters or on the use of Pidgin English or some other makeshift means of communicating with his informants. Boas recommended, as well as practiced, the recording of texts—taking down information firsthand in the native language—on all possible subjects. Once recorded, this material could later be translated and analyzed. Some topics can be approached only through language, such as poetry, prayers, oratory, and personal and local

names. Boas relied on his own skill in transcribing and analyzing Kwakiutl and other Indian languages, and also encouraged and worked in collaboration with natives who became proficient in writing their own languages. Similar training in linguistic skills was recommended for anthropology students going into the field.

(2) On a more theoretical level, Boas pointed out, there is a close connection between language and thought. There are "unconscious phenomena"—such as the classification of ideas and their expression by the same or related terms, or associations which are apparent in the metaphorical use of terms—which can only be approached through the study of language. In summary, he wrote that the study of language is important to anthropology "from practical, as well as from theoretical, points of view. . . . On the one hand, a thorough insight into ethnology cannot be gained without practical knowledge of language, and, on the other hand, the fundamental concepts illustrated by human languages are not distinct in kind from ethnological phenomena; and because, furthermore, the peculiar characteristics of languages are clearly reflected in the views and customs of the peoples of the world."

Although many anthropologists have done cultural research without making any special use of language, there are others who have pursued and developed principles similar to those of Boas. The British social anthropologist Bronislaw Malinowski (1889–1942), who is considered by many anthropologists to be a key figure in the development of methods of cultural research and description, outlined an approach which emphasized the importance of language for the field ethnologist. Malinowski, who lived for several years in the Melanesian communities on which he based his major studies, advised the coordinated use of three types of field data:

(1) *"The organization of the tribe, and the anatomy of its culture."* This would include statistical data on such things as marriage and the composition of households, the compilation of kinship charts, measurements of acreage and crop yield, and the like.

(2) The observation of *"the imponderabilia of actual life"*; that is, the detailed description of real instances of behavior, recorded by maintaining daily accounts in a field diary.

(3) The verbatim recording of *native terminology*, "ethnographic statements, characteristic narratives, typical utterances, items of folklore and magical formulae." Malinowski felt that the publication of a body of this linguistic data should be especially valuable, both as documents of native thinking, supplementing his own cultural study, and as a basis for further study and analysis by other researchers whose interests might be different from his own. Thus, linguistic study is given a role coordinate with observation and the collection of statistical data (Malinowski, 1922).

In recent years, there have been movements in both European and American anthroplogy which give a key role to language in the gathering and interpreting of cultural data. A number of American anthropologists have developed the field of *ethnoscience,* an approach to the description of culture which relies on terminology as a plan or "mapping" of culture. Investigators using the method of ethnoscience collect words and phrases and ask questions based on them in order to discover how things are classified, or to understand the relationships among them, according to the members of a speech community. The proponents of this "new ethnography" see it as a revolutionary approach, claiming that it is an "improvement of ethnographic method" which will serve "to make cultural discriptions replicable and accurate" (Sturtevant, 1964).

There are other approaches in contemporary anthropology, such as *structuralism, componential analysis,* and *cultural semiotics* which seek in various ways to demonstrate parallels between culture and language, to apply linguistic methods to the study of culture, or to analyze cultures as systems of "signs" or meanings, following the model of linguistic analysis.

These brief references to a few of the many different trends in contemporary anthropology are intended simply to demonstrate the important role which linguistic studies have played and continue to play in the discipline. At various times the study of language has served to assist (as a practical aid to fieldwork), to complement (by demonstrating parallels between language and other types of culture), and to inspire (as a model of description and analysis) other types of anthropological study. In the following chapters we will be concerned with both the study of language itself and with further discussion of its place in the broader field of anthropology.

TOPICS FOR STUDY AND DISCUSSION

1. Why is the study of language a part of anthropology? Should it also be relevant to the other social sciences, such as sociology, psychology, and history?
2. Watch portions of an adventure film, a situation comedy, a religious service, and a sports event on television with the sound turned down. Which could you follow the best? Why? How much could you comprehend if you were unfamiliar with American culture?

2

The Origin and Evolution
of Language

The word *language* is, like many of the familiar words which denote key concepts in the social sciences (such as *culture* and *society*), a word which has been used in several different ways. It has general and specific, strict and metaphoric usages. We may, for example, speak of "the Russian language," "sign language," "animal languages," "computer language," the language of heraldry," "the language of love." Roughly, *language* can serve as a synonym for any sort of communication expressed in any medium. However, linguists usually define the term *language* to apply only to *human vocal communication* (though even they are not always consistent in using it in this way).

Even with this restriction, there is still a double meaning attached to *language*. We must make a basic distinction at this point, if we are to put language into anthropological perspective, a perspective which includes the total evolutionary history of mankind. When we discuss the origins and general evolution of language, we are concerned with the first of two levels of meaning and with the fact that human beings—at all times and in all places—speak. As a species, humans have language. Language, in this sense, has a number of common fundamental properties or "universals." In the second sense, we must deal with the diversity of languages which we encounter every day, each one different from the others, and each playing a part in the social, cultural, and ethnic varieties of mankind. It may be as challenging to account for the diversification of languages as to discover their underlying unity.

HOW DID LANGUAGE BEGIN?

Attempts to answer this question, and to account for the development of language as we know it, are many; none of these answers is completely satisfactory, because there is so much to explain. We would like to understand how and why the vocal tract began to form speech sounds; how the evolution of intelligence led us to begin formulating messages in the form of words and sentences; what psychological motivation led our ancient forebears to begin naming things, asking questions, and giving instructions; and how the use of language fitted into the early social life of genus *Homo*. This is a large order!

There is, very likely, no subject about which there has been so much curiosity, so much speculation, and so much uncertainty as the origin of language. We can never really find solid evidence to tell us what early language was like, because speech is such an ephemeral thing. We cannot find the remains of ancient words the way we find potsherds or arrowheads. The earliest writing is not very old in terms of human history; written records which can be deciphered go back approximately 5000 years, and it seems likely that some sort of human language has been in use for perhaps 100 times longer.

Scholars, sages, and mythmakers have, over the millennia, developed many explanations for language. Reading the Biblical account of the Creation, we find that Adam had speech from the beginning, and, being made in God's image, he spoke to God just as God spoke to him. This original language was used by Adam and Eve and their descendants until the time of the building of the Tower of Babel, when many languages were created as a divine punishment for human presumptuousness:

> "And the whole earth was of one language and one speech. . . . And they said, Come, let us build a city, and a tower whose top may reach unto heaven; and let us make us a name, lest we be scattered abroad upon the face of the whole world. . . .
> "And the Lord said, Behold, the people is one, and they have all one language, and this is only the beginning of what they will do. . . . Come, let us go down, and there confound their language, that they may not understand one another's speech. So the Lord scattered them abroad from thence upon the face of the earth. . . ." (Gen. XI, 1–8).

Similarly, the sacred literature of many other peoples tells of, or implies, a miraculous origin for language. Very often, we find an explanation for the differences among languages occurring—as at the Tower of Babel—through an arbitrary or punitive act of the creator or a culture hero. For example, among native peoples of California (an area whose population consisted of many small tribes and a number of different languages), the mythology of the Maidu gives a typical explanation for this diversity:

> ". . . [U]p to this time everybody spoke the same language. The people were having a burning (funeral ceremony) . . . when in the night everybody suddenly began to speak a different language. Each man and his wife, however, spoke the same. Earth Initiate (the creator) had come in the night to Kuksu (the first man) and had told him about it all, and given him instructions for the next day. So, when morning came, Kuksu called all the people together, for he was able to speak all the languages. He told them each the names of the different animals . . . in their languages, taught them how to cook and hunt, gave them all their laws, and set the time for all their dances and festivals. Then he called each tribe by name, and sent them off in different directions, telling them where they were to live (Thompson, 1966).

Though we still hear accounts of the miraculous origins of languages, few educated people today accept them in a literal sense; for one thing, the evidence for human evolution makes them untenable. (However, it is still possible to believe that human language is something of a miracle if we consider, as many people do—scientists as well as laymen—that there is a qualitative difference between the intelligence of animals and that of humans.)

There are other theories which have tried to explain the beginnings of language as the outcome of a natural or rational development. Some of these, which may be said to anticipate an understanding of human evolution, imagined early man emerging from a "state of nature," essentially by use of his own intelligence. Two of the most popular suppositions, both of which have been defended by philosophers since the time of Plato and Aristotle, are the theory of *onomatopoeia* (or "Bow-wow" theory), and the theory of language originating from natural cries (sometimes called the "Ouch!" theory). The first of these suggests that early man invented language by imitating the sounds of nature. Pursuing this idea, the nineteenth-century British prehistorian, Sir John Lubbock, one of the founders of British anthropology, observed:

> "Many names of animals, such as cuckoo, crow, peewit, &c., are evidently derived from the sounds made by those birds. Everyone admits that such words as bang, crack, purr, whizz, hum, &c. . . . have arisen from the attempt to represent sounds characteristic of the object it is intended to designate. Take, again the inarticulate human sounds—sob, sigh, moan, groan, laugh, cough, weep, whoop, shriek, yawn: or of animals; as cackle, chuckle, gobble, quack, twitter, chirp, coo, hoot, caw, croak, chatter, neigh, whinny, mew, purr, bark, yelp, roar, bellow: slap, crack, smack, whack, thwack, pat, bat, batter, butt; and again, clash, flash, plash, splash, smash, dash, crash, bang, clang, twang, ring, ding, din, bump, thump, plump, boom, hum, drum, hiss, rustle. . . .
> I cannot but think that we may look upon the words above mentioned as the still recognizable descendants of roots which were onomatopoeic in their origin. . . ." (Lubbock, 1874).

The other of these theories (the "Ouch!" theory) suggests that natural instinctual cries or emotive sounds (sighs, laughter, cries of alarm, pain, or disgust) became transformed into language. In the late nineteenth century, Charles Darwin proposed a version of this theory, finding a continuity between the vocalizations of monkeys and apes and the language of humans.

A third view, distantly related to both of these, suggests that there is some sort of natural association between words and their referents. An early German linguist, Max Muller, proposed this idea (sometimes called the "Ding-Dong" theory), which suggests that the natural qualities of things called forth the instinctive invention of appropriate names by the early founders of language. This is the same sort of idea which was expressed in Plato's dialogue *Cratylus*, one of the earliest philosophical treatises on language. Cratylus, an intellectual whose views were criticized by Socrates, argued that names reflect the nature of things, and that the first "name-giver" based the names on a prior knowledge of things. He asserted that a knowledge of names was, therefore, an important part of education.

The wise Socrates replied to this by inquiring how that first inventor of names acquired the knowledge of things on which to base the names if there were no language to provide him with that knowledge. Socrates was expressing the opinion—which has been defended by many linguists in the twentieth century—that language is a human invention, and that the vocabulary of language is essentially arbitrary and conventional.

Socrates said that names were invented for human use, just as a craftsman might invent a spindle or a lathe. The Bible gives us a suggestion of this same idea: Adam becomes an inventor of language when he gives names to all the animals.

The major part of the vocabulary of modern languages is, to all appearances, arbitrary. We can easily demonstrate this by comparing the names of animals, plants, heavenly bodies, or almost anything else, in a random selection of languages. English "dog" is the translation equivalent of French "chien," Spanish "perro," German "Hund," and Russian "sobaka;" even though all these languages are related, the words seem quite dissimilar. Adding a few others, around the world, we find Navajo "łeécaa'i," Maori "kurii," Malagasy "alika," Swahili "mbwa," and Burmese "khwêi."

The point is that most vocabulary does not reveal any necessary or apparent connection between form and meaning. It has seemed obvious, from the point of view of the descriptive linguist, that the important thing is not which form stands for which meaning, but that the speakers of a language agree on the selection of forms and meanings, and that they all use words in the same way. As an insight into the way languages work, this position leaves very little room for argument.

However, the claim that language began in this way (deliberately invented or agreed upon for the purpose of communication) implies that a high degree of human intelligence developed earlier than language. It is nonsense, as Socrates pointed out, to imagine that our ancestors could have decided to use words, and could have agreed upon their meanings, without having a language to formulate their decisions and register their agreement!

This possibility can no longer be taken seriously as a historical explanation; it is outdated by the modern accumulation of knowledge about human evolution. Language did not have a miraculous origin, and it was not invented; it evolved as humankind evolved. Anthropology, which seeks an integrated perspective on human biological and social evolution, must include language in that perspective.

LANGUAGE AND BIOLOGICAL EVOLUTION

When anthropologists list the main criteria for defining humans, contrasting them with other related forms of life, they usually give a prominent place to language. The ability to speak ranks along with upright posture, high intelligence, and the manufacture and use of tools, as one of the basic differences between creatures considered human (*hominid*) and those which are related but subhuman (*hominoid*). (See, for example, Hoebel, 1972.) It might seem rather pointless even to make such a list. After all, we have no trouble in distinguishing our fellow men from monkeys or apes. But in the unlikely events that a lost colony of "yeti" is discovered on earth, or if we find strange creatures in outer space, we may yet have a need for criteria of this sort.

Such a list, however, is meant as a conceptual tool; it clarifies our thinking about the many individual finds of skeletal remains with which paleontologists deal— the fossil "men," "apes," and creatures which are sometimes referred to as "ape-men" or "man-apes." Evolution does not consist of a single, orderly series of steps; the evolution of the primates has been a slow, constant process of variation and selection over millions of years, a series of events which did not take a single path or pass through identical stages. But there is, among scientists, a general consensus on these critical mileposts in the transition from subhuman to human.

Therefore, it is worth noting that the acquisition of language is one such occurrence. George G. Simpson, an eminent biologist, calls language ". . . the most entirely unique, the most completely diagnostic characteristic of *homo sapiens*." (Simpson, 1969). Seen in this light, language is part of the biological heritage of mankind, and is functionally connected with all the other aspects of the process of *hominization* (becoming human). An early step in this process was the attainment of upright posture. The ancient australopithecines (or "man-apes") of southeast Africa, more than 2 million years ago, walked—or, rather, ran—upright, although skeletal remains indicate that they were not as completely adapted to sustained upright posture as are their modern descendants. These creatures are usually considered to be human, or at least transitional to fully human status, because of their upright posture and because there is evidence that they used simple tools.

The development of upright posture (Fig. 1) is evidenced by major changes in the lower skeleton, especially the pelvis (1). Upright posture, in turn, must have been functionally connected with the free use of the hands (2) for activities which include making and using tools; it is also associated with changes in the shape and proportions of the head and face, including the growth of the brain-case (3) and flattening of the face and jaw (4). There are several anatomical developments associated with upright posture which have been incorporated in our biological adaptation for speaking. Among these is the enlargement of the pharynx (part of

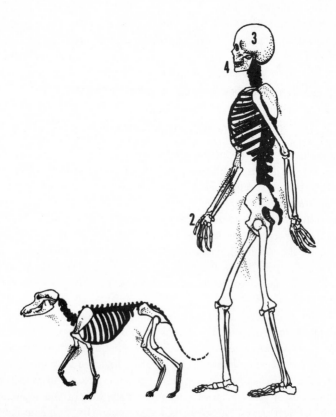

Fig. 1. Skeletal changes in the shift from pronograde to orthograde (upright) posture. Reprinted by permission from E. A. Hoebel, Anthropology, 4th ed., p. 87. Copyright © 1972 by McGraw-Hill Book Company.

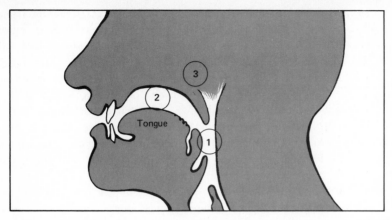

Fig. 2. The principal resonators of the speech apparatus: (1) the pharynx: (2) the mouth; (3) the nasal cavity.

the vocal tract between the back of the tongue and the larynx or "Adam's apple"), which became elongated and bent as the skull became balanced upright at the top of the spinal column (rather than suspended at the end of it). This enlarged pharynx serves as one of the important resonators used in the production of speech sounds (Fig. 2). The mouth is a second resonator: changes in the anatomy of the jaw and a gradual reduction in the size of the teeth have improved the mouth as a resonating chamber and have provided space for the movements of the tongue in articulating speech sounds. These two resonators, the pharynx (1) and the mouth (2), a third resonator in the nasal cavity (3), and the tongue, which can be moved rapidly and freely within the mouth, are the basic equipment which all humans use in shaping the distinctive sounds of speech.

Biological evolution ties in with the growth of culture, since the use of language seems obviously associated with habitual tool use (limiting the use of gestures) and with increasing human intelligence. The growth of the brain, in both size and complexity, is related—partly as cause and partly as effect—to the evolution of language. The average size of the brain increased enormously and rapidly, from 500–600 cc to more than 1400 cc in the course of approximately 2 million years of human prehistory. This growth has been paralleled by the increasing importance of speech; language and human intelligence can be thought of as two aspects of the same evolutionary development.

By the middle of the Paleolithic Age (Old Stone Age, about 100,000 years ago), we find that there were human beings who lived in caves or in open camps in groups that we might call "bands" or "tribes." Males must have worked together when hunting, for there is evidence that they killed animals by surrounding them and driving them into water or over cliffs; they also used other methods which would have required cooperation. Females may also have pooled their labor, probably as gatherers of plants, shellfish, and other foods; and, at times, all the members of a community must have joined in large-scale undertakings. For such large-scale coordinated activity, language was essential.

Individual skills were important, too. By the time the human brain had evolved to its present size, human hands had evolved in special ways, attaining a fine capacity for precision, coordination, and strength of movement. In our museums, we can see a great variety of ancient stone tools—axes, points, blades, chisels, augurs, and so forth—which testify to knowledge of intricate and complex techniques.

A wonderful thing about human knowledge, and perhaps the most important advance over the knowledge shared by other species of animals, is that our knowledge is cumulative. It has been handed down and amended through the years and centuries. It is in the developing tool and art traditions of the Old Stone Age that we can, for the first time, see striking evidences of this sharing and accumulation of knowledge, and with it see the most persuasive evidence for the growth of language.

According to physical anthropologist Bernard Campbell, "the real cultural advances that we associate with the Hominidae must almost certainly have awaited an adequate language. Speech alone made possible levels of abstraction that were necessary for the development of material culture and human society, for it is an accomplished kind of communication between individuals that makes possible a material culture and a complex economic social structure and maintains its integration" (Campbell, 1966).

The Vocal Tract   Philip Lieberman has attemped to trace the evolution of the anatomical adaption for language by studying skeletal remains of ancient human and subhuman populations. One of his most controversial studies (done in cooperation with E. S. Crelin) involved measurements of Neanderthal skulls. In this study, two complete Neanderthal skulls and an additional mandible were compared to a collection of modern human skulls, both adult and newborn. The objective of the study was to reconstruct the Neanderthal vocal tract and to calculate the range of sounds which could be produced.

Adjusted in scale (Fig. 3), the newborn skull (A) has many features in common with the Neanderthal (B); both are relatively elongated from front to back, and flattened from top to bottom; the mandible (lower jaw) is similar in shape and both lack the chin development of the modern adult (C). Seen from below, the dental arch of the modern adult is V-shaped while those of the newborn and the Neanderthal are U-shaped (a trait shared with monkeys and apes). These and other similarities are the basis for the authors' statement that "the skeletal features of Neanderthal man show that his supralaryngeal vocal apparatus was similar to that of a newborn human infant."

Because of these skeletal similarities, the newborn anatomy was used as a guide reconstructing the Neanderthal larynx, tongue, and musculature of the pharynx. The vocal tract was reconstructed with modeling clay, and from this casts were made of the air passage (Fig. 4). Comparing these with casts of the modern human vocal tract, again it can be seen that there is greater similarity to the newborn than to the adult.

Lieberman and Crelin went on to synthesize electronically the sounds which could be produced in such a vocal tract. The distinctive qualities of the vowels in human languages are the result of variations in three resonators: the oral cavity, the pharynx, and the nasal cavity. A computer program calculated the range of vowel sounds consistent with the dimensions of the Neanderthal vocal tract.

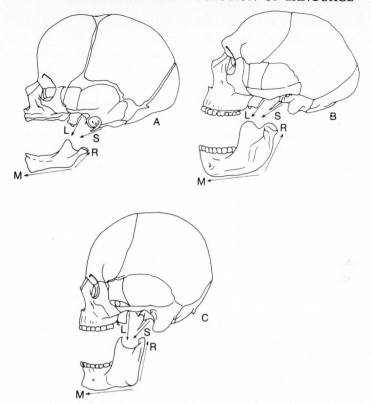

Fig. 3. Lateral view of skulls of newborn (A), Neanderthal (B) and adult man(C). Reprinted with permission of Macmillan Publishing Co., Inc. from On the Origins of Language *by Philip Lieberman. Copyright © 1975 by Philip Lieberman.*

The vowels of American English range from the high front /i/ (the vowel in *beet*), to the high back /u/ (as in *boot*), to the low central /a/ (as in *hot* or the first syllable of *bottle*) (see Chapter 5 and chart). While we distinguish a number of other vowels within the same range, these three are *extremes* of vocalic contrast used in English and in many other languages; in addition, many languages make a

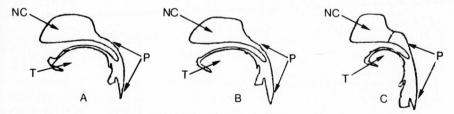

Fig. 4. Supralaryngeal air passages of newborn (A), Neanderthal (B) and adult man (C). NC—nasal cavity; T—tongue; P—pharynx (after Lieberman and Crelin, simplified). Reprinted with permission of Macmillan Publishing Co., Inc. from On the Origins of Language *by Philip Lieberman. Copyright © 1975 by Philip Lieberman.*

contrast between oral and nasalized vowels. Lieberman and Crelin were forced to conclude that the Neanderthal vocal tract "was inherently incapable of producing the range of sounds that is necessary for the full range of human speech." The Neanderthal vowels were restricted to a range including the sounds /ɪ/, /ɛ/, /ə/, and /æ/ (as in *bit, bet, but,* and *bat*). Because of the high location of the larynx, velar consonants like /g/ and /k/ would have been impossible. It is also unlikely that a distinction of nasal and nonnasal sounds could have been made.

Critics have not agreed on the significance of the study by Lieberman and Crelin; some argue that it supports a view that the Neanderthals lacked language, others, that it indicates that they were capable of language. Lieberman and Crelin's conclusions seem reasonable: Neanderthal man "was not as well-equipped for language as modern man," but "represents an intermediate stage in the evolution of language." This, in turn, supports the view that "the evolution of language was gradual, that it was not an abrupt phenomenon" (Lieberman and Crelin, 1971).

The Language-Specialized Brain   In the course of the last million years, our human brains have become much larger than those of our prehuman ancestors or of any other member of the primate order. Even in the brainiest of these, the gorillas and chimpanzees, we find a cranial capacity which is less than half the human norm. And this is only part of the story: our brains are not just larger, they are also developed in special ways. It appears that much of the specialization occurred as language evolved.

Some of the more important features of a human brain are these:

(1) There is an enlargement of the occipital (posterior) lobe, which is characteristic of all primates, including humans. This area is associated with vision, a sense which has been very important to arboreal primates, as well as to us ground dwellers. (By contrast, all primate brains are underdeveloped in the areas associated with the sense of smell.)

(2) Primate brains also show a strong development in the temporal lobes; this is especially marked in humans. Large parts of these areas are involved with the analysis of visual and auditory stimuli and with the recall and reactivation of past experiences.

(3) Frontal lobes of the brain are also enlarged in the higher primates, and greatly enlarged in humans—so much so that a high, bulging forehead is considered a distinctively human trait. The cortex, or surface portion, is folded and convoluted, which greatly increases the total surface area. Much of this cortex contains motor and sensory areas, of which those associated with the fingers, the hand, and the mouth are especially large.

In all of these developments, humans exhibit tendencies which are shared, to some extent, with other primates. However, there is one uniquely human trait:

(4) Lateralization is the localization of certain functions in either the right or left hemisphere of the brain. Unlike other species, our brains do not have complete bilateral symmetry. Lateralization may have developed after the brain reached its present size as a way to increase specialization with further increase in surface area. Speech functions, including word memory and associations, are concentrated in the left hemisphere; by contrast, spatial orientation and concepts of proportion seem to be "right-brain" functions.

Directly or indirectly, then, many of the areas which are highly developed or specialized in the human brain have some bearing on the use of language: special language areas, areas for perception and association, memory, and for fine muscular control and coordination (of the lips, tongue, glottis, and so on). There are also special neural "pathways" which link together various areas and types of function: the auditory, motor, and associational areas involved in speech, for example, are coordinated in this way.

PRIMATE COMMUNICATION AND LANGUAGE

A persistent and reasonable idea about the beginnings of language holds that there is a continuity between natural, instinctive sounds, (such as barks, screams, and calls) and human language. This is quite consistent with an evolutionary theory; however, not all proponents have argued for a direct development from animal cries to human language. For example, the eighteenth-century philosopher Rousseau is only one of several writers who have compared the early growth of human language to a child's progression from meaningless babbling to a meaningful association between objects and sounds.

However, most proponents of a "natural sound" origin of language have, as noted above, emphasized a similarity between interjections and exclamations in human languages and the cries or calls of animals. The supposition is that such instinctive sounds gradually became associated with the situations or objects which excited them and became stabilized as vocabulary. The main resistance to such suggestions has been the tremendous gap that seems to exist between human and animal communication. True, there is a general resemblance between animal cries and interjections; but interjections (like onomatopoeia and mimicry) play a very small part in language. The animals most similar to man—the monkeys and apes—produce a limited number of different cries (perhaps 40 at the most), while all human languages use thousands of different words. And animal cries are properly called "emotive," while human languages are built mainly upon symbols, sounds, and combinations of sounds which stand for things, actions, or ideas in a more or less arbitrary fashion. Linguists have tended to emphasize the gap or discontinuity between human and other animal communication, arguing that there are both quantitative and qualitative differences between them. An article by Charles F. Hockett, written in 1960, represented an important move away from this attitude and toward an effort to suggest how the gap between animal cries and human languages might have been crossed.

Hockett listed 13 "design features" of human language as shown in Fig. 5. Of these, he identified the last four (*displacement, productivity, traditional transmission,* and *duality of patterning*) as being unique to human communication; the others are shared with various animal species, especially with mammals and birds. Therefore, Hockett suggests that features 1–9 were present in prehuman vocal communication (as they are in the call system of gibbons, for example), while features 10–13 developed later and in approximately this order.

These crucial features deserve a brief discussion: *Productivity* means the ability

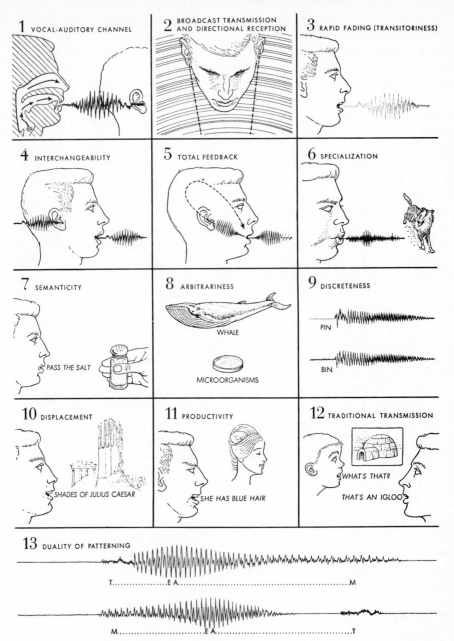

Fig. 5. Thirteen design features of language. From "The Origin of Speech" by Charles Hockett. Copyright © 1960 by Scientific American, Inc. All rights reserved.

to say new things. Species like gibbons (apes) and baboons (monkeys) typically have a small, unchanging set of a dozen or more calls, with identifiable general meanings such as alarm, danger, or discovery of food. They thus partake of features 6–8, as well as the lower-numbered features which are shared by most other mammals. However, these call systems appear to be nonproductive; that is, new calls are not invented, and the existing calls are not combined. Another way of saying this is that these are *closed* systems, while all human languages are *open* and can take in or invent new words and meanings. Hockett suggests that combinations of calls were the first, perhaps accidental, step toward an open system and thus to an increase in vocabulary.

By *displacement,* Hockett means the ability to talk about some thing or event which is not present. Certain other animals (bees, for example), exhibit what might be called displacement, but those closest to man do not; vocal calls generally occur together with the stimulus, as when the sight of a predator elicits a danger call. Hockett feels that displacement, like productivity, began to develop fairly early in human evolution and gradually increased in importance. He compares displacement to the carrying of sticks and stones, which is "like talking today about what to do tomorrow." That is, both give an indication of foresight or planning.

A productive system is one which can grow, and the feature of displacement implies an increased use of verbal signals because they can be used in more different situations. Perhaps at this point we could refer to the system as a language. But the most characteristic feature of human language may be *traditional transmission,* because it is this which links it most closely with culture. Although the potential for using languages, the general ability to do so, is biologically transmitted, specific languages are taught and learned. They are passed on traditionally, generation after generation, from older speakers (who already know the language) to younger ones (who acquire it). In turn, language enables humans to learn other things through tradition rather than by direct experience. Even in a very early stage of human development, Hockett says, such learning would have a survival value: "A child can be taught how to avoid certain dangers before he actually encounters them."

The most complex of the design features, and the one which Hockett thinks must have developed relatively late in human history, is the one he calls *duality of patterning.* This feature is common to all modern languages, but may have originated only when simpler language systems became overloaded, so to speak. If we assume, as Hockett does, that the earliest human languages were built by "opening up" a primate call system and adding additional elements to it, we can imagine that it might grow from perhaps a dozen up to 100 or more different elements. This vocabulary would be much more extensive than any known set of primate calls, and probably sufficient for a rudimentary human culture. But, says Hockett, "there is a practical limit, for any species or any machine, to the number of distinct stimuli that can be discriminated, especially when the discriminations typically have to be made in noisy conditions" (Hockett, 1960).

An improvement over this situation is a language system built from two types of elements: a small number of distinctive sounds (most languages use between 20 and 40) which combine in regularly patterned ways to form an almost limitless number of words and other meaningful units. All modern languages, structured in this way, can form many thousands of distinctive meaningful units. If we follow Hockett's view of the evolution of language, this step is the most dramatic and perhaps the hardest to comprehend.

The article by Hockett, and another larger study by Hockett and Ascher (1964), excited a great deal of interest and marked the beginning of a wave of anthropological theorizing about the problem of *glottogenesis,* the origin of language. Other scholars have partly rejected or revised Hockett's list of "design features," and he himself has added to it. One criticism of Hockett's approach might be this: his tendency is to think of language origins strictly in terms of *vocal* communication. This seems to be a rather anthropocentric view—that is, it takes the human type of communication as its standard. A truly balanced comparative view would indicate that human language is unique and very specialized in its principal reliance on vocal signals. However, it is not enough to trace a continuity between the vocalizations of other species and the vocalizations used in language by man; there must also be a continuity of a broader sort between total communication systems. Even in the relatively short span of years since Hockett's article appeared, the numerous field studies of chimpanzees and other primates have drawn attention to the complexity and subtlety of their gestures and other nonvocal communication. Detailed study of these systems may, in the future, serve to narrow further the gap between human language and its antecedents.

Experimental Studies of Primate Language Ability   An approach to human evolution of growing importance in anthropology is the comparative study of primate behavior. This has taken two main directions: the study of primate social groups under natural (or nearly natural) conditions; and the laboratory study, observation, and testing of individual animals. Both should, in the long run, give us insight into the relationship of human behavior (including language) to the behavior of primates in general.

The several experiments in teaching human language to primates is part of the history of these animals' use in psychological experimentation. The work is still done largely by psychologists, though anthropologists have also become participants in primate research. One of the most famous experiments in chimpanzee learning was conducted by psychologists W. N. Kellog and L. A. Kellog, who, in the 1930s, raised a chimpanzee in their home together with their own son. The boy and the chimpanzee were given a parallel series of intelligence tests, and their progress was described in published and filmed reports. It is of interest that the chimpanzee, Gua, was physically ahead of the child, and scored higher in most tests through the first year-and-a-half of life, up to an age when language begins to play an important role in human learning (Kellog, 1968).

The Kellogs did not attempt to teach Gua to speak, though they believed that he understood a number of English phrases. Subsequent experiments by others elsewhere have attempted to go further. K. J. Hays and C. Hays succeeded in teaching a home-raised chimp, Vicky, to pronounce three words in appropriate situations: "mama," "papa," and "cup" (Hays, 1951). The most recent experiments in chimpanzee learning, however, have concentrated on nonvocal use of language. This is, in part, a reaction to the consistent failure of the animals to learn to speak (despite an obvious intelligence and aptitude for various kinds of mimicry). It also reflects the influence of field studies of primates; these studies, as we will see, emphasize the importance of communicative gestures among primates in the wild.

There are a number of experiments now in progress which involve the manipulation of linguistic symbols by chimpanzees. It is difficult to predict what the eventual impact will be on our view of the linguistic and intellectual abilities of these primates and, indirectly, of man. One of the most interesting of these projects was the work of R. A. Gardner and Beatrice Gardner in teaching American Sign Language to the chimpanzee Washoe.

The Gardners undertook the experiment out of an interest in the processes and mechanisms of learning. Washoe, a caught-in-the-wild infant chimpanzee, was between 8 and 14 months old at the beginning of the experiment, and sociable. A gesture system, considered appropriate to chimpanzees, was selected to take advantage of Washoe's natural use of gestures and her superior ability in manipulation. "[W]e reasoned that gestures for the chimpanzee should be analogous to bar-pressing for rats, key-pecking for pigeons, and babbling for humans."

ASL (American Sign Language), the gesture system which was chosen, is a composite of signs some of which are iconic (that is, have some resemblance to their referents), and others which are quite arbitrary. It is a widely used system, though the literate deaf often supplement it with a system of finger-spelling. The crew of experimenters arranged their schedules so that Washoe had constant companionship, and they maintained a social atmosphere in which ASL was freely used. The objective was to expose Washoe to ASL in much the same way that most children experience the use of spoken language around them. Sounds such as clapping, whistling, and laughing were used, but only sounds which a chimpanzee could imitate; speech was, in general, not used.

The psychologists were relying on the chimpanzee's penchant for imitation. However, direct imitation of signs was not much in evidence; rather, she often demonstrated delayed imitation, using a sign spontaneously after observing it over a period of time. For example, Washoe's teeth were brushed after each meal, and the sign for "toothbrush" was used at this time. After several months of this, on a visit to the Gardners' home, she walked into the bathroom, surveyed its contents, and signed "toothbrush." Similarly, she had been shown many flowers and pictures of flowers before spontaneously signing "flower" in an appropriate situation.

Washoe was drilled in imitation, and games were invented to encourage it. The crew seized upon accidental movements which resembled signs, correcting them and demonstrating their meaning. Their responsiveness to Washoe's movements had the effect of increasing her manual "babbling" (random activity of the arms and hands), upon which new signs could be built. Finally, the experimenters sometimes simply guided Washoe's hands to help her learn new signs; this proved to be the quickest way of all. In the first 22 months of the experiment, Washoe learned to use 30 signs (Fig. 6).

"Come-gimme," her first sign, began with a begging gesture already used by the chimpanzee. It was modified toward the ASL signs for "come" and "give me," which include a beckoning movement of the wrist. Washoe often used this sign in combinations, such as "come tickle" or "gimme sweet." "Flower," an iconic sign made with the hand cupped to resemble a flower and touched to the nose, was acquired early and spontaneously, and generalized by Washoe to flowers of all sorts, and to pictures of flowers. When she went on to apply it to odors of all sorts (such as a tobacco pouch), the sign for "smell" was introduced. Washoe learned the appropriate distinction, but occasionally erred by using "flower" in "smell" contexts.

Washoe: "book"   Washoe: "baby"

Fig. 6. Two of Washoe's signs: "book" and "baby." From Apes, Men *and* Language *by Eugene Linden, illustrations by Madelaine Gill Linden. Copyright © 1974 by Eugene Linden. Reprinted by permission of the publisher, E. P. Dutton.*

A sign was considered to be established in Washoe's vocabulary after three different observers reported it as occurring in an appropriate context. It should be noted that, once the signs were learned, the chimp used them creatively, transferring to new contexts and extending them to new referents. Her use of "flower" was an instance of this. In another case, the sign for "open" was introduced in reference to specific doors; Washoe transferred it to other doors, containers, the refrigerator, briefcases, jars, and eventually to water faucets. The sign for "dog" was transferred both to pictures of dogs and to the sound of a dog barking but not in sight.

The Gardners concluded a preliminary report on this experiment by observing that "the most promising results have been spontaneous naming, spontaneous transfer to new referents, and spontaneous combinations and recombinations of signs" (Gardner and Gardner, 1969). Later reports on Washoe's progress indicated rapid increase in vocabulary up to at least 160 signs, and the forming of increasingly long and complex constructions. Current research in progress involves more chimpanzees, with an interest in observing the possible social use of signs, and the transmission of signs to a second generation of chimpanzees (Linden, 1974).

Other language-teaching experiments with chimpanzees have concentrated on syntax rather than vocabulary. The Gardners noted that Washoe used signs in combinations and sometimes put together long sequences of them. However, their experiment was not designed to deal with the syntactic ordering of the signs. In another pioneering experiment, David Premak, also a psychologist, taught a chimpanzee, Sarah, to use colored plastic tokens as linguistic components. The tokens, which stood for words, had to be arranged in a particular order, producing sentences. Premak used a behaviorist approach, and rewarded Sarah with treats when she constructed correct sentences or obeyed instructions. Other psychologists, at the Yerkes primate center in Georgia, have used a similar approach with Lana, a chimpanzee who has learned to write messages on a specifically designed typewriter.

Finally, though most of these experiments have been conducted with chimpanzees, a young gorilla named Hanabi-Ko (or Koko) made the news in 1978 because of her langauge ability. Like Washoe, Koko learned American Sign Language (Patterson, 1978). Her achievements may, in time, be even greater than the chimp's.

Field Studies of Primate Social Behavior   Over the last two decades, there has been an increasing interest in the study of monkeys and apes in their natural habitats. The central objective of the studies usually has not been communication; generally, the focus is on ecological adaptation and social structure. However, these modern primate studies have made anthropologists acutely aware of the integral place of communication in the total adaptation of all primate species, and this, in turn, contributes to our perspective on man.

A pioneering study, which set a standard for subsequent research, was directed by S. L. Washburn and I. DeVore. They observed baboon troops on wildlife preserves in South Africa. Baboons are Old World monkeys which share with man the distinction of being terrestrial (ground-dwelling), in contrast to the majority of primate species which are arboreal (tree-dwelling). Baboons are extremely social animals, living in compact troops of 20–250 individuals. A population of baboons were studied living in open savanna country, where they often come in contact with carnivorous predators. The strength of the baboons' social organization, which keeps members of a troop always in contact and organized for defense, is considered to be the key to the successful adaptation of this species.

Washburn and DeVore described aspects of baboon society in a number of articles, as well as in an excellent series of films. Characteristic features of primates (including man) are the dependency of infants and the critical role of learning for their eventual competence as adults. Infant baboons are constantly in contact with their mothers, carried first on the belly and, after the first month or two, on the back. An infant explores the territory as the mother travels with the troop, learns to feed by observing and imitating her, and is frequently groomed by the mother. Baboons of all ages spend time daily in mutual grooming; it is a kind of tactile communication which reinforces solidarity between individuals. Juvenile baboons play together, test their strength against one another, and establish a dominance hierarchy which is of great importance in the peaceful internal organization of the society. Although baboons have a number of vocal calls which are of special importance as signals of warning and aggression, they are generally quiet animals. This may be partly related to the danger in attracting nearby predators, and partly to the compactness of the baboon troops—members of a troop are generally in visual contact with one another. According to Washburn and DeVore, "It is not unlikely that the major system that mediates interindividual behavior for baboons is one of visual cues from facial expressions, intention movements, and attitudes, while auditory, tactual, and olfactory cues are of descending order of importance" (Washburn and DeVore, 1961).

Gorillas and chimpanzees are much closer to man, in evolutionary terms, than are baboons. Gorillas are the largest of the primates, and probably, next to man, the most intelligent. Their social groups are smaller than those of baboons and the membership is less stable, with individuals frequently leaving and joining various groups. Chimpanzees, too, appear to have a flexible organization, and their groups are scattered unevenly over a large area of forest. Frequent "hooting" calls and drumming on tree trunks serve to maintain contact among groups, keep each aware of the others' location, and sometimes are signals for a larger gathering or "carnival."

Within social groups of gorillas or chimpanzees, there is constant communication among individuals which combines vocal, facial, and gestural signals. Jane van Lawick-Goodall, who has studied chimpanzee behavior in the field, has described many instances of such behavior, and discerns a general similarity between chimpanzee and human nonlinguistic interaction:

"[O]ne significant aspect of chimpanzee behavior lies in the close similarity of many of their communicatory gestures and postures to those of man himself. Not only are the actual positions and movements similar to our own but also the contexts in which they often occur.

"When a chimpanzee is suddenly frightened he frequently reaches to touch or embrace a chimpanzee nearby, rather as a girl watching a horror film may seize her companion's hand. Both chimpanzees and humans seem reassured in stressful situations by physical contact with another individual. . . .

"When two chimpanzees greet each other after a separation, their behavior often looks amazingly like that shown by two humans in the same context. Chimpanzees may bow or crouch to the ground, hold hands, kiss, embrace, touch, or pat each other on almost any part of the body, especially the head and face and genitals. A male may chuck a female or an infant under the chin. . . .

"Many of (the chimpanzee's) games are like those played by human children. The tickling movements of chimpanzee fingers during play are almost identical with our own. The chimpanzee's aggressive displays are not dissimilar to some of ours. Like a man, an angry chimpanzee may fixedly stare at his opponent. He may raise his forearm rapidly, jerk back his head a little, run toward his adversary upright and waving his arms, throw stones, wield sticks, hit, kick, bite, scratch, and pull the hair of a victim.

"In fact, if we survey the whole range of the postural and gestural communication signals of chimpanzees on the one hand and humans on the other, we find striking similarities in many instances. It would appear, then, that man and chimp either have evolved gestures and postures along a most remarkable parallel or that we share with the chimpanzees an ancestor in the dim and very distant past; an ancestor, moreover, who communicated with his kind by means of kissing and embracing, touching and patting and holding hands" (Lawick-Goodall, 1971).

Comparing Subhuman and Human Communicative Behavior   A leading primate specialist, Jane Lancaster, comments that the communication systems of monkeys and apes are "extraordinarily complex," compared to those of birds and many species of mammals. Part of this complexity lies in the fact that communication is largely "multimodal"—it involves the simultaneous use of vocalization, body movements, facial expressions, and, at times, touch or olfactory stimuli; three or four senses may be involved in receiving a composite message. Another consideration which makes this communication difficult to analyze under any but close field conditions is the fact that social context is essential to the total meaning of a signal; a threat, for example, may be taken seriously in one situation and ignored in another. Primate signals, finally, are often *graded;* a particular type of vocalization will vary in meaning in a continuous serious of changes in volume or duration. This grading of signals, Lancaster points out, is quite different from the songs of many birds, which are unique and easily identifiable as to motivation or situation. It is also different from human language, in which complex messages are built up of separate, discrete parts. Lancaster emphasizes this difference but she also points to similarities: "[T]hese systems have little relationship with human language but much with the ways our species expresses emotion through gesture, facial expression, and tone of voice" (Lancaster, 1975).

The essential difference, the great gap between subhuman and human communication, is the fact of *environmental reference.* Language, as Lancaster puts it, "provided human beings with a tool by which they could communicate information to others not only about their own emotional states but also about social relationships and the physical environment." There is little doubt that this gap was bridged, in human evolution, by natural selection in favor of high intelligence. The particular course of development of language has paralleled, and seems to have a common basis with, the development of tool use by early humans.

Philip Lieberman has claimed that there are similarities between the cognitive patterns—roughly, the mental maps or plans—which underlie the chipping of stone tools of the sort made and used during the Paleolithic period, and the syntactic structure of human language. The parallelism which he discerns suggests that as culture, and especially technology, became more complex, language also was expanded or grew in complexity (Lieberman, 1975).

Language did not begin all at once; it was built slowly and cumulatively, out of many parts. Names, or nouns, are one basic component; like tools, they serve to separate and control the materials, things, and creatures of the environment. Language also incorporates the instinctive ways in which love, concern, alarm, fear, hatred, and other human emotions are expressed. The grammar of language codifies spatial and temporal relations, the logic of cause and effect, and the sequencing of events; it gives a means for relating the past to the present and planning for the future, for understanding relationships and weighing probabilities. The categories of language give rise to concepts and metaphors, extending knowledge of the concrete and immediate to the abstract and general, the basis for an encompassing "world view." As a finished product, language has all the complexity we need for social interaction, coordination of activities, division of labor, teaching and learning, ritual and worship, and the perpetuation of human knowledge across the generations.

TOPICS FOR STUDY AND DISCUSSION

1. Look through collections of mythology to find more examples of how various peoples have accounted for the origin and diversification of languages. Compare.
2. Compare the "Bow-wow," "Ding-Dong." and "Ouch!" theories of the origin of language. Can any of these ideas be proved or disproved? Does any of them seem especially persuasive?
3. What are the two directions that primate studies have taken? How do they contribute to an understanding of human communicative behavior?
4. Visit a zoo and pay attention to animal communication. If there is a large social group of primates—a colony of baboons or rhesus monkeys, for example—spend an hour or more in observation and see how many different types of communication you can distinguish.

3

The Acquisition of Language

How do babies begin to acquire language? Human infants are not born with the ability to speak; everywhere in the world, they cry and coo and babble. But before long their babblings begin to sound like words—words in the languages spoken around them. Words lead to sentences, and eventually they all become conversationalists, participating in verbal repartée, asking and answering. This happens in every human society—but how?

We who live in a highly literate Western society, with all of the emphasis that we put on education, sometimes have the illusion that language must be taught. It *is* an illusion. Despite the hours that school children devote to reading and writing and "language arts," these are all, in a sense, frills. The most basic knowledge, competence in one's own native language, is gained without formal instruction and, at times, under the most adverse conditions. How does this happen? One explanation holds that language is learned outright, as children listen, observe, and mimic; an opposite theory insists that there is an inborn capacity for language, which develops and expands naturally, as a child matures. We should not really have to advocate one of these views to the exclusion of the other; however, most interested scholars have tended to take a partisan position, emphasizing either the external (learned) or internal (innate) source of language.

The philosopher John Locke (1632–1704), one of the most famous and influential figures in liberal Western thought, described the human mind as an "empty cabinet." He used this simile to underline the fact that knowledge is acquired and to assert the importance of education. This was a liberal view in Locke's time, since it implied that members of both the upper and the lower classes were products of their environments; thus, it minimized the importance of birth and inheritance. One line of theory in anthropology which might be traced back to Locke regards individuals simply as the product, the sum total, of their life experiences and cultural milieu. As a theory about language, a similar emphasis can be put on environment; the indiviual is seen as playing a passive role, learning and retaining the forms which are used by those around him. Linguists who have held this view (a popular one early in the twentieth century) have been strongly influenced by behavioral psychologists such as J. B. Watson and B. F. Skinner, who propounded the concept of the *conditioned response*. According to Skinner, words and their meanings and appropriate uses are all acquired through conditioning. If a baby's babbling resembles an acceptable word ("Daddy," for example), the baby is rewarded with smiles and attention, and so that particular response is reinforced; other babbling is ignored and gradually becomes less frequent. Similarly, a child will, at first, apply words in a very general sort of way, narrowing or adjusting the meaning as his use of them meets with approval or disapproval. One child, for instance, used the word *kitty* for all small animals, *doggie* for larger; another, for some weeks, identified all men as *Daddy* (despite vigorous negative reinforcement from his mother). But children are usually eager to please, and so their behavior, including speech, is gradually shaped by social conditioning.

An all-out application of this approach is too simplistic; it is difficult to understand how individuals learn the subtleties of language, such as connotations and extensions of meaning, and, most of all, how they learn to use particular words in constructions which they have never heard. Modern linguistics, since the 1950s, has been strongly influenced by an alternative view of language and the mind, a view which also has a respectable philosophical tradition.

The French philosopher René Descartes (1596–1650), a few years earlier than John Locke, advocated the view that knowledge and perception are based on innate ideas or structures in the mind; these shape the interpretation of experience. Applied to language, this view would imply that the basic or underlying form of language is already present in the mind at birth. The particulars of individual languages must be acquired, it is true, but these are like icing on the cake; the basic patterns are innate.

The most influential modern spokesman for this viewpoint is Noam Chomsky, a linguist who bases his discussion on the study of syntax. According to Chomsky, the major categories of language (such as subject, predicate, object) reflect a specific type of mental organization which is uniquely human. This inborn "universal grammar" serves as a model or template against which the child can match and sort out the forms of the specific language which is spoken around him; he is constantly testing and discarding or modifying hypotheses until the proper set of grammatical rules is discovered. This is like solving a puzzle, and different children go about it in different ways. But it is not as laborious a task as learning, one by one, all the individual forms of a language, and it is not as complicated a feat as discovering the principles of grammar without any preliminary clues.

LANGUAGE IN EARLY CHILDHOOD

Chomsky has used the term *deep structure* for the innate part of language. Deep structure is transformed, in speech, into specific *surface structures*; the linguist formulates *transformational rules* to account for the surface structures of particular languages (see p. 77). In research on children's speech, it is interesting to discover how, and in what order, the transformations and surface structures of adult speech are acquired.

Studies of English sentences used by young children reveal a typical course of development. The first sentences are short; in many cases these are one-word (*holophrastic*) sentences, often accompanied by gestures, such as pointing. However, two-word (or two-part) sentences make up a very large proportion of the speech of young children between roughly one and two years of age; several researchers have described and compared the grammar of these sentences. Typically, sentences consist of a combination of two classes of words which may be called (A) *the pivot class* and (B) *the open class*. The pivot class has relatively few members, and new words are added slowly; one pivot word occurs in most sentences. The open class has more members, and takes in new words rapidly. A sample of one child's vocabulary included:

A (pivot)	B (open)
allgone	boy
byebye	sock
big	fan
more	boat
pretty	milk
my	plane
see	vitamins
nightnight	celery
hi	shoe
	hot
	Mommy
	Daddy, etc.

Actual sentences, then, usually have the form A + B: Big boy. Allgone milk. My shoe. Byebye celery. Byebye plane. See Daddy. Nightnight Mommy.

This type of construction is typical of children's earliest speech in English, and close parallels have been described in Russian and other languages. In time, of course, vocabulary becomes larger, sentences grow longer, and the number of word classes and types of sentence construction increases. The initial "pivot" class includes words which will eventually be resorted as adjectives, verbs, salutations, and the like; the "open" class may approximate the adult category of nouns, but these will eventually be differentiated into nouns of different types—singulars, plurals, and so on.

Another characteristic of children's speech is that it is telegraphic. That is, small words such as pronouns, prepositions, conjunctions, or even verbs (like *is* or *can*) are often omitted, and so are the endings which distinguish tenses in verbs or show possession in nouns. Thus, a child who has just begun to string two, three, or four words together may say such things as: See plane. Adam make tower. Cat stand up table. Pop go weasel. Where Ann pencil? Apparently, the words (or parts of words) which are omitted are those which are usually unstressed in adult speech; these are gradually added later, in the older child's speech (McNeill, 1966).

Several recent studies of children's speech focus on the differentiation of types of sentences and the acquisition of transformational rules. The youngest children may use only one type, or a few basic types of sentence construction; real diversification and variety come with the addition of transformations. Among the first transformations to develop are rules for producing negative sentences. Progressively, this may go through a number of stages, such as (in response to the question "Do you want some food?"): (1) No want some food. (2) I no want some food. (3) I don't want no food. (4) I don't want some food. (5) I don't want any food.

Linguists wish to discover just how, and in what order, such transformational rules develop. It may be that the priorities which affect the acquisition of language have some relationship to the processing of more complex sentences by adult speakers, and to the total hierarchical structure of language (Smith and Miller, 1966).

BIOLOGICAL FOUNDATIONS OF LANGUAGE

A psychologist whose interests overlapped those of both linguists and anthropologists, Eric Lenneberg suggested that one of the most important biological foundations for human language is the ability to generalize and form categories of phenomena. In this, he found a "discontinuity" between man and other creatures; but this discontinuity does not mean that there was an actual break in the processes of evolution. Lenneberg suggested that a number of interrelated physiological processes are involved in human *cognitive function*, a capacity which is actualized or developed as behavior during the long period of immaturity characteristic of the human species. Thus, the complex cognitive function which is the basis for language is a species-specific biological endowment, unique to man.

As a psychologist, Lenneberg based his argument primarily on studies of language acquisition by children, comparisons of normal children with those whose language ability was impaired, and clinical observations of patients with language-related conditions, such as aphasia. He found that there are uniform stages in the speech development of most children (whatever their language and the conditions under which they learn it), and that these stages parallel, and are related to, the general course of growth and motor development. A few of these "milestones" in language development are:

Age	Stage
12 weeks	"Cooing," vowellike and pitch modulated
20 weeks	Addition of consonantal sounds (fricatives, spirants, nasals), though all are still very different from the mature language
6 months	Cooing changes to babbling, resembling one-syllable utterances
12 months	Identical sound sequences are replicated, words are emerging (mama, dada, and so on)
24 months	Vocabulary of more than 50 times, beginning to join vocabulary in two-word phrases
36 months	Vocabulary of about 1000 words, intelligible utterances; grammatical patterns of adult language (with mistakes)

According to Lenneberg, this general course of development is universal and is largely a contingency of biological maturation. The particular language an individual acquires, of course, depends on the social environment, and a deficient environment may limit development. Pursuing this point, he cited studies of children in institutions and other "deficient" environments, including the physically normal children of deaf parents. In this last instance, the children were compared with a control group of children of speaking parents. "The environment of the two groups of children differed in two ways: (1) the amount, nature, and occasion of adult vocalization heard by the babies differed significantly, and (2) the baby's own vocalizations could never be responded to by a deaf mother, who, we discovered, could not even tell whether her child's facial expressions and gestures were accompanied by silence or noise. The babies born to hearing parents appeared to vocalize on the occasions of adult vocalization, whereas the babies born to deaf parents did not. Nevertheless, they made as much noise and went through the same sequence of vocalization development with identical ages of onset (for cooing noises) as the control group" (Lenneberg, 1967).

Although Lenneberg drew heavily on studies of English-speaking subjects, some observations by anthropological investigators are cited in support of his position; they indicate that progress in language development appears to parallel the acquisition of motor skills, though there may be some variation in absolute age.

Lenneberg asks rhetorically: "Why do children normally begin to speak between their eighteenth and twenty-eighth month? Surely it is not because all mothers on earth initiate language training at that time . . ." (1967). Apparently, the answer is that they are biologically programmed to begin speaking at this time, and will do so unless they are severely impaired or unless the environment is severely limiting.

It should be emphasized, however, that not all children employ the same strategies in beginning to use language. One child may build a large vocabulary of single words—used in combination with appropriate gestures—before undertaking any longer sentences; another may remain speechless longer and begin using whole sentences sooner. Some children are observed to imitate sentence intonation patterns while chattering in nonsense syllables, while others are precocious in their mastery of syntactic rules. Some seem to learn socially, but others practice the repetition of words and sentences while in bed at night or when playing alone. The general stages which have been outlined are just that; they do not apply to all children in exactly the same way (Jolly, 1972).

PLAYING THE LANGUAGE GAME

A normal child, as we have seen, is ready and eager to undertake the task, or to play the game, of language acquisition. Such a child takes the initiative in learning to speak, in experimenting with sounds and sound combinations and in discovering their meanings. In acquiring words and grammar, as well as in learning the social conditions which affect the use of speech, each child must find the solution to an endless succession of riddles, and must discover the particular set of rules which his or her society has chosen to live by.

Playing with Sounds   A babbling infant seems to be experimenting with the use of his or her vocal tract, learning to produce sounds. At the same time, hearing the speech which goes on all around, the infant has a model to work from. The problem appears to be twofold: to learn voluntary control of muscles—which movements will produce which sounds—and to learn which of these are important. Those that are important are those which carry information, of course; but the first step in determining this is the identification of contrasts among them. For example, an 18-month-old English-speaking child may use only a single medial stop—which sounds like a "d"— in words like: *Jill* [dɪə], *dear* [dɪə], *doggie* [dodi], *Tommy* [dami], *Daddy* [dadi], *Give me* [dɪmi], *stomach* [dəmi], *kitty* [dɪdi], *sticky* [dɪdi]. All these words sound very much alike—but not to an adoring parent!

As the child's vocabulary grows larger, the confusion could be greater; however, at the same time, he or she is learning to make more of the necessary contrasts in the phoneme system. Thus, the child who began speaking English, as we have described, will soon learn to distinguish medial from velar stops (*d* from *g*), voiced from voiceless (*d* from *t*), stops from affricates (*d* from *j*), and so on. The same list of words, for a two-year-old, might be: [jɪl], [dɪə], [dogi], [tami], [dadi], [gɪmi], [təmi], [kɪti], [tɪki]. Not perfect from an adult point of view, but much easier to understand and less ambiguous.

Of course, a child who is becoming a Russian-speaker has to learn a somewhat different set of phonological rules; a Navajo-speaking child, still a different set. But each one, as he or she matures, eventually masters the contrasts (or *distinctive features*) which are at work in a particular language. There is a generalized sort of order to be seen in all this. According to Roman Jakobson, a linguist who developed the analysis of language in terms of distinctive features (see Chapter 5), the contrasts such as voicing, nasality, and affrication are acquired successively in much the same order by all children. This order is, it is interesting to note, approximately the reverse order in which the features are lost by persons suffering from speech disorders, such as aphasia (Moskowitz, 1973).

The Puzzle of Syntax   The two-part sentences described above seem to rest on a universal perception of relationships which might be called *predication*: the linking of two entities as cause and effect, or means and end, possessor and thing possessed, and so forth. But beyond that, the constructions are undifferentiated, and they may be ambiguous in terms of any adult grammatical system. For example, according to one linguist, a child was heard to say "Mommy sock" in two different situations—when her mother was putting a sock on her foot (subject–object), and when she picked up her mother's sock (possessor–thing possessed). The child's speech is telegraphic; some parts are omitted, and the meaning can be interpreted only in the context of the particular situation (Bloom, 1973).

The child's further development, then, leads to the acquisition of the rules of a grammatical system. The English-speaking child would soon progress to something like "Mommy put on sock," and "Mommy's sock." Both of these are still grammatically incomplete; they will be further differentiated as question, command, or statement as the child learns to use intonation (early) and transformations (later) to form different types of sentences.

Again, the acquisition of large sets of particular rules leaves us with a picture of endless diversity among languages. However, broad generalizations can be made about the acquisition of grammatical rules cross-culturally. D. Slobin, a psychologist and specialist in language acquisition, makes the following observations, among others:

(1) Inflections at the ends of words—suffixes and post-positions—are learned earlier than prefixes and internal changes in words. Thus, *Mommy's* might occur sooner than *to Mommy*.

(2) Standard word order is learned early; deviations from standard word order may be interpreted as if they *were* in standard order. One effect of this, in English, is that young children usually misunderstand passive constructions: for example, *The girl is pushed by the boy* could be misunderstood as *The girl pushes the boy*.

(3) Present tense is learned before any other tenses or time indicators.

(4) General rules, and rules applicable to larger classes, are learned before rules for special cases. This is very noticeable in children's use of English, since almost all children seem to generalize the rules for making past-tense verbs (saying *knowed, runned,* and *hurted*) and plural nouns (such as *sheeps, childs,* and *mouses*). Typically, an unmarked form is learned first (in English, the singular noun); the most common type of marking is learned next (*key/keys, doggie/doggies*); the marking is then overgeneralized (here, applied to any and all nouns); and eventually, the exceptions are learned and the adult system is acquired (Slobin, 1973).

A Guessing Game with Words   From what has been said so far, one can probably also predict how the system of meanings (the semantic structure) of a particular language is acquired. Children must, of necessity, first learn meanings on the basis of particular examples. They generalize from these examples, and they must then correct and reformulate their definitions until the appropriate set of categories is arrived at. If a child learns—as children in our own society often do—to identify picture-book animals as *kitty, doggie, bunny,* and so on, they will generalize these terms to take in more examples and new experiences. Sometimes the name of a household pet may be the basis for terms applied to other animals. One psychologist analyzed his own child's acquisition of words for animals as shown in Fig. 7.

(1) At 21–22 months of age, the child applied the cat's name, Timothy (abbreviated as "Tee") to all animals, while (2) a toy dog was called "goggie." (3) "Goggie" was soon extended, replacing "Tee" in application to small dogs. By twenty-three months, "Tee" had been further narrowed by the successive introductions of "hosh," "pushie" and "moo-ka." Finally, at twenty-four months, a compounded term, "biggie-goggie"—first applied to a St. Bernard, then to other large dogs—narrows the range of "hosh," and completes the approximation of major adult categories (with subcategories, such as breeds of dogs and cats, still to be learned). It is interesting that one distinction which was obvious to the child from the beginning—the difference between a real animal ("Tee") and a toy (the first referent of "goggie")—has been blurred in his two-year-old vocabulary! (Lewis, 1959).

It is easy to see that a process as flexible as this can incorporate many different types of cultural knowledge. It would appear that young children typically begin with the immediate experience of objects and individuals within the family or household, and structure the larger world on the basis of this experience—with the help of the older individuals around them. Most of that help is given through language; thus, the child learns that certain things are grouped together, empha-

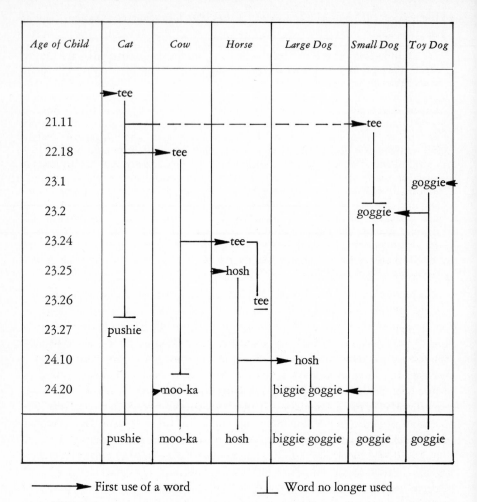

Age of Child	Cat	Cow	Horse	Large Dog	Small Dog	Toy Dog
	→tee					
21.11					→tee	
22.18		→tee				
23.1						goggie◄
23.2					goggie ◄	
23.24			→tee			
23.25			►hosh			
23.26			tee			
23.27	pushie					
24.10				→ hosh		
24.20		►moo-ka		biggie goggie◄		
	pushie	moo-ka	hosh	biggie goggie	goggie	goggie

———► First use of a word   ⊥ Word no longer used

Fig. 7. The development of one child's semantic categories. Figure 1, page 135, in How Children Learn To Speak *by M. M. Lewis, © 1959 by Basic Books, Inc., Publishers, New York.*

sizing their similarities (as toy dogs, small dogs, large dogs), while other things are set apart, emphasizing their differences (as horses and cows). Many anthropologists have emphasized the role which language plays in shaping or influencing the ways in which individuals experience and perceive the world (see Chapter 6).

Who Am I? Children never acquire language in isolation; while they are learning grammatical forms and meanings, they are also becoming familiar with some of the social settings in which speaking occurs. They may learn that there are times when children are expected to speak—even to show off their verbal skills or to dominate the conversation—and that there are times when they must be quiet, be "seen but not heard," or even be excluded entirely.

In small communities in which social roles are fairly undifferentiated, and in which numbers of people of different ages and of both sexes often work together—a peasant village, for example—a child might be able to observe and learn firsthand almost all of the speech patterns of adult life. However, in many societies the adult male and female worlds are quite segregated; little boys (cared for by women) have little or no opportunity to learn to act and speak like men. In such cases, there may be a prescribed time or an "initiation period" when boys are separated from their mothers and female kin; formally or informally, they are taught male skills, including the kinds of speeches, rituals, jokes, bragging, or recounting of history and mythology which are the cultural prerogatives of men. Girls may have an easier time of it, since they usually remain with their mothers, and learn adult women's ways of acting and speaking by imitation and participation.

In large and complex societies like our own, social roles are many and varied, and there are numerous dialects, levels, and styles of speaking. There are speech patterns which are associated with geographical area, accents which are considered urban or rural, and special vocabulary or mannerisms which might identify a person's ethnic group, social class, educational background, or occupation. There are styles of speaking appropriate to formal or informal settings, work or play, and there are often differences between men's and women's speech. Besides all this, children have a special status, not just as boys or girls (learning to be men and women) but as *children*. We provide institutions, organizations, sports, entertainment, movies, records, television, films, books, magazines, clothing, furniture, and other equipment—all designed exclusively for children and adolescents. There is much in the way of specialized knowledge, vocabulary, and verbal lore which goes along with all this, which is the special domain of children.

With all this diversity, therefore, there is a great deal of room for individual variation. Some of the reasons for this are obvious: families are on the move; the makeup of households often changes; individuals play different social roles; and children learn from a variety of teachers—parents and other family members, friends, schoolteachers, and mass media such as television. Even though a child is likely to begin speaking like his parents, he may not; and as one grows older, the influence of other models (teachers, peers) will almost surely be stronger than those in the home.

Perhaps the most important linguistic training for adult life which children can receive in a society of this sort is the experience of "code-switching." Children may learn, first of all, the language which they hear at home but in participating in different social roles and situations, they learn the forms of speech appropriate to each one. A little girl may learn to "talk like a lady," but she also learns to talk like one of the boys if she wants to be accepted on the Little League team. A boy may practice "talking tough," but he will not talk that way at Sunday school or synagogue. A family may have private phrases, jokes, or pet names which children learn to use only at home, not in public. Children learn to speak more politely or formally at school, more casually or with more slang in the playground. They may even need to learn how to switch from one language to another, if the language of the home is not that of the school or larger community.

Linguistic variety is a fact of life, and is especially marked in our contemporary society. Everyone has some ability in code switching, because no one speaks in just the same way in all situations. It seems likely, however, that children who learn to use this general ability with greatest facility can also function most comfortably in a variety of adult roles.

THE EFFECTS OF SOCIAL ISOLATION

Special insights into the development of language can be gained by looking at cases in which the normal has not occurred. For example, as Lenneberg indicated, it is of interest to observe the children of deaf parents because their development, under the most difficult conditions, so closely parallels that of children in a normal environment. Similarly, other researchers have studied the linguistic case histories of children with physical handicaps which affect their ability to speak. Such research can be oriented both toward understanding the effects of impairment on the normal acquisition of language, and toward therapeutic methods to overcome or bypass the impairment.

There are also cases in which isolation, either physical or social, has kept children from normal contact with a larger speech community. Examples of such occurrences are "feral children," children who have been found and returned to human society only after years of isolation. Perhaps the most famous of these cases is Victor, the Wild Boy of Avignon, who was found roaming the French countryside in 1797. Like Victor, such children often seem to be mute, and do not appear to recognize speech sounds as such; it is difficult or impossible for them to recapitulate the stages of development which they have missed. Two such children were found in 1920 in India; the younger, Amala, did begin to learn to speak (however, she died within a year), but Kamala, who was eight when discovered, learned only a few words. Victor eventually learned to read, but never to speak (Brown, 1958).

There are more numerous cases of social isolation, of children whose contacts with society are limited or made difficult by the restrictive social conditions under which they live. Under these conditions they may develop unusual, private forms of speech, and some go so far as to invent a language of their own. Something of this sort has often been observed with twins, who normally do learn to speak the language which they hear around them, but also—apparently because of their especially close and intense relationship with one another—develop a private system of communication.

A startling case of twin language was reported, in 1977, in newspaper and magazine accounts of twin girls who, at seven years of age, had retained their private language much longer than is usual. It is estimated that close to half of all twins do have some special code of this sort, but most lose it by around three years of age. Not only did Gracie and Ginnie have a full-fledged private language, but they did not speak English or German (the two languages which they heard at home) or Spanish (the main language in their San Diego neighborhood). When they entered school, they were at first classed as retarded; later, when the nature of their problem became more obvious, they were enrolled with speech therapists for accelerated training in speaking English.

These children appear to have been shy, relying socially almost exclusively on one another until they began school. In their home, the parents spoke English to one another, and German to a grandmother, who knew no English. Tests revealed that the twins understood both these languages perfectly well, but they seldom tried to use them. Besides *Mommy, Daddy,* and a few English nouns, they got by with nonverbal signals, lapsing most often into their private language. One of the most interesting details in this case is the report that Gracie (who is five minutes older than her sister) usually took the initiative in inventing vocabulary. Sometimes, according to their father, Gracie "would hold up an object, and after a brief exchange the girls would agree on a name for it." In this way, they developed a large vocabulary which showed little resemblance to either German or English, though some words apparently were phonological transformations of adult speech (probably originating in "baby talk"). For example, *topit* for "stop it," and *gimba* for "camper" may have come from English, but other words were unrecognizable, such as *dine* for "pen." One of the difficulties in recognizing words, or in transcribing and analyzing their conversations, lay in the extreme rapidity with which they spoke; however, samples of their speech have been recorded and will be studied further by the same speech specialists who have been helping Gracie and Ginnie begin speaking in English.

It seems clear that a multilingual environment contributed to these twins' linguistic isolation. As writers F. Davis and J. Orange (1977) point out, many children grow up in a home where two languages are spoken and learn both quite successfully; but others do not. They may confuse the two, and learn neither perfectly. *Idioglossia* (a term which includes "twin-language" and other private codes) is a common enough phenomenon, but in this case it may have been more important, and retained longer than usual, as a sort of compensation for the difficulties presented by the environment in which the two children found themselves. It would appear that they tried to deal with this environment as they perceived and understood it—a world which included three languages, each closely related to a separate social category. English was their parents' language, German was identified with their grandmother, and Spanish was the language of the outside world. It must have seemed quite reasonable to invent a fourth to serve their own special relationship.

TOPICS FOR STUDY AND DISCUSSION

1. State the opposing views of language acquisition. Try to build a case for each. What are the strengths and weaknesses of each?
2. Spend some time—in a home, playground, or other setting—listening to the speech of young children. Write down exactly what you hear. What typical constructions do you find? Discuss.
3. Does the speech of children have anything in common with the language of early man? Can research on language acquisition be used as evidence for the evolution of language?

4

The Comparative Study
of Languages

EARLY STUDY OF LANGUAGES

From the time of Plato and Aristotle, Western philosophers have discussed grammar and logic and speculated about the nature of language essentially on the basis of their knowledge of their own and other European languages. Greek and Latin, especially, have played a prominent part in establishing our ideas about language. For centuries, Greek and Latin had great cultural importance in the Western world, as languages associated with literature and scholarship, with political and judicial power, and with established religion. Latin maintained a prestigious position throughout western Europe, at least through the time of the Renaissance. Not only did learned men of the Middle Ages and Renaissance know little or nothing about the languages of pagan peoples in Africa. Asia, and the unexplored areas of the world, they also gave short shrift to the vernacular of their own countries. The Germanic, Slavic, Romanic, and Celtic dialects spoken by most of the rural population of Europe were not written or studied, and received as little scholarly attention as Zulu or Eskimo.

Latin, on the other hand, was the object of much study, both because of its literary importance and because of its practical value. There were textbooks and treatises on Latin grammar, because young men who spoke French or Spanish or English had to learn Latin in order to become properly educated and to advance themselves. Greek also was well known to scholars, since it was a language of philosophy and religion and was considered to be an older and more perfect language than Latin. This emphasis on Greek and Latin was so pervasive that by the fifteenth and sixteenth centuries when English, French, and German emerged as languages worthy of study, they were described and taught according to a plan developed with the classical languages. Centuries of study of Latin grammar set a precedent for the description of English grammar, even though the two languages are quite different from one another. (The influence of Latin grammar is still to be felt, as when we use terms like genitive, ablative, or vocative in analyzing the structure of English sentences.)

By the seventeenth century, there was also a respectable amount of study devoted to Hebrew, which had special importance as the language of the Old Testament. Some biblical scholars felt that Hebrew must have been the earliest language, or at least the direct descendant of this language, which was given to Adam and Eve at the time of the Creation and was, therefore, divinely created and perfect. Early comparative studies attempted to trace the origins of words in Greek, Latin, and modern languages to Hebrew, or to reconstruct an earlier language which might be identified with the Creation. Another view held that the languages of the world had been split apart, so to speak, at the time of the tower of Babel; all, therefore, were distorted or transformed versions of the divine language of Creation, and comparisons were undertaken with the hope of revealing some clues about the nature of the original language.

By the eighteenth century, certain European scholars had developed a substantial interest in Arabic, Chinese, Sanskrit, and other Oriental languages. All of these were literary languages of long and respectable antiquity; it was written literature which was being studied and translated, not the contemporary languages as spoken by ordinary people.

However, during the period of the Enlightenment (roughly, the late seventeenth and the eighteenth centuries) there was a great deal of curiosity about the civilizations and cultures of the world, and a growing awareness of the existing variety in the human condition. Some of the earliest speculative anthropologies were written during this time by such authors as Montesquieu, Voltaire, and Locke. Both linguistic and anthropological horizons were broadened by an increase in world travel and trade, giving Europeans a growing amount of information about the rest of the world. Interest in the variety of languages of the world is exemplified by the *Mithradates* of Johann Christoff Adelung, a four-volume work completed in 1817 which presented—as a basis for comparison—the Lord's Prayer translated into 500 languages.

Accounts of the Chinese language, beginning with the journals of Marco Polo, excited a special sort of curiosity, since Chinese was radically different from the languages of Europe. With its short, uninflected words and fixed word order, Chinese seemed to some Western intellectuals to be a more "logical" language than the familiar European tongues; one writer even suggested that Chinese might be the lost language of Creation!

Another point of interest which aroused the admiration of Western scholars was the Chinese system of writing. Unlike the alphabets of Europe, in which letters stands for *sounds*—and which can be read and understood only by persons who know each individual language—Chinese writing employs signs which stand for *ideas*. Persons who speak the several different languages of China (Mandarin, Cantonese, and so on) all learn the same written system, each pronouncing the words of his own language. Writing thus serves the function of communication across language boundaries; individuals whose speech is not mutually intelligible can communicate by writing. In polygot Europe, Latin was by this time on the wane and no longer served adequately as an international language. The idea of developing an international writing system, modeled after the Chinese, seemed an excellent one, and intellectuals of the Enlightenment (Leibniz, for one) expended much effort in analyzing and comparing languages in order to invent such a system.

These efforts failed, unfortunately; no international written language was ever widely accepted, and the efforts to devise one dissipated as a philosophical, rather than a practical, undertaking. However, the analytic approach to language which went into the effort played a part in the future development of linguistics. It led scholars to new theories of semantic structure, to a consideration of universals and variables in language, and to attempts to analyze and explain the many difficulties encountered in translation—all of which are still key problems in the study of language.

LINGUISTICS IN THE NINETEENTH CENTURY

Nineteenth-century comparative linguistics had a prevailingly historical orientation. A strong popular interest in the sources and historical relationships of the languages and peoples of Europe and the Orient inspired a substantial body of careful, detailed research. This scholarship, and the questions and insights which emerged from it, led to many of the theories and approaches which still occupy the attention of linguists in the twentieth century.

Grammarians and philologists of the Enlightenment had spoken of "older" and "younger" languages, and sometimes judged the younger languages (such as English or French) to be degraded or imperfect in comparison to Latin or Greek—as these, in turn, would have been in comparison to the divine language of Creation. The key to a new and more scientific view of language and the relationships among existing languages was a dynamic concept, a concept of linguistic change. This was the crucial development in the linguistics of the nineteenth century.

Historians of linguistics usually date the beginnings of linguistic science from 1786, when Sir William Jones, a British civil servant in India, published a paper calling attention to the similarities among Sanskrit (the classical literary language of India), Greek, and Latin. The revolutionary aspect of Jones's discussion of these similarities was his hypothesis that the three were related *by common descent* from some earlier or ancestral language. This concept of "genetic" relationship and change as an explanation for the origins and similarities among languages became the accepted one, replacing a generally static view which assumed that languages were created more or less in accord with biblical tradition.

Sir William Jones and his contemporaries broadened the horizons of European scholarship by demonstrating that Greek and Latin were related—as the descendants of a common parent—to Sanskrit and, by implication, to other, possibly more distant, kin. Following them, many other scholars advanced the comparative study of languages; among these were Rasmus Rask (1787–1832), Jacob Grimm (1785–1863), and August Schleicher (1821–1868). Rask, a Danish linguist, published in 1814 an essay on the Icelandic language, defining the interrelationships of the Scandanavian languages and, in more general terms, their relationship to other Germanic languages. It is considered one of the earliest rigorous applications of the comparative method in linguistics. Jacob Grimm, between 1819 and and 1837, published an encyclopedic German grammar, in which he traced points of similarity among all major divisions of Germanic tongues, and identified the regular correspondences of consonants in these languages to others more distantly related (in particular, to Greek, Latin, and Sanskrit, as representatives of the earlier parent language). The formula which states these regular correspondences is still commonly referred to as Grimm's Law (see next section).

Three decades later, August Schleicher, another prominent scholar of Germanic languages, undertook the task of reconstructing words and forms of the Indo-European parent language. In order to obtain more complete data for this comparative work, Schleicher wrote a grammar of Lithuanian—a language which, until that time, had not been the subject of scholarly interest. Published in 1857, this was one of the first field studies of a vernacular language, based on speech rather than on literary texts.

By the late nineteenth century, linguistic science had been inspired by developments in the natural sciences, and linguistic change was seen by some as analogous to the workings of evolution. August Schleicher characterized language as a kind of living organism which is born, lives, gives birth to offspring, and eventually dies. He charted the genetic relations among languages in the form of a family tree—a form in which they are still often presented, although many linguists have found fault with this analogy between languages and living organisms. Schleicher also propounded a typological classification of languages, based on descriptive concepts formulated by the influential scholar and philosopher Wilhelm von Humboldt. As adopted by Schleicher and other linguists of his time, it had evolutionary implications.

Following this typology, languages could be classified into three types. An *isolating* or analytic type, in which each word is a single, unanalyzable unit, was seen as the earliest and most primitive type; Chinese is an example. The next stage is the *agglutinative* or synthetic type of language. In this type, words are composed by the mechanical combination of parts (bases, prefixes, and suffixes); Turkish is an example of an agglutinative language. The third and highest types is *inflectional;* words change in form to express a variety of meanings, but are less easily analyzable than the preceding types. This type is exemplified by Latin and Greek. Following the attainment of this highest type of development, languages might fall into decay; thus, clear typological classification was not always possible.

An accumulation of evidence drawn from languages of the world, and the testimony of actual linguistic histories, soon cast doubt on such theories of universal and inevitable stages of language. However, typology remains an interest of modern linguistics, and new approaches to typology play a part in recent efforts to identify universal features of language.

THE COMPARATIVE METHOD IN LINGUISTICS

The early focus of study in comparative linguistics, following the lead of Sir William Jones and his contemporaries, was the large group of languages which includes the Germanic, Romanic, and Slavic languages and extinct languages such as Sanskrit, Latin, and Greek; today, this is called the Indo-European family of languages. Methods of comparison and standards of language description were developed in the study of Indo-European which have since been applied to many other languages.

The comparative study of a group of languages aims, first of all, to confirm or disprove the relatedness of the languages included. The proof of relationship is the discovery of regular parallels or *correspondences* in the phonemes (speech sounds) and grammatical patterns of the several languages. Beyond this, comparisons enable linguists to reconstruct the forms and meanings of earlier times, going back to the remote common ancestor of the group of related languages. A reconstruction attributes to an earlier stage those features which are shared by daughter languages, and suggests forms which seem likely to have given rise to features which are divergent but similar. Such a reconstructed language is identified by the prefix "proto-"; thus, proto-Germanic is the reconstructed ancestor of the Germanic languages, while proto-Indo-European represents a still earlier stage, ancestral to Germanic and all other divisions of Indo-European.

This procedure of comparison and reconstruction resembles, in a general way, the method a biologist might use in studying the evolution of plants or animals. For example, a comparison of the hands of various anthropoids (monkeys, apes, and humans) would lead one to the conclusion that the common ancestor of these closely related animals had a hand with five prehensile fingers, including a short, opposable thumb, and with flat nails on all the fingers—features which are shared by most existing species of this suborder. It becomes obvious, then, that the elongated fingers of the gibbon and orangutan, the atrophied thumb of the spider monkey, and the relatively long, rotatable thumb of *Homo sapiens* are all specializations or adaptations away from the general pattern. Obviously, too, these specializations developed at a later time than did the general features which are shared. A natural scientist, studying such a problem of taxonomy, can sometimes draw on the evidence of fossils which remain from earlier geological periods, and which supplement (and may revise) the conclusions which might be reached by comparison of living creatures.

Similarly, a linguist might compare French *terre,* Spanish *tierra,* and Italian *terra* (all meaning "land"), and come to the conclusion that the earlier form must have been very similar to those in the daughter languages. In this case, the existence in written documents of Latin *terra(m)* serves something of the same function as fossil evidence for the biologist. However, this kind of confirming evidence is not always at hand, and is never available when we are dealing with languages which do not have a history of writing. Therefore, the comparative linguists' reconstructions are based, for the most part, on the general evidence of grammatical parallels and the more specific evidence of cognate words.

Indo-European   Cognate words are words which can be shown to have a common origin; that is, they are descended from forms which were present in the ancestral language. The following list presents several examples of Indo-European cognates, with examples from Sanskrit, Greek, Latin, and English (as a representative of the Germanic languages).

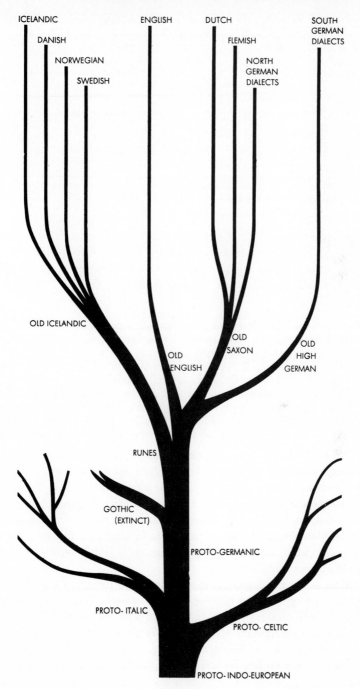

Fig. 8. Family tree of the origin of modern Germanic languages. From "The Origin of Speech" by Charles Hockett. Copyright © 1960 by Scientific American, Inc. All rights reserved.

Sanskrit	Greek	Latin	English	
1. pitár	patér	pater	father	*p
2. trájah	trejs	tre:s	three	*t
3. kravih	kréas	crûor	(O.E. hreaw) raw	*k
4. pad	póda	pedem	foot	*d
5. yugá-	zugón	iugum	yoke	*g
6.	kannabis		hemp	*b
7. bhratar	phrā:tēr	fra:ter	brother	*bh
8. vidháva	e:itheos	divido	widow	*dh
9. hári	khólos	helvus	gold	*gh
10.		porcus	pork	—

Adapted from Bruce L. Pearson, Introduction to Linguistic Concepts. *Copyright © 1977 by Alfred A. Knopf, Inc. Reprinted by permission.*

In reconstructed forms of this sort, each letter stands for a set of corresponding sounds in the cognate words. It is regularity in these correspondences, in consonants and vowels, which are taken to be the only convincing proof of common origin. Some of these, which can be noted in this list, are stated in summary form as Grimm's Law:

(1) Where the Indo-European parent language had *voiceless stops* (*p, t, k*), the Germanic cognates have *voiceless fricatives* (*f, th* [θ], *h*). Items 1–3 give examples of this set of correspondences.

(2) Where proto-Indo-European had *voiced stops* (*b, d, g*), Germanic cognates have *voiceless stops* (*p, t, k*). Note, especially, items 4–6.

(3) Where the ancestral language had *aspirated voiced stops,* (*bh, dh, gh*), Germanic cognates have *voiced stops* (*b, d, g*). Items 7–9 include examples of this type of correspondence (it is less obvious than the other types, because the aspirated voiced stops have also been lost in Greek and Latin).

Once the regular patterns of correspondences have been established, linguists can determine whether individual words which show resemblances are true cognates. Sometimes resemblances are simply coincidental. More often, words are simply borrowed from one language to another. It may prove relatively easy to spot these because they are more recent, and are apt to resemble one another more closely, than true cognates. Item 10 is an example: English *pork* is a loan from French (while the true Germanic cognate is Old English *fearh,* retained as modern English *farrow*).

It will be noted in comparing the words in the list given here that consonant correspondences appear to be more regular than vowels. This has been obvious from the time of early comparative studies. Corrections and modifications of Grimm's formulas have been concerned with explaining irregularities and apparent exceptions, and with the vocalic system. This is complex and involves changes of vowel quality, since vowels are affected by position in the word, stress, and other factors.

Karl Verner (1846–1896), a Danish linguist writing in the late nineteenth century, explained some apparent exceptions to Grimm's Law which arose from the location of stress in the proto-language. (His formulation is sometimes referred to as Verner's Law.) In 1878, Ferdinand de Saussure (1857–1913) was able to explain the seemingly erratic behavior of many vowels as responses to the influence of a type of consonant which, he asserted, must have been present in the ancestral language (but was lost in the descendants). Some of these theories are still matters of discussion and disagreement. Grimm and other founders of Indo-European study had discovered the basic patterns and rules of correspondences, and their work was the point of departure for many later modifications and new discoveries and theories.

Algonkian   In the 1920s, Leonard Bloomfield, a prominent American linguist, undertook a comparative study of the Algonkian languages of North America. This was an important step in the history of linguistics, because Bloomfield intended his study to be a test case, applying the comparative method to a group of languages which lacked the extensive written documentation found in other languages. Bloomfield made use of previous descriptive studies of Algonkian languages by other scholars, but relied primarily on his own field studies of four languages of north central North America: Cree, Ojibwa, Menomini, and Fox. Because he did not have adequate information on the more peripheral divisions of the Algonkian family, including languages of the Great Plains (such as Cheyenne and Blackfoot) and the Atlantic coast (such as Micmac, Abenaki, and several extinct languages of New England), Bloomfield concentrated on languages of the Great Lakes area and called his reconstructed ancestral language proto-Central Algonkian (or PCA) (Bloomfield, 1946).

English	Fox	Cree	Menomini	Ojibwa	PCA
man	ineniwa	iyiniw	enɛɛniw	inini	*elenyiwa
stone	asenya	asiniy	aʔsen	assin	*aʔsenya
louse	ihkwa	ihkwa	ehkuah	ikkwa	*ehkwa
kettle	ahkohkwa	askihk	ahkeeh	akkik	*axkehkwa
duck	šiišiipa	siisiip	seeʔsep	šiišiip	*šiiʔšiipa
my grandmother	noohkomesa	noohkom	noohkomeh	nookkomiss	*noohkomehsa
I place him	netasaawa	nitahyaa	nettaaʔnaw	nintassaa	*netaʔlaawa

Later Algonkianists have broadened the scope of the comparative studies which Bloomfield initiated. Other Algonkian languages, which were not a part of his data, have been found to conform well to the outlines established for proto-Central Algonkian. Proto-Algonkian is now well established, and the comparative work has been extended to the discovery of more remote relationships. Bloomfield's studies both launched a continuing tradition of Algonkian research, and also inspired similar work on other aboriginal language groups in North America: Siouan, Athabascan, Salishan, and others.

Bantu   A third group of languages which early invited, and received, comparative study is found in Africa. According to Malcom Guthrie, a leading modern scholar of African languages, the Bantu languages number at least 300; they are spread over a large part of the African continent (see Map 1). Most of these languages show such obvious resemblances that the fact of their common origin has never really been in question. But, at the same time, the distribution of features among the different languages makes it very difficult to set up neat subdivisions within Bantu, and the historical picture is obviously complex (Guthrie, 1967).

Bantu was established as a language family through studies done by pioneer Africanists such as the German scholars C. Meinhoff and D. Westermann. Westermann also noted the more remote resemblance of the Bantu group to languages further to the north, but he left the nature of this resemblance unclear. Later scholars established these more distant relationships, and the American linguist Joseph Greenberg has classified Bantu as a division of the Niger–Congo family, within the Congo-Kordofanian phylum of languages (Greenberg, 1968).

Some striking similarities among languages can be seen in the table of nouns taken from an early survey of Bantu shown below (Werner, 1919).

LANGUAGE, TIME, AND HISTORY

The demonstration of relationships among languages, with the prospect of tracing and reconstructing their common ancestry, holds an obvious interest for anthropology. In 1916, Edward Sapir, one of the most influential of anthropological linguists, wrote an important essay (*Time Perspective in Aboriginal American Culture*) which called for the use of such linguistic evidence—together with the distribution of culture traits and other types of "direct and inferential evidence"—to solve complex historical problems. There are two types of questions which historically oriented anthropologists may hope to answer with the help of linguistic data: (1) Can the prehistoric cultures studied by archeologists—which often can be assigned fairly exact dates—be identified or related to historical cultures or speech communities? (2) Can reasonably accurate dates be determined for the origins, separations, or movements of known population groups, in the absence of solid archeological data?

Such problems are often very difficult to resolve. However, there are methods which attempt to deal with them, bringing linguistic data into use along with information of other types. One of these methods is *lexical reconstruction*.

The reconstructed vocabulary of a proto-language can provide information about aspects of culture. The task of reconstructing vocabulary leads almost inevitably to hypotheses about the prehistoric culture, since words which are cognates in the daughter languages are, by definition, words which have been in existence since the time when the proto-language was spoken. If these cognates have approximately the same meaning in each language, then it seems reasonable to assume that something close to the original meaning has been retained.

Some of the most interesting and productive studies in lexical reconstruction have dealt with the terms for plants, animals, and other vocabulary which can be used as evidence for defining features of habitat or environment. Attempts have also been made to use vocabulary as the basis for inferences as to subsistence pursuits, social and kinship systems, religious concepts, political and military life, and

Noun Class	Zulu	Chwana	Herero	Nyanja	Swahili	Ganda	Giau	Kongo
1. human being	umu-ntu	mo-tho	omu-ndu	mu-ntu	m-tu	omu-ntu	umu-ndu	mu-ntu
2. human being (pl.)	aba-ntu	va-tho	ova-ndu	a-ntu	wa-tu	aba-ntu	baba-ndu	a-ntu
3. tree	umu-ti	mo-re	omu-ti	m-tengo	m-ti	omu-ti		
4. tree (pl.)	imi-ti	me-re	omi-ti	mi-tengo	mi-ti	emi-ti		
5. tooth	ili-zinyo	le-ino	e-yo	dz-ino	j-ino	eri-nyo	li-sino	d-inu
6. tooth (pl.)	ama-zinyo	ma-ino	oma-yo	ma-no	m-eno	ama-nyo	kama-sino	m-enu
7. chest/thorax	isi-fuba	se-huba		chi-fua	ki-fua	eki-fuba		
8. chest/thorax (pl.)	izi-fuba	li-huba		zi-fua	vi-fua	ebi-fuba		
9. elephant	in-dhlovu	tlou	on-dyou	njobvu	ndovu	en-jovu	i-tsofu	nzau
10. elephant (pl.)	izin-dhlovu	li-tlou	ozon-dyou	njobvu	ndovu	en-jovu	tsi-tsofu	nzau
11. wand	ulu-ti	lo-re	oru-ti		u-ti			

(after Werner, 1919)

so forth. Voluminous studies of this sort have been devoted to the reconstruction of Indo-European lexicon, and the approach is increasingly attractive to specialists in the study of other language groups. For example, a major work on proto-Athabascan kinship by an ethnologist, D. F. Aberle, and a linguist, I. Dyen, is both an important test of the method and a contribution to an issue of theoretical interest in social anthropology, the origins of matrilineal kinship in certain American Indian societies (Dyen and Aberle, 1977).

Lexical reconstruction achieves results of interest to anthropology through comparisons which make use of "cultural" vocabulary—vocabulary which can vary as culture itself varies. Reconstructed cultural vocabulary might lead us to conclude, for example, that the people who spoke a particular proto-language were big-game hunters or agriculturalists or maritime folk, lived on dairy products or meat or grain, believed in nature spirits or worshiped their ancestors—depending on the richness or paucity of cognate vocabulary in particular areas.

On the other hand, there is seldom any distinctive cultural information to be gained from the terms for eating, breathing, walking or talking, for body parts, earth, water, wood, or stone. Such things are universal or inevitable in human experience. This type of "culture-free" vocabulary, however, has proved especially valuable as the basis for the best available method of arriving at dates and time estimates for the origins of languages or the separation and dispersal of groups of related languages. *Lexico-statistical dating* (or *glottochronology*) is a method developed by Morris Swadesh, a distinguished anthropological linguist and a student of Edward Sapir. Like Sapir, Swadesh was a specialist in the study of American Indian languages, and was intrigued by the challenge of discovering clues to their origins and relationships.

Seeking a method for assessing or measuring linguistic change, Swadesh reasoned that cultural vocabulary could sometimes be stable or could change rapidly; words for plants or animals, for example, could be lost as people migrate from one area to another, and technical vocabulary might increase greatly in response to inventions or cultural contacts. On the other hand, "culture-free" or *basic* vocabulary would appear to be fairly immune to such nonlinguistic influences. If this proved to be the case, Swadesh reasoned, the rate of change would be a minimal one, and the degree of change found in any given case could serve as a sort of index of elapsed time.

Pursuing this idea, Swadesh and several of his associates formulated, tested, and refined a list of basic vocabulary (there are 100- and 200-word versions of the list) and used it to make preliminary studies of a number of languages for which more than a thousand years of documentation is available—Chinese, Egyptian, Greek, Latin and its daughter Romanic languages, and several others. It was found that in such cases, when earlier and later vocabularies could be contrasted, the rate of change of basic vocabulary was surprisingly regular; words were lost and added, or replaced, at the rate of approximately 18 to 20 out of 100 in a thousand years' time (Swadesh, 1959).

When a percentage derived from this is taken as a constant, it becomes possible to estimate the time of separation of related languages simply by counting shared or cognate items in the basic list. This calculation can be done by listing words in parallel columns, examining them one by one, and judging each pair of words as "same" ($+$) or "different" ($-$). Then, using a standard formula, the count can be translated into years of separation. The formula is: $t = \log C \,(2 \log r)$, where t = time (in thousands of years), C = percentage of cognates, and r = the constant rate of retention (.805) (Gudschinsky, 1956).

There has been much discussion and debate, pro and con, concerning the application of lexicostatistical dating. There are few linguists who would accept the time estimates at face value; yet glottochronology excites great interest among anthropologists as a method which is fairly easy to apply and which yields tangible results.

Indo-European Origins   Since the initiation of the techniques of lexical reconstruction, developed by August Schleicher in the mid-nineteenth century, linguists have done extensive research toward describing the culture and identifying the homeland of the ancient Indo-European people. There was, at first, an inclination to suppose that Sanskrit was the closest to the proto-language and that the early location might have been in India. However, the linguistic data clearly disprove this. The proto-Indo-European language had terms for trees such as birch, beech, oak, willow, and fir (but not fig, olive, or grape); for wolf, bear, lynx, and fox (but not for elephant, monkey, or tiger). There are proto-Indo-European cognates which refer to cattle, sheep, horses, pigs, and goats; to barley, bees, and honey; to the hedgehog, turtle, beaver, otter, and salmon. The weight of the evidence of such lexicon seems to point clearly to a forested environment and a temperate climate, somewhere between the Mediterranean and the Baltic Seas. The concurrence of beech trees, salmon, and turtles limited the possible choices and prompted some scholars to identify an area along the coast of the Baltic as the "proto-Indo-European homeland." Further, while the reconstructed vocabulary indicates that both domesticated plants and animals were known, the weight of the lexicon seems to be toward pastoralism; the number of words associated with cattle and sheep is especially large (Thieme, 1964).

Partly through the interpretation of early written inscriptions, partly through the use of glottochronology, and partly by assessing the relative degrees of similarities and differences among languages and proto-languages, the time of the existence of proto-Indo-European (either as a single language or as a group of closely related languages and dialects), can be estimated at about 5000 to 6000 B.C. There have been several attempts to identify the ancient Indo-European with known prehistoric peoples; some archeologists have favored a pastoral horse-raising people called the Kurgans, who migrated into Europe from the steppes of Russia in the fifth century B.C.

Another theory, which seems more likely, suggests that the Indo-Europeans can be identified with people living in the Danube basin around 6000 B.C. (exemplified by a site called Starčevo), who adopted agriculture through their trade contacts with the Mediterranean. This change in subsistence made possible an expansion in population, eventually leading to migrations in search of new lands. As farmers, they were able to make use of areas which were not productive for the smaller populations of hunting peoples already present (Claiborn, 1977). In short, it appears that the territorial expansion of Indo-European can be identified with the spread of Neolithic culture northward and westward in Eurasia (this theory says nothing about the Indo-European invasion of India and Iran, which was a separate and later movement—see Map 2).

The Proto-Algonkian Homeland   The combined efforts of a number of students of the Algonkian languages, over the four decades since Leonard Bloomfield initiated a specialization in this field, have resulted in the accumulation of a body of comparative data which may be second only to that on Indo-European tongues. In 1967, F. Siebert published a study which utilized reconstructed terms for 53 species of plants, animals, birds, and fish as the basis for locating the geographical area inhabited by the proto-Algonkians. There are terms for widespread species of temperate and subarctic North America such as the common raven, golden eagle, great horned owl, and pileated woodpecker; porcupine, squirrel, moose, skunk, and bear; and familiar American trees such as elm, white spruce, maple, and willow. The names of a few species, however, are critical for Siebert's identification of the proto-Algonkian homeland: woodland caribou, harbor seal, and lake trout are all found in the proto-Algonkian vocabulary. The community of speakers, then, must have lived in an area where all three were present, a requirement which narrows the search to areas adjacent to the upper St. Lawrence River, Hudson's Bay, and the Great Lakes. On the basis of these and other considerations, the core area appears to be, at around 1200 B.C., an area ". . . between Lake Huron and Georgian Bay and the middle course of the Ottawa River, bounded on the north by Lake Nipissing and the Mattewa River and on the south by the northern shore of Lake Ontario, the headwaters of the Grand River, and the Saugeen River" (Siebert, 1967). From this early homeland, the Algonkian peoples expanded through the larger northern Great Lakes area by 900 B.C.; by 1500 A.D., a diversity of Algonkian languages covered much of the northeastern quadrant of North America (see Map 3).

Another Algonkian specialist, Willard Walker, has recently contributed to the reconstruction of proto-Algonkian material culture and social life, and has attempted to relate Siebert's localization of proto-Algonkian to known archeological horizons. Tentatively, the Middle Woodland culture called Early Point Peninsula, which archeologists date as early as 3000 to 2500 years ago, can be identified—in time span, spatial location, and overall culture content—with the proto-Algonkians (Walker, 1975).

The Early History of the Bantu Peoples   The close similarities among languages of Bantu peoples over a very large part of Africa suggests that they, like the Algonkians, spread out at a fairly recent time. This is especially true of the southern and eastern parts of the Bantu area. Swahili, a Bantu language of the east coast of Africa, has been much used for centuries as a trade language; this has been facilitated by its general similarity to many other languages of east Africa, making the learning of one by speakers of the others a relatively easy task. Comparisons of Bantu with other African languages led J. Greenberg to the conclusion that Bantu is a subfamily, a part of a larger family which he has called Niger–Congo. The greatest diversity within this family is in west-to-central Africa, between the west coast and Lake Chad; the eastern and southern languages, on the other hand, are the most uniform. These facts alone would suggest that the direction of movement of Bantu was from the northwest toward the southeast.

Close examination of Bantu vocabularies has led specialists, such as D. Dalby and M. Guthrie, to divide the languages into several groups and to suggest the routes by which migrations may have taken place: (1) The suggested early center of dipersal was located in the vicinity of Cameroon, and the direction of movement was from west to east, limited on the south by the dense equatorial forest; the extreme point reached in this movement was an area in northeast Zaïre near Lake Albert. (2) A separate expansion carried Bantu speech southward, along the coast or by river routes to the southern margins of the equatorial forest; here, a center of dispersal for the western half of the modern Bantu area (Angola and southwest Africa) developed. (3) A later wave of movements from the area of Lake Albert sent Bantu to the south, southeast, and southwest. (4) A late center of activity in south central Africa (Zambia) brought together elements of the western and eastern areas, and sent out a wave of languages ancestral to most of those now known in southeast Africa (Kenya to Zimbabwe-Rhodesia and the Republic of South Africa).

One sign of the ultimate northern origin of these languages is the existence of words for cattle and sheep, common to the different divisions of Bantu, which prove to have been originally borrowed from non-Bantu languages of the Sudan. This suggests that the knowledge of pastoral pursuits was acquired in the Sudanic area, one of the early Neolithic centers in Africa. Other widely dispersed Bantu vocabulary includes several terms associated with metallurgy—items such as "iron," "forge," and "bellows."

The time span within which linguists place the dispersal of Bantu, roughly the last 3000 years, is matched well by the archeological evidence for the beginnings of African iron-working. The earliest metal tools are found in the Sudan and date from the first millennium B.C. From here, the working and use of iron, as part of a culture complex which includes a distinctive type of pottery, spread eastward. Important Early Iron Age sites in the Lakes area date from between 300 B.C. and 100 A.D. Along the west coast also, iron-working was developing at this time.

A later wave of Iron Age cultures, which superseded the earlier and simpler horizons, came in the eleventh century A.D. This led to the merging throughout southeastern Africa of eastern and western metallurgical traditions. Drawing together the linguistic and archeological evidence, D. W. Phillipson comments that there is ". . . a marked degree of similarity . . . between the archeological sequence of the Iron Age in subequatorial Africa and the linguistic evidence for the spread and development of the Bantu languages and their speakers" (1977).

The complex pastoral and agricultural societies of these Iron Age Bantus, then, outnumbered and replaced simpler societies, Bantu and non-Bantu, which preceded them. Some remnant groups of the latter type still survive in the Bushman and other Khoisan-speaking peoples of South Africa (see Map 1).

TOPICS FOR STUDY AND DISCUSSION

1. How did the concept of an Indo-European family of languages develop? How was it extended to other groups of languages?
2. Go through several pages of a German–English dictionary and write down all the German words which you recognize as resembling English vocabulary. Do the same with Latin, French, Spanish, and/or other languages. Compare the results. Can you tell the difference between cognate words and borrowings?
3. Make a word-by-word comparison of a passage written in an older form of English (a section of Chaucer's *Canterbury Tales*, for example) with its translation into modern English. How much has the language changed, over how many centuries? What general types of change do you find?
4. What are some of the noticeable differences between British and American English? American and Australian? Can you explain these differences?
5. How can languages be used in reconstructing the history of a people? Discuss, with examples.

5

Description and Analysis of Languages

It has been the concern of most linguists to study and describe the existing variety of languages. This includes, first of all, the identification and notation of speech sounds and the recording and analysis of the forms of language in objective fashion. If this much is accomplished, the materials collected by one scholar can be reused, classified, and compared by others at other times; they can even be reinterpreted or used for purposes unconnected with the original study. Languages are, first and foremost, to be described in and of themselves, as self-contained systems without reference to any other standard. Most of all, it is this approach to language which modern linguists have come to regard as a scientific approach, since they feel that the methods which have been developed are as rigorous and objective as those physical or mathematical sciences.

SPEECH AND LANGUAGE

Ferdinand de Saussure (1867–1913), a famous and influential Swiss linguist, epitomized in his own work a major change which took place from the historically oriented linguistics of the nineteenth century to a somewhat different orientation in the early twentieth century. This change amounts to a turning away from the comparative approach—which had accomplished so much in the study and reconstruction of Indo-European, Ural-Altaic, and other language families—to give a priority to methods of recording and describing individual languages. There was, in other words, a shift in emphasis from comparative to descriptive linguistics.

Saussure has been mentioned as a prominent student of Indo-European languages who was able to formulate rules which explained a number of apparent irregularities in the vowels of the reconstructed proto-language. He was also a general theorist of language, and he was dissatisfied with the piecemeal way in which languages were usually compared, often simply as words and isolated forms taken out of context. It was Saussure's view that languages should be analyzed as systems in which each part is related to each other part. Accordingly, he perceived change to be a process affecting the whole fabric of language, a process which cannot be understood satisfactorily by comparing sets of cognate words. In a famous analogy, Saussure compared language to a game of chess, commenting that ". . . if I use ivory chessmen instead of wooden ones, the change has no effect on the system, but if I increase or decrease the number of chessmen, this change has a profound effect on the 'grammar' of the game." At any given moment, the chessboard is in a state of equilibrium; each piece has a particular value in relation to all the others, and a move has far-reaching effects. "A certain move can revolutionize the whole game and even affect pieces that are not immediately involved." In a similar way, according to Saussure, a language can be viewed as an intact system at any time, without regard to its history; what may have seemed to be a small change (such as a shift of stress) will prove to be related to many other things (such as the length of words, the phonetics of neighboring syllables, and so on).

As a renowned teacher, Saussure had a great deal of influence on the linguistics of his time; his *Course in General Linguistics* (1958; orig. 1916), a book based on his lectures and compiled after his death by several of his students, is one of the classics of modern linguistic science. One reason for an eager acceptance of innovations in linguistic method and theory was the need felt by many researchers (especially anthropologists) for standard procedures to deal with languages which, unlike those of Europe, do not have a written literature. Franz Boas was one of these; as an anthropologist, he was determined that the study of language should play a part in the study of culture, and that languages should be recorded and described objectively (see Chapter 1). Boas's linguistics put great emphasis on the need to approach "primitive" languages without preconceptions based on a familiarity with European languages. He wanted his students to be aware of the great variety of sounds, grammatical processes, and meanings to be found in languages, and to be able to discover and record any of these in any language. Under the impetus of field research, then, attention turned from dictionaries and documents to the phonetic transcription and interpretation of speech sounds.

In emphasizing the fact that language is a *system,* Saussure was indicating that it is the contrasts, or *oppositions,* among the sound units of language shared by the speakers, rather than the particular sounds of individual speakers, which have fundamental importance. Individual speakers may vary among themselves, and the same individual will not even pronounce the same words in the same way; yet this does not interfere with communication. We hear and interpret speech, the particular utterances of particular speakers, within a framework provided by our general knowledge of a given language. Thus, for example, speakers of English vary greatly in their pronunciation of the sound /s/; some pronounce it forcefully, with a lot of frictional noise; some more lightly: some with the tip of the tongue near the teeth; some with the blade of the tongue near the hard palate (an important difference in some languages but not in English); and some even produce /s/ with an accompanying whistle—but none of this is important for understanding. The important thing is that the /s/ contrasts with the sounds that resemble it most closely, that is, /z/, /š/ (the *sh* sound) and /θ/ (the voiceless *th* sound), so that "sip" and "zip," "sin" and "shin," and "sink" and "think" all remain distinct.

According to Saussure, *parole,* or speech, is individual and particular; it provides the raw material from which the linguist can determine the system of a language. *Langue,* language, is a social fact, a convention agreed on by a community of speakers. The fact that we have such a conventional understanding enables us to use our language quickly and automatically as a tool for transmitting information.

In other words, we do not have to think about forming and interpreting speech sounds; as we learn the language this becomes automatic—and so we can think about formulating and interpreting the messages conveyed by the sounds.

The distinction between speech and language has been generally accepted in twentieth-century linguistics, and is basic to the ways in which languages are described and analyzed. The American linguist, Leonard Bloomfield (1887–1949) was influential in developing the principle of the autonomy of language as an object of study. This means that the patterns of language operate with regularity and can be studied in a scientific way, as laws. Following Bloomfield's ideas, as developed in his major work, *Language* (1933), the points of agreement in grammatical form and the shared system of meanings which constitute a linguistic system are the bases of linguistic study. For most purposes, a linguist does not need to describe all the individual variations among speakers, much of which can be ignored. (In Section 6, it will be seen that some modern linguists depart from these assumptions, turning attention to variation rather than to shared features of language.)

It might be noted that the linguistic assumptions under discussion here are very similar to those made by most cultural anthropologists. In the traditional anthropological approach to behavior, it is regular, habitual, and shared patterns of behavior which are of interest, and it is these which are put forward in a cultural study. (For those interested in exploring this resemblance between linguistic and cultural theory, it might be noted that there is a close connection between Saussure's ideas and those of the French sociologists of his day, the most prominent of whom was Émile Durkheim, an important figure in the history of anthropology as well as sociology.)

Another way of viewing the distinction between speech and language is to see the latter as a plan or design, a mental abstraction shared by members of a speech community, and manifested in their individual acts of speaking. (Such a view also has its parallels in theories of culture.) This mental construct is developed, in the individual, partly on the basis of clues which he finds in the speech of others; it may also be based in part on an inherent human capacity for language. As we noted above (Chapter 3), some linguists have come to advocate the view that the most basic properties of language are, in fact, inborn rather than acquired.

This is, essentially, the view of language developed by Noam Chomsky, a linguist of great influence during the period since the publication of his book, *Syntactic Structures,* in 1957. Referring to the importance of a native speaker's linguistic knowledge, or competence, Chomsky attempts to discover the abstract form of language, *deep structure,* through introspection. That is, he bases his analysis primarily on his own knowledge of his native language, English, and discounts the efforts of others to study languages on the basis of a *corpus,* or collection of speech data.

Chomsky's position is a complete reversal of the approach to language study which has been advocated by most anthropological linguists. However, it does attempt to shed light on aspects of language structure which the more traditional approach does not deal with. It has been especially influential in leading to a discussion of general characteristics of language (rather than the distinctive characteristics of individual languages) and to a positing of universal properties of language.

APPROACHES TO LINGUISTIC DESCRIPTION

Analysis and description of the systematic features of any language can proceed in either of two ways. First, the larger units of speech can be taken as the starting point. These might be whole utterances, or the segments of utterances marked by pauses, by change of speaker, shift of topic, and so on. Such large segments can be progressively broken down into component units such as sentences and phrases, and these into still shorter units, such as words, or groups of words with identifiable functions; and so one can go on to identify progressively smaller "building blocks" of language, including the components of individual sounds. This approach, which gives priority to the study of syntax—the broad, logical relationships among words and phrases—is most conveniently applied to the analyst's own language. It rests on a "native speaker" competence in the language, and certainly does not resemble the approach which a foreigner would take in learning a language new to him.

An opposite approach would be to start with the minutiae of speech, to become proficient in identifying vowels and consonants (recognizing, pronouncing, writing them down), using them in single words or short utterances, and learning how these are built up; and, finally, learning the rules for combining these units into longer grammatical sentences and utterances. This more closely parallels the way in which a foreigner's learning of languages is usually undertaken.

Both of these methods—the method of "working down" and the method of "working up"—are useful approaches for gaining certain types of insight into linguistic problems. Anthropological linguists, when doing research which involves fieldwork, have usually studied languages which are foreign to them and of which they often have no prior knowledge. They have, therefore, tended to follow the procedure of "working up," discovering the structure of the language bit by bit and, in the process, gaining both increased competence in communicating with the native speakers and a valuable source of insight into the culture of these same people.

For this kind of situation, linguists have developed field methods which are equally applicable to any natural language, and which can be relied on to provide an adequate and complete description of the *phonology* (the system of sounds), *morphology* (the meaningful units and structure of words), and *syntax* (the structure of phrases, sentences, and larger units of language). These are the three levels of structure usually included in a descriptive grammar.

PHONOLOGY: LANGUAGE AS SOUND

Phonology is the most general term for the study of speech sounds. Two other terms are often used to distinguish two different types of study, each of which has its own methods and objectives: phonetics and phonemics.

Phonetics includes methods for identifying and describing sounds which enable the linguist to make an inventory and arrive at an objective description of the sounds of any language. This requires a skill in hearing, identifying, and writing down the small details of speech; recordings and laboratory equipment for the instrumental analysis of sound are also sometimes used. On the phonetic level of analysis, languages may resemble or differ markedly from one another; but all the sounds of human speech can be identified and described according to the same basic principles.

Phonemics consists of, most importantly, a concern with the system, or internal organization, of the sounds of any particular language. Phonemic analysis involves the use of methods aimed at discovering this system, identifying the *phonemes,* or functional units and categories of sounds, and the variations in these and the rules of order, combination, and selection which are unique to a particular language.[1]

Phonetics: An Inventory of Speech Sounds   As long as linguistic scholars were chiefly occupied with the languages of Europe and the rest of the civilized world, they were able to rely primarily on written documents. They tended (as many people in our own society still do) to identify *language* with *writing.* However, most non-Western languages did not have, and many still do not have, an established form of writing. Moreover, those languages which have a long history of writing employ a variety of traditional orthographies, many of them highly conventionalized and each with its own particular quirks of spelling and punctuation. Comparison of these is an art in itself. Spelling rules may vary considerably, even between very closely related languages such as Spanish and Portuguese. There is no "natural" association between speech sounds and written symbols; writing systems are, at best, only imperfect ways of recording spoken language. Most of us who have learned to read and write English as our first language are aware of some of the inconsistencies of our spelling system. For example, the letter *o* stands for three sounds which most speakers can (if they listen) distinguish as different in the words "No, not now," and for a fourth in the second syllable of "button" (a vowel similar to but lower than that written as *u* in the first syllable).[2]

We are accustomed to such oddities as the *gh,* which a spelling reformer might want to replace by *g* in *ghost,* by *f* in *enough,* and leave out entirely in *bright* or *slough.*

These conventions of our writing system (*orthographic conventions*) do not really trouble us once we have grown accustomed to them. But it would be quite another thing to attempt to use our orthography to transcribe words of a completely unfamiliar language, or to try to read back those words as written down

---

[1] Some cultural anthropologists have used these linguistic terms, *phonetics* and *phonemics,* as the basis for terms which distinguish different types of cultural description. One linguist, K. Pike, was the first to develop this parallel between linguistic and cultural analysis, coining the terms *etics* and *emics* to apply to levels of cultural description. The current adaptation of these terms, as by anthropologist Marvin Harris, has departed somewhat from their implications for linguistics.

[2] [o^w], [a], and [æ] in the author's pronunciation. In *button* the first vowel is [ə], the second [ɨ].

by someone else, perhaps a Frenchman or German with different rules of spelling and pronunciation.

When travelers and explorers from various Western countries have attempted to record the names of places, peoples, and other vocabulary (such as the terms associated with plants and animals) from the native languages of the Americas, Africa, and the Orient, there has often been a great deal of inconsistency and confusion. For example, the northwest coast American Indian tribal name which is now usually written as *Tlingit* is found in various sources (German, French, Danish, English) as *Thlinkit, Tlinkit, Thlinkeet, T'linkets, Klen-e-kate,* and *Klen-ee-kate.* The neighboring Chinook of Washington and Oregon have been called *Chinuk, Tshinuk, T'sinuk, Tschinuk,* and *Cheenook.* And the Cherokee, of the southeastern United States, have been variously identified as *Tschirokes, Chirokis, Chelekee, Shannaki* and *Tsalagi* (Powell, 1891).

In part, such lack of agreement obviously reflects the different spelling conventions of the reporters. The consonantal sound which an English writer would record as *ch* (as in *Cherokee* or *Chinook*), would typically be written as *tch* by a French and *tsch* by a German writer. But in part also, there are differences which simply derive from the efforts of the reporters to deal with speech sounds which may resemble, but are not identical with, sounds in their own languages. This undoubtedly accounts for the variant spellings of the initial part of *Tlingit* (*tl, thl, t'l,* and *kl*), and the variation between a medial *r* and *l* in *Cherokee.*

One truth which emerges from these efforts is that there is an almost endless variety in the sounds of languages. As Franz Boas observed: "The number of sounds that may be produced . . . is unlimited. In our own language we select only a limited number of all possible sounds. . . . A comparison of the sounds of the well-known European languages—like English, French, and German; or even of the different dialects of the same languages, like those of Scotch and of the various English dialects—reveals the fact that considerable variation occurs in the manner of producing sounds, and that each dialect has its own characteristic phonetic system . . ." (Boas, 1911). In other words, the human speech organs can produce great variety in sounds, from which any individual language or dialect uses only a fractional part. Because of this variety, one of the most essential steps in the history of linguistics was the development of an accurate, objective method for identifying and transcribing sounds. The need for this *phonetic transcription* is perhaps most obvious when one is dealing with remote or "exotic" languages which do not have accepted, standardized writing systems to guide the foreign student. However, as Boas pointed out, there also is variation among the dialects of the same language, which could hardly be studied with any accuracy if one relied on a single written form.

Boas went on to describe certain speech sounds which are characteristic of American Indian languages but are quite different from those common to European languages—sounds which (like the examples given above) had proved difficult to analyze and transcribe. However, this interest which anthropologists have in the variety of languages is balanced by an interest in the discovery of basic principles shared by all languages. Languages are, Boas pointed out, different in particulars, but are also, in a broader sense, very much alike. Similar types, or classes, of sounds are found in all languages, though each may differ in some details from the others. Like most modern linguists, he recommended that speech sounds be described and classified on the basis of their *articulations*—the ways in which they are produced by movements of the body.

The sounds of speech are produced by: (1) the flow of air exhaled from the lungs; (2) the *voice,* the harmonic sound of the vibrations of the vocal cords, which are set in motion by the flow of air; (3) modifications of this sound in three resonating chambers: the pharynx, the mouth, and the nasal cavity; and (4) articulations which obstruct or constrict the passage of air through these chambers.

(1) In all natural languages, most of the sounds of speech are produced with the help of egressive, exhaled, air. Only a few—the languages of the Bushmen and neighboring peoples of South Africa are the best known examples—makes use of a few ingressive sounds, sometimes called *clicks,* along with the more usual egressive sounds. With the help of muscular movements which close and open the vocal cords, this flow of air causes a vibration of the cords and produces voice. And with the help of articulations, which constrict or partially block its passage, the egressive air produces frictional or explosive *noise.* Voice and noise are the two kinds of sound used in speech.

(2) The vibration of the vocal cords is controlled by a complex system of muscles in the laryngeal area of the throat. The degree of tension and speed of vibration of the vocal cords affect the pitch and quality of the voice. There can be rapid alternation between tensing, with accompanying vibration of the cords (voice) and relaxation, with lack of vibration (voicelessness). All languages make use of this distinction. Vowels, for example, are usually voiced (though they may also be modified by devoicing, or whispering); consonants may be either voiceless (as English *p, t, k, f,* and *s*) or voiced (as *b, d, g, v, z, m, n,* and *r*).[3]

(3) The greatest flexibility of the speech apparatus is found in the supralaryngeal vocal tract, the parts between the larynx and the lips. It is in this area that the human vocal tract has its greatest biological adaptation for speech. The supralaryngeal tract is divided into three main resonating chambers: the pharynx, the oral cavity (which are the most important and the most flexible), and the nasal cavity. The size and shape of the first two of these resonators can be varied in a number of ways, but most importantly by the movement of the *tongue.* The body of the tongue, a large muscular mass, can be pushed forward and back, changing the size and proportions of the pharyngeal and oral cavities. When the tongue is drawn back, the pharynx is constricted and the oral cavity is enlarged; when the tongue is pushed forward, the relationship is reversed. The tongue can also be raised and lowered. Pushing the lips forward or drawing them back is another way of enlarging or restricting the size of the oral cavity.

These movements are responsible for most of the distinctive differences in the quality of vowels. The vowel in *feet,* for example, is produced by pushing the

[3] The reader may become aware of the presence and absence of voice by placing the fingertips lightly on the larynx ("Adam's apple") while pronouncing several words containing these sounds. The vibration of the larynx can be detected in this way. For a start, contrast a long "Sssssss!" (voiceless) with "Zzzzzzz!" (voiced); then go on to compare voiced and voiceless consonants, pronouncing them between vowels and in other environments.

tongue to the front and raising it high in the mouth; the pharyngeal cavity is enlarged, the oral cavity is small, and is constricted even more by drawing back the lips. The reader may form the articulation of this vowel, and then contrast it with the vowels of *foot, fought,* and *fat;* notice the movements of the tongue and lips, which change the size of the oral cavity.

Another change in resonance is brought about by opening or closing off the nasal cavity, by muscular movement of the *velum* (the soft palate). The velic valve can be open or closed; it is open for consonants like *m* and *n,* and for other sounds, usually vowels, which are "nasalized" (French has a number of such vowels).

(4) So far, we have seen that speech sounds are ordinarily formed with exhaled or egressive air; that voice can be present or absent, as can nasal resonance; and that the shape and proportions of the main resonators can be varied a great deal, mainly by gross movements of the tongue. Additional smaller movements of portions of the tongue and of other *articulators,* which obstruct or interfere with the flow of air through the pharyngeal and oral cavities, account for most of the distinctions among consonants. The tip, blade, and back of the tongue, and the lips are movable articulators, touching or forming a narrow constriction with the teeth, alveolar ridge (just back of the teeth), palate, or velum. These articulations are usually described by naming the point of articulation (rather than the articulator): for example, an *alveolar* consonant is formed with the tongue touching, or almost touching, the alveolar ridge, as in the initial sounds in *tip, dip, sip, gyp,* or *zip*).

Thus, consonants can be partly identified by naming the place or *point of articulation;* they are further identified by *type of articulation.* The main types are: (1) *stops,* in which the air passage is completely closed; (2) *nasals,* with a closure of the oral cavity and opening of the nasal cavity; (3) *trills* or *flaps,* characterized by a series of brief closures (like the tongue-tip trill [r] of Spanish, or the uvular flap [r] of French or German). These are often grouped together with (4) *laterals,* in which the tongue is in contact with some point of articulation, while air escapes on one or both sides (as in the initial and final sounds of l and t in *little*). A lateral may have some frictional noise, depending on the force with which the air escapes—frictional noise is generally light for English *l*; it is stronger for [ʎ], the initial sound in the native pronunciation of *Tlingit* (as we noted above).

(5) *Fricatives* are formed by narrowing the air passage. There is audible frictional noise caused by this narrowing, as in the initial sounds of *fit, sip, ship,* and *thin* (f, s, š, θ: voiceless fricatives), and *vine, zip,* and *then* (v, z, ð: voiced fricatives).

(6) The term *affricate* is used for speech sounds which are a combination of stop and fricative—a complete closure released with frictional noise. English examples are the initial and final sound in *church* (č) and the initial in *jam* and *ginger* (ǰ).

Besides single-letter phonetic symbols, linguists frequently use diacritic marks for close, or detailed, phonetic transcription; in the above chart, the subscript caret and dot are examples of this (as in t̬ and x̣). Use of diacritics enables the field-

PHONETIC SYMBOLS

CONSONANTS

	BILABIAL	LABIODENTAL	DENTAL	ALVEOLAR	ALVEOPALATAL	VELAR	UVULAR	GLOTTAL
Stops								
(voiceless)	p		t̪	t	tʸ	k	q̣	ʔ
(voiced)	b		d̪	d	dʸ	g		
Affricates								
(voiceless)			c	č				
(voiced)				ǰ				
Fricatives								
(voiceless)		f		s	š	x	x̣	h
(voiced)	ƀ	v		z	ž	l		
Nasals								
(voiceless or devoiced)	m̥			ṇ	ñ̥	ŋ		
(voiced)	m		n̪	n	ñ			
Flaps, Trills				ř, r			r̥	R
Laterals				l			ḷ	

Semivowels

	w			r	y	(w)		

VOWELS

Tongue in Front	Tongue in Center	Tongue in Back
i (beet)	ɨ (just)[4]	tongue high
ɪ (bit)	ə (about, butt)	u (boot)
e (bait)[1]	a (pot, car)[3]	ʊ (book)
ɛ (bet)		tongue mid
æ (bat)		o[2] (boat)
		tongue low
		ɔ (bought)

[1] bait ([béit] or [béyt]) contains a rising glide from [e]; like [o], [e] does not occur as a simple vowel in most dialects of English.

[2] [bout] or [bówt].

[3] Low vowels are particularly variable in English; for some speakers car may have the same vowel as bought.

[4] Only in unstressed syllables; compare [jist] "Just a minute," [ǰəstis] "Justice."

worker or interviewer to record whatever distinctions or variations he finds of interest in a particular language, or even in a particular individual's speech, while still requiring a fairly limited number of basic symbols. The specific diacritic marks which are used vary considerably, and may even be invented ad hoc to deal with specific languages. However, it is common practice to use the following: ʌ below a letter indicates articulation further forward; . indicates articulation further back; raised ʸ means palatalization ("y-off-glide"); raised ʰ or ' indicates strong aspiration; raised = indicates definite lack of aspiration; raised ʷ stands for labialization (simultaneous lip-rounding); . below the letter (or use of capital letter) stands for voicelessness (m̥ or M).

Skilled phoneticians rely on a combination of experience in perceiving speech sounds (listening to and comparing the sounds of languages), and in mimicry (imitating the sounds) which, in turn, helps them to analyze articulatory movements and identify new sounds. Linguistics students usually receive phonetic training of this sort, working with native speakers or with recordings of various languages and in courses in phonetics, field methods, or other advanced linguistics courses. However, a beginner can practice phonetic transcription by recording his own speech or noting the pronunciation of varieties of English or other languages spoken at home, in the classroom, or on radio or TV.

If you listen to, compare, and attempt to transcribe a list of words as pronounced by several different individuals, you will become aware of the variations which can be found in different speakers of the same language, variations which may usually go unnoticed (though we are usually aware of certain distinctions which mark national and regional dialects). The following words are part of a longer list which has been used in studying regular patterns of variation among regional varieties of English (Trager, 1972). Here we can see differences which might be found in individuals from three different geographical areas A, B, and C (the reader may attempt to identify these, and compare them to his own speech).

	A	B	C
"merry"	mɛri	mɛri	mɛri
"marry"	mæri	mæri	mɛri
"Mary"	meri	meri	mɛri
"wash"	wɔš	wɔiš	waš
"water"	wɔtər	wóʌtər	watər
"greasy"	grisi	grizi	grisi
"penny"	pɛni	pɪ̈ni	pɛni
"about"	əbæut	əbæut	əbaut
"park"	pæˇrk	paək	park

Phonemics: The Systemics of Speech Sounds   Phonetic transcription is an important practical skill for anthropological fieldworkers, whether or not they are primarily interested in language. Phonetic transcription is also basic to most linguistic research since it is essential for obtaining a first objective record of spoken language. This record, however, is raw material, preliminary to further linguistic analysis. Such a preliminary record gives one an inventory of the individual sounds used by speakers of a language; but further analysis is needed to show the relationships of these sounds to one another, similarities and differences among them, and their grouping into functional classes which reflect the patterns of particular languages.

One of the exciting discoveries of twentieth-century linguistics has been the fact that the sounds of languages vary not only in number and selection but also in their structure—the ways that they are organized. The units of language on this level of analysis are called *phonemes*.

In a passage referred to above (p. 58), Franz Boas commented on the variations in the sounds of any language, observing that "each sound is nearly fixed, although subject to slight modifications which are due to accident or to the effects of surrounding sounds" (Boas, 1911). With this observation, he anticipated the concept of the phoneme, a concept which was later developed by linguistic scholars such as Leonard Bloomfield, Edward Sapir, and Morris Swadesh.

The two types of variation to which Boas alluded are those which modern linguists call *free* and *conditioned variation*. A phoneme can be defined as a class or group of sounds (*allophones*) which vary in either of these two ways. As an example of conditioned variation, we might use some of the sounds of English. If we are native speakers of English, we are aware of the voiceless stop consonants (*p, t, k*) as separate and distinct units of sound; we do not usually notice the variations which we make in the pronunciation of these consonants. However, it is easy to detect some of this variation; pronounce each of these stops at the beginning of a word, followed by a vowel: *pot, top,* and *cop*. If you hold your hand or, better still, a piece of paper in front of your mouth, you can detect a fairly strong puff of breath, or *aspiration,* as the initial *p, t,* or *k* is released. To specify this fact, a phonetician might write them as [pʰ], [tʰ], and [kʰ].

Now put the three consonants in a different environment, with each of them as the second consonant (*spot, stop* and *Scot*), and you will find that there is less aspiration as the stops are released. To show the contrast, we might write them phonetically as [p⁼], [t⁼], and [k⁼].

In these examples, the variation between [pʰ] and [p⁼], [tʰ] and [t⁼], and [kʰ] and [k⁼] is automatic; the choices are *conditioned* by the phonological environment—in this case, the conditioning factor is the position of the consonant in the word. Because the variation is automatic, native speakers of English are seldom aware of these choices or, indeed, that there is variation in the sound at all.

The other kind of variation, *free variation,* may also be observed in the sounds of these same words, as they might be pronounced by different speakers or at different times. All of the words have voiceless stop consonants in *final* position; some individuals, when reading a list like *spot, stop, Scot* will strongly release or aspirate all the final consonants, and some will not. Thus, *spot* could have a final [tʰ] or a [t⁼]. Again, the variation would probably not be noticed, unless called to our attention; but is it not automatic (though it probably would be found to relate to rate and style of speaking).

English, as we know, also has a set of voiced stops: *b, d, g;* these occur in fewer environments and show less variation than do the voiceless stops. A distinction between voiced and voiceless phonemes is important in English, characteristic of affricates and fricatives as well as stops. Therefore, a contrast is maintained between voiceless *p, t, k,* and voiced *b, d, g,* in all environments in which both sets may occur.

	ENVIRONMENTS		
Phoneme	Initial, before Vowel	After /s/, before Vowel	Final
/p/	[pʰ]	[p⁼]	[pʰ] or [p⁼]
/t/	[tʰ]	[t⁼]	[tʰ] or [t⁼]
/k/	[kʰ]	[k⁼]	[kʰ] or [k⁼]
Voiceless Stops	Conditioned Variation		Free Variation

When these and other examples of regular allophonic variation in the sounds of English are first pointed out, it may seem that the variation is natural and inevitable. One might expect that the same variation would be found among the sounds of any language. But this is not the case. It is true that various types of allophonic variation are found in all languages, but not the *same* patterns of variation. Languages differ from one another both in the selection of sounds which are used and in the ways that those sounds are organized in relation to one another. In other words, the differences are not only phonetic, but also phonemic.

To explore this concept a bit further, let us compare these English stops with those of another language, Seneca, as written (a) nonphonemically, by a nineteenth-century social anthropologist, and (b) phonemically, by a modern linguist:

Seneca is a native American language which was spoken by one of the five tribes of the powerful Iroquois confederacy, and is still spoken by numerous individuals, especially in reservation communities in New York State and Ontario. The famous nineteenth-century American anthropologist, Lewis Henry Morgan, studied the Seneca and provided a valuable body of information on their kinship system, social organization, and traditions. In Morgan's description of the League of the Iroquois (1851), there are numerous Seneca terms, including the following:

	L. H. Morgan (1851)	W. Chafe (1963)
"my father"	hä-nih	haʔnih
"my grandfather"	hóc-sote	haksoːt
"my grandson"	ha-yä-da	heyaːteʔ
"my aunt"	ah-gá-huc	ʔakeːhak
"my son"	ha-áh-wuk	heːawak
"my daughter"	ka-áh-wuk	kheːawak
"my nephew"	ha-yá-wan-da	heyEːwɔːtEʔ
"my mother"	no-yéh	noʔyEh
"my younger brother"	há-ga	heʔkEːʔ
"they are twins"	da-géek-hä	tekiːkhEh
"we are siblings"	da-yä-gwä-dán-no-dä	teyakwatEːnɔːtEːʔ

Morgan, making a commendable effort to write down the Seneca forms as he heard them, used letters of the English alphabet, plus a number of diacritic marks to indicate variation in vowel quality; stops are indicated by the letters *t, d, k, c,* and *g*. His *k* and *c* are used inconsistently (since both stand· for the phoneme /k/ in English). There is, one notices, no sign of a *p* or *b*—and in this, Morgan's transcription is accurate, since Seneca has no labial sounds except for the semivowel /w/. Seneca does have one stop phoneme which is not matched in English, a glottal stop (/ʔ/), which Morgan seems to have overlooked completely and probably did not hear.

Aside from these points of difference, one would conclude from Morgan's transcription that the Seneca inventory of speech sounds resembles the English by including both voiceless and voiced stops (voiceless *t* and *k*, voiced *d* and *g*). Almost any native speaker of English would agree with Morgan in hearing and recording the Seneca stops in this way. However, in phonemic structure, the English and the Seneca systems differ; the voiced and voiceless sounds *are not in contrast* in Seneca, as they are in English. Therefore, in Seneca, the alternation between [t] and [d] is as automatic and unconscious as that between English [tʰ] and [t⁼]; and Morgan's transcription is in error from the point of view of modern linguistics.

If we compare Morgan's transcription with one made by a linguist and Iroquois specialist, Wallace Chafe, we can also note that Morgan sometimes did not hear [h] when it followed another consonant ([kh]), that he did not distinguish between short and long vowels (indicated here by colon [o:]), and that he did not recognize nasalized vowels E and ɔ, though he sometimes heard the nasal quality and included an *n* in his spelling. So we can see that, as many other amateur linguists, Morgan overlooked phonetic features which were not found in his own language, and imposed a phonemic distinction (between voiced and voiceless stops) which was important in his own language but superfluous in the other (Seneca).

Wallace Chafe writes three Seneca stop phonemes, /t/, /k/, and /ʔ/, and states the rules for variation as follows (1967):

Phonemes	*Allophones*	
/t/	[t]	before consonant (h,s,t, or ʔ) or word-final
	[d]	before vowel or semivowel
/k/	[k]	before consonant or word-final
	[g]	before vowel or semivowel
/ʔ/	[ʔ]	in all environments

A General View of Phonological Systems Speech sounds can be identified and distinguished on the basis of their articulation and production, as discussed above. They also can be identified by means of analysis of sound waves. This approach to the study of sounds is called *acoustic phonetics*.

Whichever approach is taken, it is found that the distinctive phonemes of any language differ from one another in a limited number of ways. There are, in other words, *classes* of sounds, each of which has certain features in common; these features can be taken as the basis for comparing languages. Looking at the labels which we put on phonetic charts, we can speak of *stops, affricates, nasals,* or *laterals;* we can compare languages as to the number of labial or dental or alvolar consonants, front or back vowels, voiced or unvoiced stops or fricatives, and so forth. The fact that sounds and sound systems can be compared in this way makes it possible to have a general science of phonology, to know what is possible or impossible, typical or unusual in languages of the world.

DISTINCTIVE FEATURE ANALYSIS   The most influential attempt at such an all-encompassing view of languages is *distinctive feature analysis,* which was given its definitive formulation in the book *Fundamentals of Language,* by Roman Jakobson and Morris Halle (1956). The terminology which is used by Jakobson and Halle (and by other members of the "Prague School" of linguistics) is difficult, and is based primarily on acoustic, rather than articulatory, phonetics. The theoretical approach to the study of language exemplified in their discussion has been compared with (and, in fact, may have inspired) the structuralist approach in anthropology. In brief, the goal of analysis is the discovery of contrastive features, or oppositions, which serve to differentiate the phonemes in any language. Twelve such features were named by Jakobson and Halle; some or all of these twelve, they suggested, underlie the phoneme systems of all languages in the world. They claim that the "supposed multiplicity of features" which characterizes different languages has been shown to be "largely illusory," since this mutiplicity can be interpreted as just so many manifestations of the same limited stock of oppositions.

As an example, P. Postal analyzes the consonants of Mohawk (an Iroquoian language very similar to Seneca) in terms of seven distinctive features: *consonantal, sonorant, vocalic, grave, nasal, compact,* and *interrupted.* Each consonant differs from (is in contrast with) all the others in at least one of these features (Postal, 1964).

	n	r	w	y	k	p	t	s
consonantal	+	+	+	+	+	+	+	+
sonorant	+	+	+	+	−	−	−	−
vocalic	+	+	−	−				
grave			+	−	+	+	−	−
nasal	+	−						
compact					+	−		
interrupted							+	−

The seven features listed here, plus roughly half a dozen others (the numbers and the names given several of the features have varied slightly in the work of different scholars), are found to underlie the phonemic inventories of all languages. What is revealed most strikingly, then, are universal principles in the way such systems are built.

SUBSYSTEM TYPOLOGY   A rather more practical approach, which preserves the distinctiveness of individual phoneme systems while still aiming at compari-

sons and generalizations, was developed by C. F. Voegelin and several of his associates. Their analysis resulted in an inventory in the form of a series of brief statements which included: 1) the total number of consonants and of vowels, and the
ratio of the two; 2) the distribution of phonemes in terms of articulatory positions
and phoneme series (stops, nasals, vowels, and so on); and 3) a notation of the
separate components (such as voicing, nasalization, or length) which occur in each
phoneme series (Voegelin, 1958). With all of this information codified, it is possible to make rapid comparisons and to speak of the types of systems and sub-
systems which actually do occur in some frequency, and the distribution and vari-
ance within each type (Voegelin and Voegelin et al., 1963).

MORPHOLOGY: LANGUAGE AS MEANINGFUL UNITS AND SEQUENCES

Beyond the analysis of the sounds of language, units of structure can be defined
by isolating stretches of speech (of one or more phonemes' duration) and determining their meanings. These meaningful units (*morphemes*) are delimited, and
the meanings identified, by essentially simple procedures of comparing and contrasting. However, a statement of the distribution, variation, and rules which
govern the occurrence of morphemes may become quite intricate. After the
initial identification of segments, there may be problems in determining whether
those which are similar in form have meanings in common, and vice versa—decisions which, in turn, will lead to treating them as the same morpheme or as separate morphemes. Most major points of difference among linguists, however, are
found in their interpretive statements of grammatical structure, or in the principles
which they follow in formulating ordered series of rules for the building of larger
and more complex grammatical structures out of simpler ones. For present purposes, we will not present an extended discussion of material of this sort. Students
who continue in the study of linguistics will become familiar with current modern
approaches to language description, preferably with the assistance of exercises and
applications of methods to specific language data.

An emphasis on descriptive methods which are appropriate and equally applicable to all languages is essentially a twentieth-century concern. It accompanies the
tremendous growth of modern travel and communication around the world, and
reflects the interest of Western scholars in the languages—as well as the cultures—
of the peoples of the world.

Fieldwork: Obtaining a Corpus of Data   For an anthropological linguist in the
field, initial stages of work may concentrate on phonetic transcription and a preliminary analysis of the phonemes of the language. Some problems of a phonological nature may be left unresolved for future study; therefore, a practical working transcription might be partly phonemic, partly phonetic (with close phonetic
transcription of points which remain to be resolved). From the beginning of
phonological study, however, the linguist is also collecting a body of texts, word

lists, and other speech data with which one can begin study of the morphological and syntactic systems. Any division or separation of these "levels" of analysis is, to a degree, arbitrary. No matter how restricted the specific problem on which the linguist is concentrating, data are also obtained which may be used for other studies by the linguist or by others.

The starting point for grammatical study is the matching of segments which are similar in form and have (or appear to have) similar meanings. The methods used can vary greatly, depending, for example, on the fieldworker's fluency in the language, the degree of bilingualism of the persons who may be serving as informants, and/or the possible need for interpreters to help in translation. The methods that anthropological linguists have typically used, even under favorable conditions, assume little or no initial knowledge of the language being studied, and aim for improved knowledge by defining and exploring both the formal organization and the semantic structures of that language (see Gudschinsky, 1967).

Imagine that you have, either your own fieldwork or from someone else's earlier research, a number of texts with parallel translations in English. If you go through these carefully, you will eventually find some words and phrases which recur in the translations and which will help you recognize (hypothetically, at least) a few words or parts of words in the text. These will serve as the point of departure for further eliciting.

The following example is part of a text which I jotted down early in my study of Arawak. Like many other linguists in the field, I began by asking for single words and phrases, sometimes pointing or asking "How do you say ————?" In order to go beyond this (and to avoid problems which sometimes came up because my informant's Guayanese English and my North American dialect were not completely intelligible), I fell into the habit of asking her to tell me a story, to reminisce, or simply to recount what she had been doing before I arrived that day. I would write this down phonetically, as rapidly as I could from her dictation, and then would read it back phrase by phrase, guided by the pauses (here indicated by diagonal lines) which I had noted in her original rendition. As she repeated and translated each phrase, I would make a few corrections in my original transcription (it was easier to identify word boundaries the second time through), and write down the English translation which she gave me; this is, it should be noted, a whole-phrase or sentence-by-sentence translation, and not in itself sufficient for the analysis or close translation of words and morphemes.

Here is part of a brief text which was acquired in this way:

	1. depéroŋsa (a) buaka/ 2. makotáičita/ 3. čičikidónua maosúañi/
first	4. dáičiŋ tokáritua/ 5. baríka akotáhu dàšikiŋ tómuŋ/
transcription	6. abúaŋdomaŋ makotáičita/ 7. mabúaŋbenàŋ/
	8. úsa tókoton tóra/ 9. hamáiroŋ dašikiŋtoŋ tekénoma

	1. My puppy sick. 2. He don't want to eat.
	3. He does fall often. 4. I think he hurt himself.
informant's	5. Withall I does give food to him,
translation	6. because he sick he don't want to eat. 7. When he ain't sick
	8. he does eat good. 9. Anything I give him, he does eat.

And here are a few comments, which touch on some but by no means all of the points of interest in this text:

1. The transcription is not completely phonemic; there are points I changed my mind about later, and some which have never been completely resolved. The č, for example, which occurs only before the vowel *i*, was later interpreted as a variant of the phoneme /t/; thus čičikidonua can be rewritten as titikidonua. Similarly, the ñ could be rewritten as /n/, and the š as /s/. These variants also occur only before /i/. The vowel segments *o* and *u* were often hard to distinguish; thus *usa* might have been (and in other texts was) written as *osa*. (The best resort, as long as there are any doubts of this kind, is to try to write down exactly what one hears, and even to make note of any indecision.)

There is also some doubt about the status of ŋ in this transcription. Some linguists who have studied Arawak would have written these words with nasalized vowels rather than a nasal consonant (deperǫ rather than deperoŋ). I prefer to consider ŋ a variant of the phoneme /n/. This was a matter of interpretation which I certainly needed to bear in mind if I wanted to compare this material with another linguist's work on Arawak.

2. At first glance, perhaps the only guess one might make about the meaningful elements in this text would be that -pero-, (in deperoŋsa, "my puppy . . .") is a possible loan from the Spanish perro, "dog." It is, but the rest of this compound word is tricky and aroused my curiosity. The first questions I asked after transcribing the text concerned this word; I do not remember just what the questions were, but I wrote down the following in my notebook:

"dog"   péro   "puppy"   perósa
"my dog"   deperóŋ   "my puppy"   depéroŋsà

I recognized the final segement (-sa) as probably the same morpheme which I had elsewhere recorded as osa and -sa, "child," as in dasa, "my child." A little later, in another text, I discovered a parallel in kárina, "fowl," and karinása, "egg."

3. Continuing to compare the transcription and translation, one would be able to discover several segments which recur, such as akotá-, -akota-, and -okoto-, which can be matched in the translation to references to food or eating:

makotáičita   "he don't want to eat"
akotáhu dašikiŋ   "I does give food"
úsa tókotoŋ   "he does eat good"

I could, at this point, have asked questions about eating, to try to obtain forms to compare to these. I did not, but later found examples in other texts: dákota, "I eat"; bokóta, "you eat"; úakota, "we eat"; uakotófa, "we will eat"; dakotáičika, "I want to eat"; wajìli makotáičika, "the man don't want to eat."

4. Another set of words, containing the segment -abua-, appears to refer to sickness:

		Compare:
abúaka	"(he) is sick"	wajili abúaka "the man is sick";
abúaŋdomaŋ	"because he sick"	abúaŋdomade "because I'm sick";
mabúaŋbenaŋ	"when he ain't sick"	mabúaŋbenade "when I ain't sick"

A preliminary examination of texts can be the basis for a tentative list of vocabulary, some hypotheses about word classes, and the inflectional system (like the *de-* and *da-,* which can be tentatively identified as marking the first person singular; *to-* and *ti-,* which is a third-person prefix; and *ma-,* a negative prefix). A number of segments can also be extracted which are similar but not identical in form and meaning. Undoubtedly, other passages will remain which are completely unanalyzable. Some of the linguist's guesses and intuitions can be followed up on the spot; some must be held in abeyance until a later date.

Usually, a fieldworker will try to follow up the translation of a text by working closely with an informant, asking questions directed at clarifying the text by identifying all of the forms. It is helpful to obtain words and phrases which are minimally different from one another in meaning, in order to isolate the corresponding formal differences (as I began to do in (4) above). At about this point I might have rewritten the text, tentatively segmented into morphemes, as follows:

1. de-pero-n-sa abuaka
   my-dog-(poss.)-child is sick
2. ma- (a)kota-iti-ta
   (neg.) eat (desid.)-it
3. t-itikid(a) -on-ua maosuani
   it-fall- (?-intrans.) often
4. da-(a)it(a)-in t-okarit(a)-ua
   I-know (subord.) it-hurt (intrans.)
5. barika akota-hu da- isik(a)-in, to-mun
   Although eat (gerund) I-give-(subord.) it-to
6. abua-n-doma-n ma- (a)kota-iti-ta
   sick (subord)-because-it (neg.)-eat (desid.)-it
7. ma-(a) bua-n-bena-n
   (neg.) sick (subord.) when-it
8. usa to-(a)kot(a)-(h)o-n tora
   good it-eat (gerund) (subord.) that one
9. hama-iron da-(i)sik(a)-in-to-n t-eke-noma
   anything I-give (subord.)-it-to it-eat-does

From this point on, work would be directed toward obtaining a complete inventory of morphemes, their variants, the rules which govern variation, and the relative order in which they occur to make up words and sentences. (For analysis and translation of a longer Arawak text, see Hickerson, 1954.) In practice, eliciting could continue for some time on the basis of a single text. However, one would wish to obtain a variety of materials. Many fieldworkers would begin to collect vocabulary by identifying material objects, artifacts, plants, body parts; asking for these words in different contexts; and working up from single words to longer utterances. Eventually, however the process of eliciting begins, one wishes to record, translate, and analyze folktales, oratory, jokes, religious stories, anecdotes, and various sorts of normal conversation in order to obtain idiomatic constructions and vocabulary not discovered in earlier questioning—things one would not know how to ask for, or for which there is no English equivalent (Samarin, 1967).

Linguistic Diversity The rapid development of methods of collecting and analyzing linguistic data, in the first half of the twentieth century, took the fact of linguistic diversity as a point of departure. Anthropological linguists seem to have been persuaded that anything is possible in language, and that they must be able to discover and deal with the unique or unexpected. In the article discussed below, Edward Sapir (1884–1939) compared the types of morphemes and sentences typical of seven native American languages. In doing this, he was able to build on previous research, by himself and others, devoted to the study of many individual languages. Sapir was an influential figure in a historical period in which there was a strong emphasis on methods in linguistics—methods which should enable the linguist to analyze and describe objectively any and all human languages.

Sapir began his discussion of "American Indian Grammatical Categories" (Sapir and Swadesh, 1946)[4] with the observation that ". . . within the confines of the United States there is spoken today a far greater variety of languages—not dialects, not slightly divergent forms of speech, but fundamentally different languages—than in the whole of Europe." In fact, Sapir comments further, even the state of California contains a wealth of native languages of greater diversity than any comparable area in the Old World. Unlike most of the languages of Europe, these American Indian languages are not known to have a common origin, and in both sounds and structures they present "the most bewildering diversity of form."

Because of this variety, Sapir felt that studies of American Indian languages had, even as early as the 1920s, contributed greatly to knowledge, to a sampling of the total range of variation in the phenomena of language, and to an eventual understanding of the psychology of language and thought. All human languages, he asserted, can be reduced to "a common psychological ground"; but the ground cannot be adequately understood or mapped "without the perspective gained from a sympathetic study of the forms themselves."

Sapir noted the existence of several very widely distributed linguistic features. All the familiar patterns of European languages, he wrote, can be found in those of aboriginal America—but none are universal, and some are encountered which are unique or rare. In order to explore the diversity which he found so impressive, Sapir used the device of translating a single English sentence into several American Indian languages, pointing out some of the characteristic grammatical features of each. The languages used here are Wishram, Takelma, Southern Paiute, Yana, Nootka, Navaho, and Yokuts—all languages of the west or southwest, and all languages which Sapir had studied in the field.

English:	He will give it to you.
Wishram:	ačimlúda (a-č-i-m-l-ud-a)
	will-he-him-thee-to-GIVE-will
Takelma:	ʔóspink (ʔok-t-xpi-nk)
	WILL GIVE-to-thee-he or they (in future)
S. Paiute:	mayavaaniaakʔanaʔmi (maya-vaania-aka-ana-ʔmi)
	GIVE-will-visible thing-visible creature-thee
Yana:	baːjamasiwaʔnuma (baː-ja-ma-si-wa-ʔnuma)
	ROUND THING-away-to-does or will do-unto-thou- (in future)
Nootka:	ʔoyiːʔaːqƛateʔic (oʔ-yiː-ʔaːqƛ-ʔat-eʔic)
	THAT-give-will-done unto-thou art

---

[4] The article was written by Sapir in 1929, but edited and published by Morris Swadesh in 1946, several years after Sapir's death.

Navaho: neido:ʔáːɬ (n-aː-yi-diho-ʔáːɬ)
            thee-to transitive-will-ROUND THING (in future)
Yokuts: ma-m waːn-en taːni
            THEE obj. GIVE-will THAT-at

In comparing these examples, Sapir emphasized (as had his teacher, Franz Boas) the contrasts in *obligatory* categories. The psychological unity of mankind is evident in the fact that the English sentence *can* be adequately translated into all the others; but each language must include information which may be omitted in others. In English, for example, we must indicate *gender* for the actor (masculine) and the object (neuter), *number* for actor and object (both singular), and must also specify the time when the action occurs by the *tense* of the verb (future). We do not need to indicate, as speakers of some languages do, the size or shape of the object, whether or not it is visible, or whether the action was observed by the speaker. Some of Sapir's commentary on each of the translations is summarized as follows:

Wishram: The construction is highly *agglutinative*—that is, it is easily analyzable into a number of separate elements. The order of these elements is fixed. Wishram has pronominal gender distinctions which are sometimes arbitrary (as in French or German); thus, the third element is "him" (the referent being defined as a stone). The base of the Wishram construction is the sixth element "give;" note that tense is marked twice, both initially and finally.

Takelma: As in Wishram, a number of elements are strung together, but Takelma is more *fusional*. The separate elements are, so to speak, fused together so that the boundaries are obscured. The verb base is the first element; the base ("will give") includes the idea of future time, as does the final pronominal element. Gender and number are not indicated; this could be done by adding independent pronouns but, according to Sapir, this would also amount to an unusual emphasis on these facts. Finally, the third person object is not formally indicated, but is simply assumed (in the presence of a transitive verb).

Southern Paiute: As in Wishram, the construction is agglutinative, but allows more flexibility in order. Two obligatory distinctions determine the choice of object and subject pronominals (the third and fourth elements)—that is, animate versus inanimate, and visible versus invisible.

Yana: The base is the initial element of the construction (as in Southern Paiute and Takelma); it indicates both movement and a classification of shape (a stone is classified as a "round thing").

Nootka: The initial element "that" or "that one" refers to the thing which is given (the stone). The second element is chosen to indicate aspect, an obligatory category; the aspect here is *momentaneous* (other possible choices might indicate greater duration or repetition of the action). Tense, indicated by the third element, is an optional category.

Navaho: The base is the final element in the word and, as in Yana, it indicates a classification ("round object") as well as movement. Future time is indicated both by the verb base as well as by an affix. Note that the actor is not formally indicated; a third person actor is implied by the absence of a first or second person pronominal element.

American Indian languages, Sapir noted, are often characterized as *polysynthetic*. All six of the examples so far discussed illustrate this general tendency; that is, they combine a large number of meaningful elements into a single word. However, the last example, Yokuts, was chosen to illustrate an opposite tendency. Here again, the third person actor is normally omitted. Sapir paraphrases the meaning of the construction as "will present thee at (or with) it" (Sapir and Swadesh, 1946).

Morphemic Analysis   We might recall that Charles Hockett, in his discussion of the origins of language (see Chapter 2), named "duality of patterning" as a distinctive design feature in language. According to Hockett, it was the emergence of this type of organization that made possible the level of complexity characteristic of existing human languages. All languages are built on this plan, which makes use of two types of structural elements. The first of these are the units of sounds, or *phonemes,* treated above. The second level consists of the meaningful elements, or *morphemes,* which in turn combine to form larger units (words, phrases, sentences, and so on).

Morphemes may be short—at times only a single phoneme—or may be made up of several phonemes, but they are the "minimal building blocks" of meaning which cannot be reduced or analyzed further. All languages can be analyzed in this way—that is, they are made up of small, irreducible units of meaning which occur in sequence and combine according to definite rules of order. However, even though this definition is simple in principle, it can be difficult to apply. For example, most speakers of English would probably agree with the author of a recent linguistics textbook (Gaeng, 1971) in his analysis of the English sentence: *Yesterday John ran away with the baker's younger daughter.* This is broken down into morphemes as follows:

yester + day + John + ran + a + way + with + the + bake + er + s +
  1   2   3   4   5   6   7   8   9   10   11
young + er + daughter.[5]
 12   13   14

Those of us who are native speakers of the language would have no difficulty with the composition and meaning of this sentence. However, a few of us might suggest that (1) *yester-* (which otherwise occurs only in *yesteryear*) cannot be separated, and that *yesterday* should be considered a single element. Most linguists would insist that (4) *ran* includes a past tense morpheme marked by the change of the vowel of the present tense form (*run*). And it is likely that some speakers of English would refuse to divide (5) *a-* and (6) *-way*, considering *away* to be an irreducible unit (despite the fact that a similar initial vowel also occurs in *aground, afloat, ahead,* and so on). Conversely, some individuals would surely

[5] This analysis divides the sentence into *segmental* morphemes; actually, it is incomplete as it does not include *suprasegmental* morphemes such as intonation and stress. The overall meaning of the sentence would be affected, for example, by using a final rising intonation (questioning), rather than the expected falling intonation (statement). It would also be changed by putting strong stress on the third segment (emphasizing *John*) or the twelfth (emphasizing *younger*).

argue that (14) *daughter* should be divided into *daught-* + *-er,* since the final -er also occurs in parallel terms, such as *father, brother, sister,* and so forth.

In any language, the morphemes, the basic set of meaningful units, are limited in number. They may be counted in the thousands, but in any case they are fewer than the words and other constructions which can be built from them. Thus, a list of morphemes would always be shorter than the lexicon, or dictionary, of a language, though languages differ in the freedom with which morphemes can combine productively to form new vocabulary.

It is typical that most morphemes can enter into a variety of combinations. Let us return to our English sentence, *John ran away with the baker's younger daughter.* We quickly recognized most of the morphemes in this sentence because we are familiar with them in many different contexts; for example, *day* occurs alone and in words such as *days, daylight, midday, half-day, Saturday.* We know *bake* as a verb (*bakes, baked, baking*) and in other words like *baker, bakery,* and *half-baked.* We make comparisons with other words and recognize the *-er* of *baker* as the same ending (the "agentive") which occurs in *miller, teacher,* and *player;* we know the *-er* of *younger* to be the same (the "comparative") as in *older, fatter,* and *jollier.* We find *baker's* to resemble, in form and meaning, other "possessives" such as *cook's, captain's, boss's,* and *George's,* while past tense forms such as *baked, wanted, cooked,* and *laughed* can be juxtaposed to *ran* (which resembles the others in meaning but is dissimilar in form).

If we compiled long lists of this sort, written phonetically, some regular variations would soon become apparent. For example, the *-s* of *baker's* (phonetically /-z/) differs from the final /-s/ of *cook's* and the /-ɨz/ of *George's.* These are identical with three alternate forms (or allomorphs) of our plural morpheme; one of the key problems in the morphemic analysis of language is to discover and state the rules for such regular alternations. Many linguists use special symbols for this purpose; for example, [-Z$_1$] might stand for the possessive and [Z$_2$] for the plural morpheme in English, and the rules for the occurrence of allomorphs can be stated by a formula such as:

$$\{\text{-Z}\} \rightarrow \begin{cases} /\text{-ɨz}/ & \text{following s, z, š, ž, č, ǰ} \\ /\text{-s}/ & \text{following other voiceless consonant} \\ /\text{-z}/ & \text{elsewhere} \end{cases}$$

Such rules should simplify the description of a language by relating the variant forms of morphemes to the environments in which they occur.

Another more awkward problem concerns the status of "irregular" forms, such as the sizable number of English plurals which do not follow these automatic rules (such as *geese, oxen, mice, children, radii,* and so forth). Some linguists might treat all of these as additional variants of [-Z$_2$], determined or selected by the particular bases with which they co-occur. Others would leave such forms out of the description of the grammatical system and list them as exceptions; the description would focus, then, on the regular, productive formations.

In English, as in other languages, the thousands of morphemes from which the lexicon is built can be divided into two main groups: *bases* and *affixes.* The bases are numerically the larger group; individually, these are apt to occur less often than most of the affixes, some of which are used again and again with great frequency. Bases are said to carry the "basic meaning" of any word, which may be modified or changed by various affixes. In our sample sentence, some of the bases might be identified as: *John, run, way, bake,* and *young.* The affixes include the *-er* and the *-s* in *baker's,* the *-er* in *younger,* and (according to our analysis) the *a-* of *away* and the infixed *-a-* in ran.

Affixes can be classified into three general types according to their sequential position in combining with the bases. It is convenient to speak of *prefixes, suffixes,* and *infixes.* Many languages use all three of these affix types, but most seem to have a preference for one and may make little or no use of the others. English makes frequent use of both prefixes and suffixes; suffixing, however, is more common and is more productive in forming new vocabulary.

As we have seen in the example above, English affixes may be divided into those which are productive (freely used in new combinations) and those which are non-productive. Many of the elements which we can identify, at least tentatively, as affixes (like the *a-* in *away* or *afar;* some of the uncommon plural forms, like *ox/ oxen* and *child/children;* or the *de-* and *per-* in *deceive* and *perceive*) come down to us from earlier historical periods, and now occur in only a handful of words; they are not apt to be used in new combinations. On the other hand, the *-s* plural suffix and several others which can form new verbs or adjectives (like *-ize, -ify,* and *-ish*) are used much more freely. We know immediately how to form the plural of a noun, even though we may never have heard the word before. When a new word is coined or is borrowed from another language—like *sputnik* from Russian, or *igloo* from Eskimo—one can immediately speak of *sputniks* and *igloos* (though the plural forms are *sputniki* and *iglut* in Russian and Eskimo respectively).

The productive resources of any language are limited, but by using them, it is always possible to form new words, to talk about novel experiences or flights of fancy, and to name inventions or discoveries. For these needs, the regular patterns of derivation, compounding, or other processes of word formation normally suffice.

On the other hand, it is unlikely that any language is completely regular and consistent in its rules and patterns. As in English, languages generally have loose ends and outdated or atrophied parts (such as the *a-* of *away,* or the *-en* plural in oxen). Irregular forms such as these are testimony to the fact that languages change, and can sometimes be used as evidence of earlier stages in the history of a language, or may provide clues to its remote relationships with other languages. In *oxen,* for example, we have a form which was, at one time, a common type of English plural; in *men* and *geese* we find traces of ablaut (internal change) which is a characteristic way of forming plurals in Germanic languages related to English; and *radii* and *fungi* are evidence of a time when English was strongly influenced by Latin. Latin plurals are especially likely to be replaced by plurals which follow the regular pattern; people say *radiuses* and *funguses* rather than using the "correct" Latin plurals.

Morphemic Typology   The distinction between bases and affixes and the limited number of operations by means of which they are combined to form words are very similar from one language to another. There are many languages in the world which make exclusive (or almost exclusive) use of suffixes: Turkish, Basque, and a few other European languages as well as Eskimo and a number of other Native American languages. Languages which rely exclusively on prefixing are much less numerous; Thai, in Southeast Asia, is one example. Russian, English, and other Indo-European languages—and, in fact, most of the languages in the world—fall between these two extremes, and employ both prefixing and suffixing in word formation.

The sort of internal change that we have seen as a minor component in English vocabulary (as in *run/ran* and *goose/geese*) can be interpreted as infixing, the insertion of an affix into a discontinuous base. This is an important type of word formation in only a few languages of the world—Arabic, Hebrew, and other Semitic languages, for example; but, like the other types, it is actually worldwide in occurrence.

Languages differ considerably in the number of morphemes which make up a word and in the changes which they undergo in the process. As noted above, one of the oldest and most general typologies classifies languages as *isolating, agglutinating,* and *inflecting.* This typology is based both on the number of morphemes combined in a word and the degree of fusion among them. The theoretical extreme of one morpheme per word in the totally isolating type is not matched in any living language (though some, like Chinese, come close); and there are limits on the number to be found in any language which would be classified as agglutinating or inflecting.

Edward Sapir, in his famous book *Language* (1921), developed a more refined typology based on these two variables. He attempted to include both the type of concepts which are formally expressed in language and the morphological processes through which this is done. In classifying the processes, Sapir took into consideration both the number of morphemes included in a word—here he used the terms *isolating, agglutinative,* and *fusional*—and in addition, the degree of synthesis. The terms *analytic, synthetic,* and *polysynthetic* refer to the welding together of separate concepts into a single form. Thus, the English words *goodness* and *depth* are similar in being made up of a base plus a suffix; but the second exhibits a higher degree of synthesis (Sapir considered the first more typical of English).

Of contemporary linguists, Joseph Greenberg has displayed a continuing interest in linguistic typology. Like Sapir, Greenberg has been interested in the relationship between words and morphemes, and has devised a simplified way of measuring this relationship, which can be given the form of a numerical index. Greenberg's index is derived by taking a sample of text, counting the words and the morphemes, and dividing the number of morphemes by the number of words; the resulting figure is, obviously, the average number of morphemes per word. The highest figure which he has discovered is 3.72, for Eskimo; the lowest possible would be 1.0. Using the same terms as Sapir, Greenberg suggests that languages in the 1.0–2.2 range be defined as analytic, 2.2–3.0 as synthetic, and those above 3.0 as polysynthetic (Greenberg, 1968). Chinese is the classic example of an analytic (and isolating) language. English would also fall into this type, though it is not such an extreme example as Chinese. Bantu and Turkish are two of Sapir's examples of synthetic languages, while Eskimo and several other North American languages (including Nootka and Southern Paiute) can be characterized as polysynthetic.

The main caution in making such assessments is the fact that not all linguists agree on criteria for defining the *word* as a universal unit of structure for purposes of making counts and comparisons. It is easy to count words in English since we learn to recognize them when we learn to read. But it is not easy to segment an uninterrupted flow of speech into words (try this when you are listening to someone speak a language which you do not understand), and there may be differences of opinion on how to do it or once it is done, whether the results should be relied upon in comparing languages.

SYNTAX: SENTENCES AND THEIR TRANSFORMATIONS

There are traditional approaches to the study of syntax which treat sentences simply as sequences or groupings of words. According to this type of analysis, *morphology* treats the structure of words and *syntax* the structure of sentences. However, the most influential contemporary approach to syntax, *transformational-generative* (T/G) analysis, takes the sentence as the basic unit of study.

Transformational-generative grammar, which has had a strong impact on linguistics during the 1960s and 1970s, employs the approach of "working down," describing languages in terms of rules for the production of sentences. These rules are found to be similar in type from language to language, and are limited in number in any language. A T/G analysis is a concise statement of the rules which a native speaker must follow in order to produce acceptable sentences. The number of sentences which may be produced is, in theory, infinite. In principle, the emphasis is on the creative aspect of language; a grammar should not be limited to description of a particular corpus of data, since speakers of any language are always capable of producing new grammatical utterances.

T/G grammarians rely on Noam Chomsky's distinction between *competence* (an individual's intuitive knowledge of the rules of grammar) and *performance* (what individual speakers actually say). (This distinction is obviously related to the older distinction between language and speech, though Chomsky states the distinction somewhat differently.) Another important aspect of the T/G view of language is the distinction which is drawn between *deep structure* (the abstract form of a sentence) and *surface structure* (its realization as morphemes and phonemes). It is on the level of deep structure that differences among languages appear to be minimal, or nonexistent, since the relationships here are conceptual and are, in theory, determined by the structure of the human mind. Chomsky has developed a series of models for the conversion of deep structure (which is made up of a syntactic and a semantic component), through several stages of syntactic processing, to the phonological processing of actual speech.

Transformational-generative analysis begins with the largest syntactic units (S, sentence) and proceeds to break them down into successively smaller parts (NP, noun phrase; VP, verb phrase; N, noun; Adj, adjective; and so on) through a series of "rewrite" rules (symbolized by an arrow, →):

$$S \rightarrow NP\ VP$$

$$NP \rightarrow \begin{cases} (Det)\ N \\ Pn \end{cases}$$

$$VP \rightarrow \begin{cases} V\ (NP) \\ is\ Adj \end{cases}$$

Det: the, this
N: student, girl, clerk
Pn: it
V: saw, remembered, wrote
Adj: energetic, pretty, impossible

A formulaic statement of this sort can serve to generate several acceptable English sentences: *The student saw the girl. The student remembered the girl. The student remembered it. The clerk remembered the girl. The clerk wrote it. The clerk is pretty. The girl is pretty. The girl is energetic.* One can easily add more words which can be used in the same ways and which would increase the productivity of such a *phrase-structure grammar.* Generative rules of this sort are called *phrase-structure rules.*

A further series of *transformational rules* serve to derive other sentences of various types from the simple declarative type shown above: questions, exclamations, negative sentences, and complex or compound sentences which are interpreted as the combination of simpler ones. Thus: *Did the student see the girl? The clerk did not remember the girl. The clerk remembered the pretty girl. The girl the student remembered was pretty.* The objective is to discover the set of rules which are known and used by speakers of a language to produce sentences which are understood and accepted by other speakers. (These procedures are outlined in numerous textbooks; for example, Pearson, 1977, Chapters 5–6.)

Transformational-generative studies have suggested that there is an overriding similarity among languages in their use of syntactic rules and structures. Since a great reliance is placed on the insight of the native speaker (in assessing the acceptability of sentences and in explaining how derived sentences are related to the simpler ones), many linguists who have done this kind of study have dealt primarily with their own use of language. However, as the transformational-generative approach has grown in importance, studies have increased in number and variety, and it has had a significant impact on anthropological writings on language. Syntax, rather than morphology, is increasingly a focus of interest in linguistic journals, with more attention paid to the structure of sentences and less to the phonological systems of various languages.

Universals in Syntax   An innovator in the comparative study of languages, Joseph Greenberg has conducted extensive research directed at identifying universal features of language. Toward this end, he and other researchers have assembled data on a selected sample of language. This approach might be compared to the method of cross-cultural comparative study in social anthropology.

Some of the generalizations which have come out of this study concern the order of syntactic elements within sentences. Greenberg has classified languages in a typology based on the relative order, within sentences, of three grammatical components: nominal subject (S), verb (V), and nominal object (O). According to his observations, sentences such as *The boy drank the water* can be found in all languages. Thus, in seven languages:

English: the bóy dránk the wáter
          S   V   O

Russian: mál'čik výpil vódu
         S   V   O

Turkish: çoçúk suyú içtí
       S   O   V

Arabic: šáraba lwáladu lmāʔa
      V   S   O

Hausa: yārō yášā ruwā
     S   V   O

Thai: dègchaaj dyym nàam
     S   V   O

Quechua: wámbra yakúta upiárqan
        S   O   V

As in these examples, subject, verb, and object can be identified and abstracted from other ideas (such as tense, gender, number, and so on) which may or may not be expressed in each language. As Greenberg points out, logically there are six possible orders in which these three components might occur: VSO, SVO, SOV, VOS, OSV, and OVS. But in fact, only the first three do occur as normal word order in the languages sampled.[6] These three (VSO, SVO, SOV) differ from one another in the placement of the verb; their common characteristic is the fact that the subject precedes the object (and never the reverse). Universals of this sort, Greenberg believes, must derive from "a general set of psychological and physiological preferences" which are genetically determined and found in all humans.

Beyond this generalization, the importance of Greenberg's typology becomes apparent when we learn that it has predictive value. That is, if it is known that a language is Type I (VSO), Type II (SVO), or Type III (SOV), then other features of its grammatical system can be predicted. For example, languages of Type I employ prepositions exclusively, while those of Type III (which seems in most respects to be the "polar opposite" of Type I) usually have postpositions. Similarly, there are positive correlations between the three syntactic types and the relative order of nouns in a genitive expression, the position in the sentence of interrogative particles or affixes, and the relative order of main verbs and subordinate verbs (Greenberg, 1966).

Greenberg's work demonstrates the fact that there are many features in language which can be studied on a comparative basis and that there are general principles which underlie the diverse rules of individual languages. It might be noted that Greenberg, with his comparative approach, has the same objective as Noam Chomsky,

---

[6] Most languages do permit some variation in word order, often expressing variation in emphasis.

who prefers the depth study of an individual language: a delineation of general properties of language and, ultimately, of the human cognitive capacity which is expressed in language. Of the two approaches, Greenberg's is more compatible with the general perspective of anthropology, since it maintains a balance in interest between universal properties and the unique patterning of individual linguistic systems.

TOPICS FOR STUDY AND DISCUSSION

1. Summarize the contributions to descriptive linguistics of the following: Franz Boas, Edward Sapir, Leonard Bloomfield, Ferdinand de Saussure, Roman Jakobson, Noam Chomsky. (Consult a good encyclopedia, such as the *Encyclopedia Britannica*, or a history of linguistics, to supplement the information you have in this book.)
2. What is the basic difference between comparative and descriptive linguistics?
3. What are the three levels of structure in a descriptive grammar? Define each of them.
4. Explain the difference between phonetics and phonemics. Compare with *etics* and *emics* in the study of culture.
5. What is a phoneme? In what ways may allophones vary?
6. How does a fieldworker obtain an inventory of morphemes? What are the alternative forms of morphemes called?
7. What is the basic unit for transformational-generative analysis? How does this approach differ from traditional analysis?
8. Why is there a need for phonetic transcription?
9. How are language universals discovered? Why would such universals be of importance to linguistics?
10. With your instructor's help, identify the 12 single vowels and the common diphthongs of American English (see p. 61). Now listen carefully as each student reads the following list. Write exactly what you hear; there should be some points of disagreement.

rich	latch	his	race	cheese	barred	language
bush	them	hiss	raise	chair	have	congress
mush	thumb	peas	shout	ought	halve	garage
dumb	hod	peace	do	more	machine	finger
hook	gem	ice	due	tour	seizure	singer
box	has	eyes	dew	bird	adjourn	throw

11. Turn back to the example of phrase-structure grammar given on page Now (a) add the following words to the lexicon: a, messenger, librarian, boy, them, us, sees, remembers, ugly, untidy, dangerous. (b) Write some of the new sentences which can be generated by applying the phrase-structure rules. (c) State new rules for negative and interrogative transformations of the sentences. (d) Which sentences can be rewritten in passive form? State a rule for the passive transformation.
12. For additional practice in the linguistic analysis, students could attempt some of the simpler exercises in H. L. Gleason, *Workbook in Descriptive Linguistics*. However, the present textbook does not provide a sufficient theoretical orientation for undertaking more difficult problems. Your instructor may wish to assign additional reading, if this is within the scope of your course.

6

Language and Society

Twentieth-century linguists have generally been guided by the distinction which Saussure expressed as *parole* (or "speech") versus *langue* (or "language"), and have given priority to the latter as the subject matter of linguistics. When working with and gathering material from the individual speakers of languages, they have directed their efforts toward defining the system shared by all speakers, and have been less interested in the variation which distinguishes speakers from one another. Yet variation is always present and is in itself a fascinating and important topic for study. *Sociolinguistics* is a developing subfield of linguistics which takes speech variation as its focus, viewing variation in its social context. Some types of speech variation are of special interest to social scientists, because speaking is almost always a social act, and because much of the variation can be seen as related to other social phenomena. Individuals do not simply differ from one another as individuals, they also differ from one another as members of groups (based on age, sex, religion, interest, occupation, and so on.); they can be identified by social status, education, and geographical provenience. Sociolinguistics is concerned with the correlation between such social factors and linguistic variation.

THE SPEECH COMMUNITY

The framework in which these factors can best be studied is the speech community. Sociolinguistics takes the community, rather than the broader and more diffusely defined language, as the basic unit for study. A speech community is a real social unit within which speakers share a repertoire of "ways of speaking"; that is, they share a set of rules for using and interpreting speech in all the special settings, nuances, and cultural meanings unique to a particular community. The speech community may include one or several languages; it is localized, crosscutting the wider distribution of national and world languages.

In many U.S. communities, for example, English and Spanish co-occur and are part of the experience of all members of the community to some degree. Familiarity with local varieties of English and Spanish and of the situations in which one or the other is normally used must be part of the linguistic competence of members of such a community. In certain western Texas communities, where English is the dominant language, several local varieties of English are heard. Most speakers can be identified as "Anglo" or "Chicano." Many Chicanos are functionally bilingual in English and Spanish, while few Anglos are (though some Anglos have undoubtedly acquired a limited passive understanding of Spanish). Since English is the language of official functions and of education, and has a higher status than Spanish, Chicanos are apt to overestimate their knowledge of English, while Anglos tend to deny any knowledge of Spanish.

The relationship between these two languages, English and Spanish, is obviously linked to the occupations and status relations of Anglos and Chicanos in the community. Since unskilled and semiskilled workers (public service workers, custodians, short-order cooks, clerks, and so on) are often Chicanos—who speak Spanish to one another on the job and to obviously Hispanic customers—Anglos are accustomed to hearing (and disregarding) Spanish as "background noise," and they find it natural that certain individuals in certain roles should speak Spanish. They are, in other words, conditioned to a "third-party" role when Spanish is spoken; their relationship to it is passive. While Anglos would be taken aback to be addressed in Spanish by a store clerk or receptionist, Chicanos need to have active control of both languages (though their English may be specialized for use in a limited set of situations). However, they are, in the status structure of the total community, rewarded or penalized according to their mastery of an Anglo variety of English, rather than for bilingual ability.

This is a very generalized picture; a more satisfactory analysis would require the identification of several varieties and styles of English, a treatment of the position of blacks in the community, the identification of dialect variation in this group, and the distinction among Mexican Spanish, Border Spanish ("Pachuco"), and a local ("Tex-Mex" or "Texican") variety which appears to be heavily influenced by English.

The relative prestige of English and Spanish, the numbers of speakers of each, and many other factors vary from one community to the next. The sociolinguistic situation in the Southwest differs from that found in California or in northeastern urban areas as New York City; in the latter, the majority of Spanish speakers are of Puerto Rican rather than Mexican origin or ancestry. There is a large potential for comparative research toward an understanding of bilingualism and multilingualism in our own national society, involving not only English and Spanish but also other languages such as French, German, Italian, and a large number of native American languages.

With modern tendencies as world travel, interethnic marriages, and mixture of populations, language contacts are worldwide in their occurrence and are frequently associated with social problems of pressing interest. There are many parallels to the problems which, in the United States, seem especially associated with Spanish–English bilingualism; the relations between French and English in Cañada, and Finnish and Swedish in Sweden offer remarkable parallels.

Diglossia   Charles A. Ferguson initiated the study of complex speech communities when he described and compared several examples of a linguistic situation which he called *diglossia*. As he used it, this term refers to speech communities in which "two or more varieties of the same language are used by some speakers under different conditions." In such a community, it is typical that there are significant numbers of bilinguals—indeed, most of the population may be bilingual—and that these bilinguals feel that each language is appropriate in certain situations. It seems especially typical that one variety of language is associated with education and literacy.

In writing about diglossia, Ferguson described his own experience in Arabic countries, where the classical Arabic of the Koran coexists with diversified local forms of Arabic (the Arabic of Baghdad or Cairo or Tunis, and so on). He compared this with examples drawn from Switzerland (standard German and Swiss-German), Haiti (French and Haitian Creole), and Greece (standard and colloquial dialects). All of these, Ferguson emphasized, are areas in which there is a long-standing stable relationship between markedly different linguistic varieties, a relationship which endures, apparently, in a stable social situation.

Ferguson labels the two language varieties in each case as H ("high") and L ("low"). He lists some of the special situations in which each is used:

	H	L
Sermon in church or mosque	x	
Instructions to servants, waiters, workmen, clerks		x
Personal letter	x	
Speech in parliament, political speech	x	
University lecture	x	
Conversation with family, friends, colleagues		x
News broadcast	x	
Radio "soap opera"		x
Newspaper editorial, story, caption, on picture	x	
Caption on political cartoon		x
Poetry	x	
Folk literature		x

In every case, it might be noted, speakers generally agree in regarding H as superior to L, and educated persons may even deny the existence of L (even though they themselves use L). This value of superiority rests partly on the basis of an established body of literature written in H, and partly on the association of H with religion: H is the language of the Bible, the Koran, and other sacred literature.

Predictably, Ferguson feels, the established relationship of H and L varieties may change as social conditions change. Widespread education and the need for ties with other communities where H is in use have in some cases established H as a universal standard. On the other hand, in an increasingly democratic society, L almost inevitably rises in prestige and displaces H, coming to be considered appropriate in any situation (though borrowing heavily in vocabulary from H in the process) (Ferguson, 1959).

Bilingualism Another way of viewing the relationship of languages in contact puts the focus on the linguistic skills of individuals. In a community in which two or more languages are spoken, there are, of necessity, a number of individuals who could be called bilingual; but not everyone is bilingual, at least not to the same degree. In the western Texas community described above, many Chicanos use both English and Spanish; some appear to be coordinate or "balanced" bilinguals, with good control of both languages, while some have only active control of English words and phrases for a few necessary transactions (at work, on the bus, and so forth). Proportionally, far fewer Anglos know any Spanish at all. Bilingual education programs—which are receiving increasing emphasis—underline the necessity for Spanish speakers to learn English, but not the reverse. Even though some Anglo educators pay lip service to the advantages of dual language skills, only a marked increase in the economic and social power of the Mexican-American population will make it seem really desirable for Anglos to learn Spanish.

Some linguists define *bilingualism* as "nativelike" control of two languages; however, this is a very narrow definition, and one which would be hard to apply. (After all, how can "nativelike" control be evaluated?) Most linguists now treat bilingualism as a gradient; there are degrees or stages of bilingualism, based on performance—the ability to understand and to produce meaningful utterances in the second language.

In a small village in western Mexico, Richard Diebold investigated an early stage in the development of contacts between the national language, Spanish, and a native language of the region, Huave; he termed this stage *incipient bilingualism*. Over 80 percent of the Indian population in this area had been counted in the official census as monolingual in their native language. Six percent were found to be coordinate bilinguals, and about twice as many were classified as subordinate bilinguals (that is, they could use Spanish, but imperfectly and with a strong Huave accent). Diebold knew that as a general trend, native languages in rural Mexico are giving way to Spanish. His study is directed toward understanding the process of change and the place of individuals who vary greatly in their language abilities in this process.

Using a 100-item list of Huave words, Diebold found that men who had been classified as fully bilingual were able to give Spanish equivalents for 90 percent or more of the words. Those in the subordinate bilingual group ranged from 61 percent to 94 percent with a mean of 89 percent. However, even the monolinguals could translate a large number of the words; they ranged between 11 percent and 68 percent, with a mean score of 37 percent. Diebold notes that many Spanish loan-words have been borrowed into Huave and are known, as Huave vocabulary, to monolinguals and bilinguals alike; but other Spanish vocabulary has also been learned by monolingual speakers of Huave, probably indirectly from those who are bilingual.

All of this goes to show that contact between languages (linguistic acculturation) is a complex process which involves the speech community as a whole. It can also be seen to involve every individual; even those who are functionally monolingual are found to be in an "initial learning stage" of bilingualism and are thus more than passively involved.

The Huave community of San Mateo, which Diebold studied, is located in a remote rural area, but it is coming into increasing contact with and participation in national life. Men from San Mateo must use Spanish on the occasions when they visit a nearby Spanish-speaking community which serves as a regional administrative and marketing center. The use of Spanish is largely a male skill; Huave is uniformly the language of the home, and the women need not speak Spanish. Indirectly, however, they are being programmed for change.

Diebold has predicted that this change can lead to either of two outcomes: (1) the extinction of the native language; or (2) a stable coexistence, with Huave and Spanish both in use (comparable to the diglossia situation described above). This prediction could be extended far beyond the Huave villages, and far beyond the borders of Mexico, since native peoples in all parts of the world are subject to similar pressures and must cope with similar necessities, affecting both the way they will live and the languages they will speak (Diebold, 1961).

THE SOCIAL CONTEXT OF SPEAKING

The contact between two or more languages is the most obvious type of linguistic diversity in which individuals ordinarily participate. As shown in Ferguson's study, bilingual individuals can be observed to switch, in different situations, from one language to the other; a person may speak one language at home, switch to a second at school or work, switch back to the first while lunching with friends, and so on. But monolinguals also switch codes (or styles of speaking) in different situations, though the changes are less noticeable because the codes which are used are fairly similar to one another. The study of diglossia and bilingualism has helped call linguists' attention to the more general phenomenon of situational variation, or "code-switching," as a normal part of social behavior.

For practical purposes, it seems impossible to record and explain *all* the variation found in speech, even in the speech of a single individual. Every individual has a unique speech repertoire which reflects his or her own experiences—the languages used in the home, school, and community, the changes in moving from one community to another, personal acquaintances and the amount of influence each has on the other, the effects of books, movies, and so on. Out of this repertoire—which makes up the individual's competence or general knowledge—he selects the speech behavior appropriate to each situation. In other words, an individual's performance shows a range of variation, since he is able to switch from one style of speaking to another.

The reasons for switching are obvious. We use speech to convey two types of message simultaneously. One of these might be called the purely "linguistic" message, the sum of the information contained in the morphemes—the raw material—from which an utterance is built up. The other, more personal, type of message is conveyed by the ways this raw material is selected, combined, and delivered. It includes information on the identity of the speaker, his feelings about other individuals, his mood and attitudes. And since each individual plays different roles and acts in different situations, the verbal clues which he gives are changeable.

Dell Hymes, a leading anthropological linguist, has worked to turn linguistic attention to, as he terms it, the "ethnography of speaking," the study of culturally significant variation in speech. Hymes points out a number of variables which influence speech by means of an acronym based on the word *speaking*:

S —*Setting* and *scene*: the time, place, and psychological setting.
P —*Participants*: the speaker, listener, audience, and any other participants.
E —*Ends*: the desired or expected outcome.
A—*Act sequence*: how form and content are delivered.
K—*Key*: the mood or spirit (serious, ironic, joking, and so on).
I —*Instrumentalities*: the dialect or linguistic variety used by the speech community.
N—*Norms*: conventions or expectations about volume, interruption, hesitation, and the like.
G—*Genres*: different types of performance (speech, joke, sermon, and so forth).

Hymes' acronym calls our attention to the complexity of speech behavior and to its interrelatedness with its social setting. We might hope that, once it has been determined just how, and to what degree, speech variation is conditioned by social variation, we can then use speech as an aid for the study of society. At times, the way people talk to one another is the social scientist's most obvious and most accessible clue to their social relationships (Hymes, 1972).

Complexities   Some of the complexity which Hymes calls to our attention can be sampled if we take a familiar speech situation and consider the ways in which it can be varied. For example, an exchange of greetings is the most ordinary, everyday sort of occurrence; it requires little thought and seems almost automatic. Most of us greet anyone we recognize, or think we recognize, and some even greet complete strangers.

a. "Hi, Mr. Jones!"
   "Hello, Tommy. How are you?"
   "Fine, thanks."
b. "Good morning, Mrs. Goldman."
   "The same to you, Dr. Stevens. Nice weather."
c. "How's it going, Sam?"
   "Not bad. How's it with you, Mike?"
   "Could be worse."
d. "Good morning, Jenkins."
   "Good morning, sir."
e. "Hello, Louise."
   "Oh. Hi."
f. "Mary! How are you? You look wonderful!"
   "Nancy! It's so good to see you!"
g. "Bill."
   "Dick."
h. "Morning, Dr. Brown. Nice day, isn't it?"
   "Oh, hello, Susan. Yes, it's nice—going to be a scorcher, though."
i. "Mommy! Mommy!"
   "Hello, Johnny! Have you been a good boy?"
j. "Good evening, Senator."
   "Hello there. Nice to see you."

Any of these could be taken as an example of what the British anthropologist, Bronislaw Malinowski, termed "phatic communion." That is, they are exchanges of words and phrases which are important less for their literal or referential meaning than for their social functions. Malinowski emphasized the key role of social context in his discussion of meaning in language; this becomes especially critical when translating from one language to another. Malinowski's work with the "primitive" languages of Pacific islanders had convinced him that words cannot be translated in any absolute sense, but are meaningful and can be understood only in the context of a particular society (Malinowski, 1923).

In our own society, we use verbal exchanges, such as an exchange of greetings, to establish or reaffirm social ties, to show that we are aware of and value one another. We know, in our own familiar social context, that "How are you?" or "How's it going?" is not a serious request for information about the condition of one's health or the state of world affairs; rather, the inquiry is an acknowledgement of one's existence and importance, and it would be very upsetting to find oneself ignored. Exchanges of greetings are often accompanied by a wave or nod, a smile or other gesture of recognition; such nonverbal salutes can sometimes suffice to serve the same functions.

Phatic communion, then, is a social function of language which can easily be separated or abstracted from the literal meaning of the words used in any individual act of communication. But there is more information contained in these brief verbal exchanges than might seem obvious at first glance. One can guess, among other things, that in (a) and (i) the speakers are an adult and a child; that in (d) and (h) there is a difference in status and that the speakers may be employer and employee; that in (c) and (g) they are well acquainted with one another, and probably friends; while in (e) and (j) the second speaker either does not know or does not remember the first. In short, from such brief and fairly "meaningless" snatches of conversation, something can usually be inferred about the relative age, status, and social relationship of the participants.

We can do this because we, as well as they, are privy to a code which is expressed through the use of names and other terms of address. The intricacies of this code have been explored in a number of studies. One of the earliest and most perceptive of these, by psychologists Roger Brown and Marguerite Ford, examined the use of terms of address in business firms and other social settings in the United States. The system which they described seems widely applicable, though variations can undoubtedly be discovered in different regional and social settings.

Brown and Ford dealt especially with status ranking in American society. This is a feature of American life which everyone is aware of, though the awareness may be heightened in certain settings, such as military organizations or business firms, where status is often emphasized. Relative status, or "pecking order," affects the way individuals behave toward one another—who does a favor for whom, who pays the luncheon check, who asks for advice and who gives it, and so forth. Perhaps the most explicit recognition of relative status, and the best source of information about status for an observer or outsider, is found in the terms of address which individuals use in speaking to one another. There are not a great many of these in English; as Brown and Ford point out, the main choices are the use of first name (FN) or a title combined with a last name (TLN). There are three possible ways these terms can be used in an interaction of two individuals:

(1) reciprocal use of FN as in example (c) above; (2) nonreciprocal use of FN and TLN, as in (a); and (3) reciprocal use of TLN, as in (b).

What determines our choice among these three options? There are two reciprocal patterns, TLN/TLN and FN/FN. Of these, the first is certainly more formal; two people are apt to move away from it and assume the FN/FN pattern as they become better acquainted. For example, they will go from "Mr. Smith"/"Ms. Campbell" to "Mike"/"Sue," rather than the reverse. Both of the reciprocal patterns might be said to assume relative equality of status; or at least, they do not express inequality.

The nonreciprocal pattern, TLN/FN is used: 1) when there is a marked difference in age, as between children and adults or between younger and older adults; 2) where there are differences of rank or status within an organization, as between a supervisor and a clerk, or an officer and an enlisted person; or 3) when someone in a service occupation wishes to express helpfulness or subordination to the wishes of a customer. In American society, any of these relationships may move toward the reciprocal FN/FN pattern. However, it is considered appropriate that the older person or the one with higher status should take the initiative in making such a change—otherwise it might be considered overly familiar or "pushy."

There are many deviations away from these general patterns, of course, and there are also other terms of address. A title alone (T)—such as Sir or Ma'am, or Professor, Judge, Colonel, and so on—is usually felt to be less intimate and somewhat more formal than TLN. Last name only (LN) is often used as a substitute for FN, but may be more formal; in this sense, it is common in military usage (Brown and Ford, 1961).

A student might find it rewarding to spend a little time observing the use of terms of address in his home town, or at his college or university. You would probably find that usage still conforms to the patterns outlined in 1961 by Brown and Ford. But you also might find exceptions or differences in pattern which are typical of a particular setting. Colleges and universities seem especially variable; standard usage between faculty and students at different institutions seems to range all the way from reciprocal TLN/TLN ("Professor Brown"/"Mr. Higgins") in conservative eastern colleges, to the more widespread TLN/FN ("Professor Brown"/"Michael"), to a reciprocal FN/FN ("Charles"/"Mike"). The last of these is quite acceptable in the western university where I am located, though all three patterns are present. The FN/FN pattern may be more common between professors and graduate students, and the nonreciprocal pattern between faculty and undergraduates, though not exclusively so. Individual professors appear to be adept at manipulating this system, making themselves seem more accessible or less accessible to their students by regulating (through approval or disapproval) the use of terms of address.

SPEECH CORRELATES OF SEX AND AGE

Most children begin to talk in a family environment, and their speech resembles their parents' in certain respects, but they are also very much influenced by other children. Children below the age of 10 or 12 who move into a community usually adapt fairly completely to the speech of the new area; peer group pressure can be quite influential, affecting choice of vocabulary and even phonetic features.

Linguists who have studied the processes of change within speech communities have found that innovations, or variants which are becoming fashionable and increasing in importance, are usually rare or absent in the speech of older persons and occur with increasing frequency in successively younger age groups. For example, W. Labov, an innovator in methods of studying speech variation, made tape recordings of speech data from New York City residents of different ethnic backgrounds and social strata. One of the features he was interested in was the occurrence of /r/ after vowels in words like *bird, tired, beer,* and *car.* An "r-less" pronunciation of such words was, according to Labov, a prestigious innovation in the 1800s which imitated the London pronunciation of the time; since World War I, however, it has been in a decline and is considered old-fashioned. In his recorded samples of New Yorkers' speech, Labov found the highest occurrence of the current innovation—the presence of /r/—in the group between ages 8 and 19, and found it to be virtually absent in those over 40 (Labov, 1967).

Many studies have revealed such differences in the use of language which are at least partly associated with age differences. Variation of this sort appears to be universal. We can easily get some sense of these differences by observing our own families; children speak differently from their parents, and still more differently from their grandparents. I notice, for example, that my children use familiar words in ways which seem new to me. The word *gross* occurs in my vocabulary, but I use it infrequently and might even have considered it a little old-fashioned. For members of my children's generation, however, it has made a comeback and is a current word, something of a fad. They use it as I might, as an adjective ("That's a gross thing to do," or "How gross!"), and also in constructions which seem new, as a verb ("That grosses me out") or a noun derived from this ("Gross-out!"), used as an exclamation of disgust. I hear them use other words which seem completely new (*grokey*, which seems to be a synonym for *gross*; *dunksey* which means "okay" or "just fair"); they also mention the names of songs, performers, and products which I am not familiar with (all associated with areas of culture which do not involve or interest me). The differences in our speech are, one might observe, a reflection of our different cultural interests and they also serve as a badge of distinctive social identity. However, parents and children do ordinarily find their speech to be intelligible to one another. Similarly, the practical necessity for grandparents and grandchildren to be able to communicate may set a maximum limit on the rate of linguistic change.

It seems self-evident that no one, young or old, speaks in exactly the same way at all times and with all people. We choose different styles of speaking—for example, students may use vocabulary and types of sentences in the classroom which they would not use with their friends, and which also differ from their ordinary speech at home.

Variations   In one of the few studies which deal with individual variation of this sort, John Fischer examined recordings which he had made when interviewing a group of school children. These recordings included responses to a questionnaire and a section in which children were asked to tell a story or encouraged to talk informally. Fischer noticed that the children frequently alternated between final -ing and -in' (reading versus readin') during the interviews, and he attempted to discover the reasons for his alternation. There were marked differences between individuals; for example, girls used -ing more often than boys, and one boy whom teachers called a "model boy" used -ing much more often than others who were considered "typical." But almost all of the children (21 out of 24) did use both. The choice, said Fischer, "appears to be related to sex, class, personality (aggressive/cooperative) and mood (tense/relaxed) of the speakers . . . to the formality of the conversation, and to the specific verb spoken." In other words, the children were more apt to say "singing," "reading," or "interesting" if they were girls, if their families were above median income, if they had dominating or assertive personalities, and if they were tense—as they might be at the beginning of the interview. As the interviews went on, and during the time when the children were asked to tell a story, they became more relaxed and were more likely to say "singin'," "readin'," or "interestin'." Finally, the alternation was clearly related to subject matter: one boy, especially, used -ing with "formal" verbs like "criticizing," and "reading," and used -in' when talking about "informal" activities such as "punchin'" or "swimmin'." Fischer's study does not tell us whether these forms became even more common when children were speaking to one another, rather than to an adult interviewer; we might guess that they would (Fischer, 1958).

Male and Female Differentials   Besides variation related to age, another type of variation which is probably found in all speech communities is a differential between the speech of men and women. All societies prescribe different roles to men and women, and this is reflected in different norms for male and female speech. The variation which has been described, however, is of several types—in some cases it is a matter of choice and selection, while in other languages the differences are part of the grammatical structure. It is tempting to speculate that further research will reveal direct connections between social structure (the division of labor between men and women, whether or not men are dominant, the restrictions placed on women's activities, and so on) and the structured differences between men's and women's speech; much of this remains to be investigated. Many traditional grammatical studies have been based on data collected from a small number of informants, and sometimes only a single speaker has been employed. In such cases, little or nothing can be learned about sex differences; what we know rests mainly on the insights of a few astute observers, such as Mary Haas, whose study of Koasati is cited below.

In certain languages, there are formal differences between male and female speech. This is the case in Yana, a native language of California. Particular verb endings must be chosen, depending on the sex of the speaker. This amounts to a kind of gender system in which grammatical forms are chosen to match the sex of the speaker rather than the referent (as is the case in several European languages). Mary Haas has described a fairly elaborate system of this sort in Koasati, another American Indian language. As in Yana, the differences are mainly in verb forms, which differ systematically according to the sex of the speaker (Haas, 1944). For example,

	Women say:	Men say:
he is saying	ka:	ká:s
don't sing!	tačilawân	tačilawâ:s
lift it	lakawhôl	lakawhós
he is building a fire	ó:t	ó:č

In other languages, there are observable differences between male and female speakers in the choice of vocabulary. This may always be true to a degree, since the cultural knowledge and activities of men and women always differ. However, in these languages the vocabulary differences are not just a matter of selection and relative frequency of usage, but are prescribed. A classic example is found in the language of the Island Carib, a native people of the West Indies. Here (and in several related languages of Central and South America), there are a large number of *doublets*, pairs of words with the same meaning; thus, for many meanings, there is a choice between "women's words" and "men's words":

	Women say:	Men say:
rain	kuyu	kunobu
sun	kači	hueyu
canoe	kuriala	ukuni
manioc	kawai	kiere

In sixteenth-century Island Carib, such doublets were so numerous that early explorers reported that men and women "speak different languages!" They did not, of course; much of the vocabulary and almost all of the grammatical system were shared by all speakers. The differences lay in the first and second person pronouns, and in many of the most common nouns. Comparative research reveals that the women's vocabulary and the basic grammatical structure identify the language with the Arawakan language family (see Map 6). The prominence of Carib loan words in the men's vocabulary are a clue to close, and probably fairly recent, historical contacts between the Arawaks and their Carib neighbors—and it is this vocabulary which led to a misidentification of the language, as is still reflected in its name (Taylor, 1977).

Sex differences in speaking also can involve intonation, the use of pitch and loudness of the voice, and variation in the rate and rhythm of speech—features which are difficult to identify, but all of which seem to play a part in popular ideas about men's and women's speech in the United States. A psychologist who deals with speech communication, Cheris Kramer, collected information on this topic. Kramer noted that women are often characterized as talkative (the subject of many jokes), and that female speech is sometimes described as "weaker" or less effective than male. Women are said to speak less forcefully than men, to use fewer exclamations, less profanity, and to weaken the impact of what they say by using qualifiers before expressing an opinion ("I may be wrong, but . . .) or by following it with "tag questions" (such as ". . . isn't it?" or "don't you think so?"). A rising, or questioning, intonation may accomplish the same thing.

Kramer confirmed the existence of such stereotypes of women's speech by showing the captions taken from a number of magazine cartoons to a group of college students (25 men, 25 women), asking them to identify the sex of the speaker in the cartoon; they were able to do this with general success. She then went on, in a second test, to ask a group of male and female students to write paragraphs describing two photographs; she then asked judges to identify the writers as male or female. The judges were not able to do this task with any success, though they sometimes called on their own stereotypes to justify their decisions, finding "sensitivity" in a paragraph judged (incorrectly) to have been written by a woman, or "objectivity" and detailed description in one attributed to a man (Kramer, 1974).

Kramer's study, then, both demonstrates the presence of certain stereotypes about the way women use language, and also tends to cast doubt on their validity. Written description, which was used in the second part of her study, is not the same thing as speech, of course; it is a more formal medium than speech, and it gives us no information about the intonation and emphasis used in speaking. The study does suggest, at least, that no regular and obvious differences are found in the way college men and women use English *in writing*. We would guess, too, that Kramer's college-student subjects were at the very age and in the very situation in which we should expect them to show few differences in the use of language. As students, their interests and activities are very much the same.

In other words, it seems to be the case that when and where women's interests and occupations are separate and different from men's, their speech will also be different. If there is less segregation of roles, speech is found to be more similar. The speech of suburban housewives, then, should come closer to the popular stereotype of women's speech than the speech of female college students or of women in business or industry.

It can also be suggested that the "weakness" which Kramer found to be a stereotyped feature of women's speech is a reflection of a subordinate social position; it will, predictably, disappear when women, as a group, are socially equal to men.

LANGUAGE, NATIONALISM, AND ETHNIC IDENTITY

Finally, it should be recognized that language has an important value as a symbol of national and ethnic identity. In the United States, we should be especially aware of this function of language, since ours is a nation made up of a great variety of peoples, with the English language as our common, official, language. For much of its history, this nation has maintained its reputation as a "melting pot." This image reflects not only the diversity of the peoples who have come into it, but also a process of change which tends to reduce differences and produce uniformity. It has seemed almost inevitable, in the past, that immigrants would rapidly lose their old ways and accept new ones. They would be "Americanized"— if not immediately, then at least in the course of a couple of generations. A prominent part of this process has been the learning of English and, along with that, the loss of the immigrants' original languages. It was the policy of the American government to insist that English be the only language of instruction in the schools, and adult immigrants were expected to learn English (often by attending night schools) as quickly as possible. President Theodore Roosevelt expressed a widely held opinion when he said: ". . . it would be not only a misfortune but a crime to perpetuate differences of language in this country" (Gonzales, 1955).

Roosevelt proposed that immigrants be given a period of five years to learn English, with deportation as the penalty for failure. No such policy was ever put into effect; however, many immigrants were eager to learn English. Since they were gaining a new nationality and leaving behind their old, they often insisted that their children speak only English. Thus, many of us who have German or Italian or Russian names, and who know when and from what foreign place our grandparents or great-grandparents came to America, do not know one word of the language which they spoke. We are the product of the melting pot. For those immigrants and for their descendants, the English language—American English— has been a symbol of our identity as Americans.

However, there is another side to this picture. The United States of America still contains more diversity than the image of the "melting pot" would suggest, and this ethnic diversity has its expression in linguistic diversity. There are some groups in our society who never wanted to become completely "Americanized," and others who have found a need to rediscover or reassert their own traditions and cultural heritage. Similar movements are going on in many areas of the world outside the United States. Colonial peoples have asserted, and achieved, a desire for self-government in Africa and Asia, and minority groups in many nations also speak of the right to self-determination.

Such movements are a powerful political force in our time, one which has increasing momentum. Recent political separatist struggles—by the Irish Republican Army, the Quebeçois in Canada, Basque separatists in Spain, and Walloon nationalists in Belgium (to name only a few)—all express the desires of minority peoples to maintain a separate identity, and *not* to be completely absorbed or assimilated into a larger nationality. In each of these cases, language plays a prominent role. In fact, these separatists are struggling, to a considerable extent, for the right to retain and use their own languages, and to teach them to their children.

American society is a pluralistic one, and many of our familiar social problems involve some type of conflict or disagreement over cultural tradition and language. When large numbers of people of the same nationality immigrated into the United States, they often settled in the same general area and retained their language, at least for several generations. There are pockets of this sort—ethnic and linguistic enclaves—throughout the United States: Germans in eastern Pennsylvania and central Texas, Scandinavians in Minnesota, "Cajun" French speakers in Louisiana, Japanese and Chinese in California, and many others. One of the largest ethnic blocs is made up of the Spanish-speaking population which is concentrated most heavily in the southwestern border states, and is increasingly represented in urban areas elsewhere. In such homogeneous ethnic areas, German or Japanese or Spanish may be used in the home, in shops, and in other local settings; but English is the language which must be used with outsiders, the official language, and the language of most media (though there may be local radio stations and newspapers which use the subordinate language). It is also, for the most part, the language of the schools, although bilingual education programs have been developed in some areas.

Typically, in ethnic enclaves, children learn to speak English more fluently and with less "foreign" accent than their parents. Children may tend to lose fluency in their parents' language, especially if jobs or higher education attract them away from their home communities. However, there is also a resistance to complete assimilation by many members of distinctive ethnic communities, a conservative movement to maintain their traditions, cultural identity, and language.

Native American peoples (American Indians) have a special position in relation to the larger national society. In most cases, their communities are small, economically depressed, and culturally marginal to dominant groups in American society; and their cultural traditions are generally ignored or misunderstood by other Americans. During the past three centuries, some Indian tribes disappeared, and many others suffered military defeat at the hands of the advancing European population of North America. In the nineteenth century, some tribes, like the Cherokee and Creek, were forcibly removed from their homes; others, like the Hopi and Pima in Arizona, found themselves confined to only a small portion of their ancestral lands. Along with this, populations were much reduced in numbers, often decimated by disease. Defeated Indian tribes were subjected to restrictive and discriminatory legislation which limited their freedom, including the freedom to use and maintain their own languages.

The United States government, through the Bureau of Indian Affairs, has consistently favored the assimilation of native peoples. Government policy has promoted the breakdown of tribal lands, integration of native communities into the larger society, and learning of "American" ways. Indian schools are usually conducted in English, with the objective of reinforcing its use and hastening the extinction of native languages. Many American Indian languages have been lost; of perhaps 500 spoken in 1600, less than 200 are in use today. But most of these persist stubbornly, and in some cases the number of speakers is even increasing. Since the 1930s, something of a renaissance movement has grown. Native Americans have organized to resist cultural assimilation; their efforts to preserve their languages are, in this case as in others, just one part of a larger struggle for human rights and self-determination.

Most American anthropologists, whatever their own national or ethnic origins might be, feel that they have a vested interest in the survival and well-being of minority cultural groups and languages, in this country and elsewhere in the world. One reason for this feeling is found in the training and professional involvements of anthropologists: most of us have lived and worked (sometimes almost as adopted members) in minority communities, and have learned to understand, respect, and value their traditions. Valuing them, it becomes our duty to assist in maintaining them, and many anthropologists have undertaken to do so. One way in which anthropological linguists have contributed is seen in the work toward developing practical writing systems, teaching materials, and the promotion of literacy in Native American languages.

Kenneth Hale, one of a number of anthropological linguists who have worked with Navajo educators in developing teaching materials for use with Navajo-

speaking children, emphasizes the important role of native knowledge in this part-
nership (Hale, 1974). I. Goosen, another linguist, has developed a series of introductory lessons in the Navajo language, a simplified Navajo orthography, and
has helped to prepare textbooks and other materials for Navajo schools (Goosen,
1967; Hall, 1971). The objectives of this work include, on the one hand, the
preservation of the Navajo language by increasing the situations in contemporary
American life in which it can be used. On the other hand, both Navajo and non-
Navajo teachers are encouraged to make education more rewarding and useful for
Navajo children by drawing on the knowledge of their own language and culture
which they bring into the classroom.

Similarly, linguists Dean and Lucille Saxton have worked together with several
Papago collaborators in publishing a dictionary, collections of myths and tales, and
other cultural materials. Their work is printed in a practical Papago orthography,
and is designed to be of use to the Papago people as well as to scholars in anthro-

Fig. 9. Cover illustration from Kee's Home *by Mrs. Bradley J. Hall. Copyright ©
1971 by Mrs. Bradley J. Hall. Mrs. Hall is a teacher in the Many Farms Navajo
School. This bilingual Navajo-English primer involves the cooperation of an
artist, Vera Drysdale; a linguist, Irvy Goosen; and a Navajo consultant, Loretta
Begay.*

pology and linguistics. Some scholars in these fields have, in the past, been drawn from native communities, and more will be in the future. It is of interest that the Saxtons dedicated their publications to, and see them as the continuation of the work of, an earlier scholar, Juan Dolores, who was himself a native speaker of Papago (Saxton and Saxton, 1973).

LANGUAGE AND WRITING

Despite the prevalence of print in our own lives, writing has not always been a characteristic of our culture. As we have seen, speech is everywhere and at all times a part of human life; our specialized nervous systems and vocal tracts testify to our evolution as *speaking* animals. But *writing* is a fairly recent achievement. It is an artifact of culture which meets the needs of human life in certain times and places, but is absent in others. Anthropologists sometimes classify human societies historically as *preliterate* (or uncivilized) and *literate* (or civilized). It has also been suggested that, with increasing reliance on computers and electronic communications media, we may be entering a *postliterate* stage of history.

In other words, there are social conditions under which writing has been invented and is of use, and there may also be conditions under which it will fall out of use. (Though, surely, there will still be literate specialists who can decipher the ancient records of our civilization!) Writing is, in origin, an elaboration or specialization of a much more ancient and universal type of human activity: graphic representation, including drawing and the use of marks for counts and tallies. People in other times and places have used conventionalized drawings—pictographs—as signs of identity, sacred symbols, records of historical events, and the like. In a study of Paleolithic artifacts, A. Marshack has shown that evidence of such activities—pictographs and tallies which appear to record the passing of seasons, phases of the moon, and number of days—can be traced far back in prehistory(Marshack, 1972). Graphic representations of events and concepts may be almost as ancient as *Homo sapiens*.

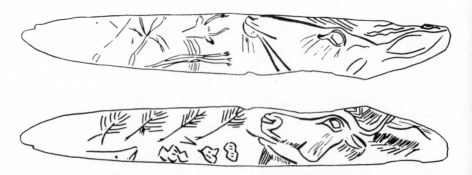

Fig. 10. Two sides of an engraved bone "knife," Magdalenian culture, Upper Paleolithic. The designs are animal heads, serpentine lines, branches, and other vegetation forms; the meaning is, of course, unknown. © *Alexander Marshack 1972.*

Fig. 11. Signpost in the National Zoo, Washington, D.C. Designed by Wyman & Cannan Ltd.

We still make use of signs which resemble pictographs, to give

warnings,   information,   or directions.

Such signs may be, as these are, simplified and highly conventionalized, but they encapsulate complex messages. These conventionalized signs resemble writing, but there are basic differences: in writing, there is a one-to-one relationship between structural units of language (words, syllables, or individual sounds) and the drawn or printed symbols. There is a linear order which follows that of speech. And while only selected information can be encoded in pictographs, a real writing system can transmit anything which can be put into words.

Still, writing must have had its origin in conventionalized drawings. Both the "letters" of our European alphabets and the "characters" used in Chinese and Japanese writing can be traced back to pictorial origins: the letter A, for example, is descended from ⱶ *aleph* ("ox"), apparently a stylized drawing of the head of an ox. Similarly, the Chinese character 日 *rì* ("sun," "day"), was earlier written ⊖, which is interpreted as a drawing of the sun. In both cases, early writing comes closer to pictorial forms than do more advanced systems, when the symbols have become more conventionalized and abstract (Gelb, 1963).

From its beginnings in pictorial representation, writing has followed two diverging lines of development. Modern writing systems can usually be placed in one or another of these traditions, although the two have often merged and influenced one another in a variety of ways. Writing systems of the first type are *logographic* (or *ideographic*); essentially, they employ symbols which stand for lexemes, whole words or units of meaning. In the evolution of such a system, pictures of things (the sun, for example) may be generalized or extended to stand for related and associated things or qualities (such as day, light, or brilliance). Chinese is perhaps the best modern example of a writing system which is basically logographic (though it also incorporates elements of other types).

In a logographic writing system, the individual symbols are whole units which have meaning; they cannot ordinarily be analyzed into smaller parts, and there is no direct connection between the writing and the sounds of speech. Such a writing system is difficult to learn since there must be, roughly, one written symbol for each item in the vocabulary; an erudite knowledge of classical Chinese literature requires control of several thousand characters—there are said to be around 50,000 in all. However, this type of writing also has its advantages. The greatest advantage is perhaps the fact that, since the characters stand for meanings and not for sounds, the same writing system can be used by speakers of different dialects or even different languages. What is required is cultural similarity and a shared system of meanings. As we have noted, the main "dialects" of Chinese (Mandarin, Cantonese,

彊克其萬年子子孫孫永寶用
畯臣天子克其日易休無
口口口降克多福眉壽永令
其用朝夕享于皇且皇且考其
用獻于師尹朋友昏溝克
不顯魯休揚用作旅盨克惟
田人克拜稽首取對天子
令尹氏友史趞典善夫克
吉庚寅王才周康穆宮王
惟十又八年十又二月初

Fig. 12. Modern Chinese writing. Reprinted from A Study of Writing *by I. Gelb by permission of The University of Chicago Press. Copyright © 1963 by The University of Chicago Press.*

Suchow, Hakka, and others) are really quite different from one another, and not mutually intelligible when spoken; however, the use of a common system of writing facilitates communication and cultural diffusion and has, over the centuries, helped to maintain the unity of the Chinese cultural sphere.

The second line of development appeared first in the western Orient, and has given rise to most of the writing systems of the modern world (outside of Southeast Asia). In this case, pictorial signs came to stand for phonetic units, rather than for units of meaning. In principle, signs of this sort resemble the kind of modern word-puzzle called a rebus.

The two kinds of signs—logographic word-signs along with those of the rebus type—are found together in Egyptian, Hittite, and other early writing in the eastern Mediterranean area. However, the rebus idea eventually won out, and in turn was the basis for a more economical and flexible system of writing, the syllabary. By about 5000 years ago, there were a number of written languages of the syllabary type in use in western Asia; the most famous of these is the West Semitic syllabary, the ancestor of modern Hebrew and Arabic scripts.

In a perfect syllabary there would be a written symbol for each different syllable used in a language. The number of these varies from language to language, but most would be in the vicinity of 100—a larger number of signs than in our alphabet, but much lower than is required in a logographic system, when signs represent individual words or concepts. The Hittite syllabary, used in Syria between 1500 and 700 B.C., exemplifies this principle.

In the course of time, some syllabaries were simplified by reducing the use of separate signs to only the most common syllables; additional consonants or vowels were then indicated by diacritic marks. This actually anticipated the idea of the alphabet, since some individual phonemes are separated out of the larger unit, the syllable. Most of the ancient writings of the Near East, which survive in the form of cuneiform inscriptions on baked clay tablets, represent this type of syllabary. In the Old Persian writing system, for example (600–400 B.C.), there are separate signs for three vowels (a, i, u); there are signs which can be used for consonants followed by a (the most common vowel) or for the consonant alone; and there are signs which stand for consonants followed by the other vowels. The total number of signs is 36.

The West Semitic syllabary used by the Phoenicians was still more condensed than the Persian in that most of the signs stood for consonants *with or without* a following vowel. In the Semitic languages, vowels are dropped or added, depending on the grammatical or syntactic function of the word in which they occur, and can often be predicted on the basis of context. Therefore, it was a convenient shorthand or simplified form of writing to omit them, at least in recording business transactions (the main context in which Phoenician writing is known). The signs were as few in number as in an alphabet, and they became the basis for alphabetic writing when borrowed by and adapted to the Greek language. This happened some time before the eighth century B.C. (Gelb. 1963).

The Greek writing system is the first which is considered truly alphabetic; that is, there is a separate written symbol for each vowel and each consonant, a total of 22. There were further modifications when the alphabet was later adapted to Latin and other western Mediterranean dialects. Greece and Rome were the centers out of

	a	e	i	u
Vowels				
Nasals				
ḫ				
i̯				
k/g				
l				
m				
n				
p/b				
r				
s				
š				
t/d				
w				
z (=ts)				
Syllables of unknown value				

Fig. 13. The Hittite hieroglyphic syllabary. Reprinted from A Study of Writing *by I. Gelb by permission of The University of Chicago Press. Copyright © 1963 by The University of Chicago Press.*

which alphabetic writing diffused to northern and western Europe, through trade, conquest, and administration. Latin was the official language of the Roman Empire, and the Latin alphabet was adapted to the writing of other languages as well. Later, under the aegis of the Christian religion, knowledge of the Latin alphabet was carried far and wide by missionary priests of the Roman Catholic Church, while the Greek alphabet was adopted in the parts of eastern and central Europe (the Balkans and Russia), where the Greek Orthodox denomination prevailed.

In the Far East, the logographic Chinese system has been, over the years, modi-

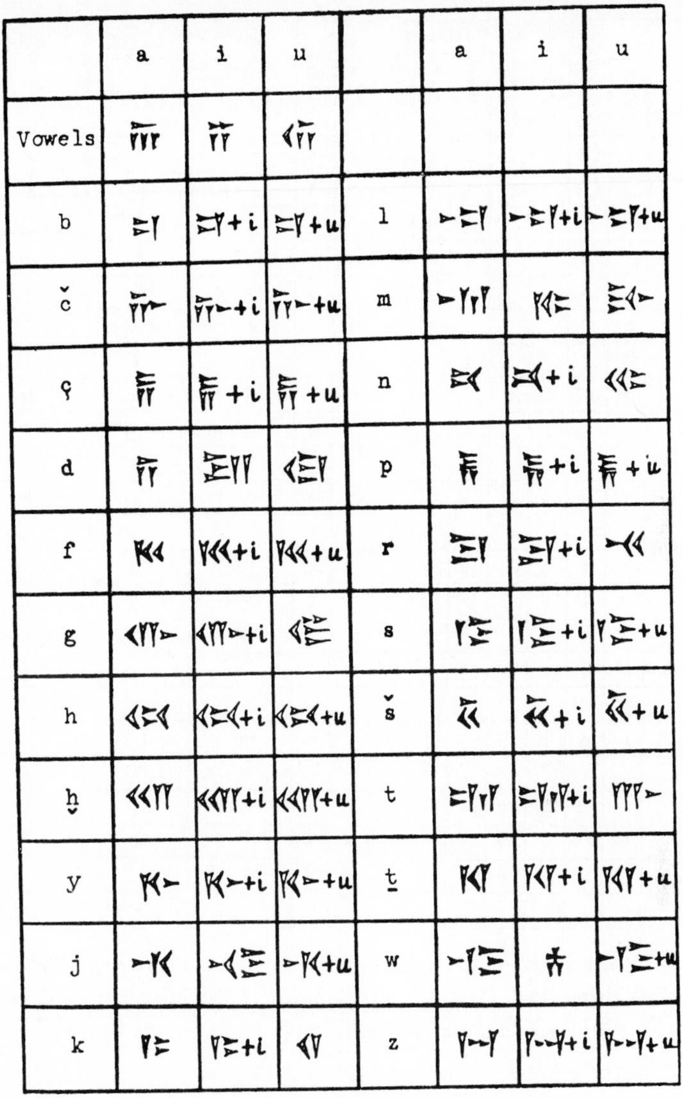

	a	i	u			a	i	u
Vowels	𒀀	�că	�că					
b		+i	+u	l			+i	+u
č		+i	+u	m				
ç		+i	+u	n			+i	
d				p			+i	+u
f		+i	+u	r			+i	
g		+i		s			+i	+u
h		+i	+u	š			+i	+u
ḫ		+i	+u	t			+i	
y		+i	+u	ṯ			+i	+u
j			+u	w				+u
k		+i		z			+i	+u

Fig. 14. Old Persian syllabary. Reprinted from A Study of Writing *by permission of The University of Chicago Press. Copyright © 1963 by The University of Chicago Press.*

fied in a number of ways; for example, there are "phonetic" signs which may be used in combination with logographic signs in order to distinguish between the several possible meanings which these might have. Syllabic and alphabetic orthographies have also been developed, but the system in general use is still the logographic. Japanese writing was also derived from the Chinese by adapting Chinese characters to stand for phonetic segments; thus, the originally logographic system was converted into a syllabary.

Of the three main types of writing—logographic, syllabic, and alphabetic—the syllabary seems somehow the most "natural," to judge by the fact that this type

| WEST SEMITIC | | | | | | | | | | | GREEK | | LATIN |
AHIRĀM	RUWEISEH	AZARBAʕAL	YEHIMILK	ABIBAʕAL	ELIBAʕAL	SAPATBAʕAL	MESAʕ	ZINCIRLI	CYPRUS	SARDINIA	OLD	LATE	
K	K	K	K,K	K	K	K	K	K	K	K	⸮, A	A	A
ꟻ	ꟻ	ꟻ	ꟻ,ꟻ	ꟻ	ꟻ	ꟻ	ꟻ	ꟻ	ꟻ	ꟻ	ꓘ, 𐌁	B	B
⅄		⅄	⌃	⌃	⌃	⌃,⌃	⅄	⌃	⌃	⌃	⅂, ⌃	Γ	C (& G replacing Z)
◁	◁		◁		△	△	◁	△	△,△	△	△	△	D
⅂			⅂				⅂	⅂	⅃	⅃	⅂, ⅂	E	E
Y	Y	Y		Y	Y	Y	Y	Y	Y	Y	⅂, Y, V	(Y at end)	F (& U,V,Y at end)
I	I	I		I	I	⊥	⊥	I			I	Z	(Z at end)
⊟	8	8	H,8		8	8	⊟	⊟		8	8	H	H
⊕						⊖	⊗	⊕		⊕	⊗, ⊕	Θ	
⟨	⟨	⟨	⟨		⟨	⟨	⟨	⟨	⟨	⟨	⟨, ⟩	I	I
⅄	⅄	⅄	⅄	⅄	⅄	⅄	⅄	⅄	Ж	⅄	⅂, ⅄	K	K
⅃		⅃	⅃	⅃	⅃	⅃	⅃	⅃	⅃	⅃	⅂, ⅃	Λ	L
ᛞ		ᛞ	ᛞ	ᛞ	ᛞ	ᛞ	ᛞ	ᛞ	ᛞ	ᛞ	ᛘ	M	M
ч	ч	ч	ч		ч	ч	ч	ч	ч	ч	ч	N	N
Ⅎ		Ⅎ					Ⅎ	Ⅎ			Ⅎ	Ξ	(X at end)
o	o	o	o	o	o	o	o	o	o	o	o	O	O
⌐		⌐	⌐		⌐	⌐	⌐	⌐	⌐	⌐	⌐, ⌐	Π	P
	ᚺ		ᚼ	ᚺ			⊢	⊢		ᚺ	ᛘ, ᛘ	(M)	
		φ				φ	φ	φ	φ		φ, φ	(φ)	Q
⍰		⍰	⍰	⍰	⍰	⍰	⍰	⍰	⍰	⍰	⍰, P	P	R
w	w	w		w	w	w	w	w	w	w	⟨, ⟨, ⟨	Σ	S
+,X		+	X		✝	+	X	✝	✝	X	T	T	T
												Υ,Φ,Χ,Ψ,Ω	U,V,X,Y,Z

Fig. 15. Comparative chart of Greek and West Semitic writings. Reprinted from A Study of Writing by I. Gelb by permission of The University of Chicago Press. Copyright © 1963 by The University of Chicago Press.

has been invented again and again. Full-fledged logographic systems are few, and it would appear that the principle of the alphabet has arisen only once.

New writing systems of the syllabary type, such as the Cherokee "alphabet" invented by Sequoyah in 1821, are built on the same general plan as that of the ancient Hittites. The Cherokee syllabary has 85 symbols, many of them adapted from the shapes of the English alphabet; they correspond almost perfectly to the syllable structure of the Cherokee language. When introduced to the Cherokee people, the syllabary was quickly accepted, since only a few hours of instruction were required for a speaker of Cherokee to learn to use it. This writing system was widely used in publications by the Cherokee nation, for official documents and a newspaper, until the destruction of the Cherokee printing press during the American Civil War. Since that time it has been used largely in private correspondence and in connection with religious affairs. Recently, there have been new efforts to promote the use of the Cherokee language and publications in Cherokee have increased, especially for educational purposes.

Another ingenious syllabary was invented in 1840 by J. Evans, a missionary, for the writing of Cree, Ojibwa, and neighboring Algonkian dialects; it also has been modified for use by Canadian Eskimo. The Evans syllabary spread widely in Canada, and is still much used in personal correspondence and other private functions, though it is no longer used in official publications since the Canadian government has adopted an orthography based on the Latin alphabet for the writing of native languages (Walker, 1975).

In contrast to the syllabary, the principle of the alphabet was invented only once. All alphabetic writing systems are, directly or indirectly, derived from the Greek and Latin alphabets and are thus related to one another; all of them have diversified within, roughly, the last 2000 years.

	e	i	o	a	nonpre-vocalic
Vowel only	▽	△	▷	◁	
p	∨	∧	>	<	‹
t	∪	∩	⊃	⊂	⸦
c	˥	ſ	∪	∪	∪
k	٩	P	d	b	▸
m	˥	Γ	⅃	L	L
n	•	σ	●	₰	▴
l	⊃	⊂	⊋	⸧	⸦
s	↖	⌁	⌁	↖	↘
š	٢	ʃ	↝	↪	↪
y	↙	↗	↙	↳	•
r	⌣	⌢	ʔ	ς	⸤

Fig. 16. The James Evans syllabary as adapted to Moose Cree by John Horden in the 1850s, reproduced from Willard Walker, "Notes on Native Writing Systems and the Design of Native Literacy Programs," Anthropological Linguistics (May 1969), which was based on a chart of the Cree syllabary in C. Douglas Ellis, Spoken Cree West Coast of James Bay, Part 1, The Department of Missions (M.S.C.C.), The Anglican Church of Canada, Church House, 600 Jarvis St., Toronto 5.

It would seem obvious that no set of written symbols or type of writing system has any necessary association with any particular language or family of languages. In fact, the distinctive characteristics of individual orthographies have developed as they have been borrowed and adapted or modified. In this way, new letters may be invented while others fall out of use, signs have been converted from representing syllables to single phonemes, diacritic marks are added or dropped, the phonetic value of a sign changes over time, and so forth.

Writing begins in the context of politically complex, centralized societies; it may have served commercial interests first, but has been intimately associated with the hierarchies of both church and state. Writing has usually diffused from one geographical area to another with the spread of empires and/or world religions. Although a need for literacy may be stimulated by technological changes and economic growth, writing itself has been more directly linked with religion. In the present century, many Catholic and Protestant missionaries have devoted themselves to the study of native languages in Africa, Oceania, and the Americas. Their first objective is the development of alphabets for translating the Bible and other religious literature into native languages; linguistic study is thus an essential part of the religious mission. The Summer Institute of Linguistics is one major organization which prepares missionary linguists for the work of linguistic study and Bible translation; the training of these missionaries emphasizes phonemics as the basis for practical writing systems.

Even though writing may be introduced in the service of a particular religious sect or denomination, its introduction can mark the beginning of other changes; literacy promotes modernization and enables isolated communities to participate in national and international political movements. For this reason, political leaders often welcome the help of missionaries in developing alphabets and introducing literacy programs, even though they may not share the religious orientation of the missionary organization. The Summer Institute of Linguistics, for example, has worked in collaboration with governmental agencies in Latin American countries such as Peru and Mexico in promoting common educational goals.

TOPICS FOR STUDY AND DISCUSSION

1. Monitor the variation in your own speech behavior, with attention to the sociocultural factors outlined in this chapter. How is your selection of vocabulary (in salutations, or in the use of slang, for example) affected by the presence of older people? younger? strangers? male or female companions?
2. What are the main varieties of language in use in your community? What patterns of code-switching are you familiar with? Try to make a summary statement about this which takes into consideration the ethnic and socioeconomic diversity of the community.
3. Discuss the social and political advantages and disadvantages of promoting literacy in minority languages.
4. Take a sampling of opinion to learn what stereotypes exist about differences between men's and women's speech. Can you observe such differences in styles of speaking?
5. Who coined the term *phatic communication*, and what did he mean by it? Collect some examples of this kind of communicative behavior by listening as

you ride the bus or elevator, stand in line in cafeteria or supermarket, sit at a lunch counter, and so on. Compare; do you find much variety?

6. What are the differences among logographic, syllabic, and alphabetic writing systems? Find examples of each of these types, using nontextbook sources, if possible.

7. Using several of the Case Studies in Cultural Anthropology (published by Holt, Rinehart and Winston), compare the social settings and functions of speaking. Pay attention to the internal divisions and groupings in each society. Try to discover which categories of persons would be in intimate association; which would be distant; which relationships are relaxed and might permit joking; which are reserved and formal. What are the occasions for discussion, and who participates? When and how do children learn to take part? What does the ethnographer say about special styles of speaking? verbal formulas for different occasions? women's and men's speech? verbal etiquette between different statuses?

You might want to go further and use your analysis as the basis for writing a proposal for a sociolinguistic study. What questions remain unanswered, and how could you go about answering them?

7

Language and Culture

A language enables its speakers to relate to their environment, to describe and identify natural and cultural objects, and to organize and coordinate their activities. However, no language is in any sense an exact and perfect copy of the real world. This is inevitably the case because the range of stimuli and sensory experiences encountered by any individual is vast in number and to some extent unique (differing from the experiences of every other individual). Every apple or snowflake, every butterfly or human being can be distinguished from every other; however, the vocabulary of each language names classes of such items. The English word *apple*, for example, is ordinarily applied to fruit which may be large or small, ripe or unripe, and includes many varieties which differ in shape, taste, and color. It might not be obvious to someone unfamiliar with this fruit that all varieties, green, yellow and red, are apples; it is conceivable that another language might use two or more labels to cover this range of variation, or might distinguish the several varieties (Rome, Delicious, Winesap, Jonathan, and so on) without a more inclusive term. In any event, the names that are applied stand for generalizations; they lump together an unlimited number of individual specimens on the basis of selected characteristics.

We can go further than this; since such categories are generalizations based on only a part of the observable characteristics, there can be differences between languages in the way the categories are defined. In fact, there *are* many such differences, and they contribute to the difficulty we often experience in translating from one language to another. This difficulty is not very great when we are dealing with such things as apples or axes, birds or fish, or the sun, moon, and stars—all of them are limited by definite boundaries. There is more striking variety in the ways in which continuous or unlimited areas of experience are broken up and categorized in different languages. Wholes (like the human body) are divided into parts, time and space are broken into units for counting and measuring, and sensory experiences like sounds, tastes, and colors are grouped and classified. The verbal "maps" for this kind of reality may be remarkably different with the kind of incongruities which have made some philosophers claim that real translation between languages is impossible.

A basic similarity as well as obvious differences can be seen in comparing the anatomical vocabulary of English with other languages, for example, Arawak (of South America) and Papago (North America). All of these (as probably all languages) have a special set of terms which segment the body into areas and parts. But there seems to be no natural or inevitable way to accomplish this segmentation. The division between "hand" and "arm," which seems natural and obvious to the speaker of English, is contrary to the distinction made in Arawak, where -*kabo* refers to the hand and lower arm, and -*duna* to the upper arm and shoulder. It is also contrary to the Papago *nowi* which includes the whole arm as well as the hand (Fig 17).

It might be noted in passing that differences of this sort are easily overlooked. An Arawak who has learned English is likely to simply equate his *dakabo* with *my hand*, and to translate it regularly that way. The difference in meaning, then, cannot usually be learned by direct questioning which is apt to produce such an exchange as:

Q. "What is the word for 'hand'?"
A. "*Dakabo.*"

Or, perhaps:

Q. "What does *dakabo* mean?"
A. "It means 'your hand'."

The author has elicited anatomical terms in Arawak simply by touching or pointing to various areas of the body and recording the words given in response. Other fieldworkers have been known to use such aids as anatomical diagrams or

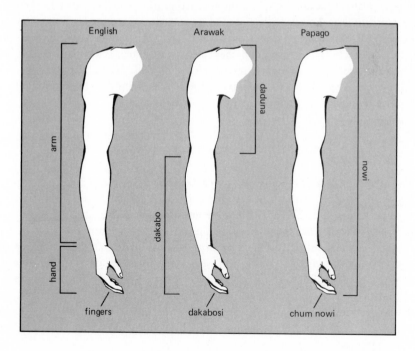

Fig. 17. English, Arawak, and Papago terms for the hand and arm.

models such as the "Visible Man" kit in an effort to get at the meaning of terms without the influence of one language on the other which intrudes with bilingual questioning or the use of a translator.

Many anthropologists who have learned languages in the process of studying the culture of the speakers have commented on the close connections between particular languages and cultures. Franz Boas, who encouraged anthropologists to study both the languages and the cultures of native peoples, did his first field study in 1883–1884 among the central Eskimo of Canada. He published a book on Eskimo culture as well as a study of the language. Boas had noted that there are a large number of words available in this language for naming and referring to such important features of environment as snow, ice, and seals. Some years later, in his Introduction to the *Handbook of American Indian Languages*, he cited such an example: in the Eskimo language ". . . the SEAL in different conditions is expressed by a variety of terms. One word is the general term for SEAL; another one signifies the SEAL BASKING IN THE SUN; a third one, a SEAL FLOATING ON A PIECE OF ICE; not to mention the many names for the seals of different ages and for the male and female" (Boas, 1911). In other words, while English has a single term *seal* and must use compounds (*seal-calf, bull seal*, and so on) or descriptive phrases, the Eskimo use a larger, specialized vocabulary.

Boas's characterization of the Eskimo language has become a classic example, often cited to show a close connection between language and the content of culture. However, it simply illustrates a tendency which can be seen, to some degree, in all languages: points of cultural emphasis are usually directly reflected in language through the size, specialization, and differentiation of vocabulary. That is, there are more separate terms, more synonyms, and more fine distinctions made in reference to features of environment or culture with which the speakers are the most concerned. There are fewer terms and they tend to be more generalized when they refer to features which are given less cultural emphasis. "Cultural emphasis" may indicate environmental or economic factors which are critical to subsistence; it can also comprehend esthetic, religious, or other kinds of values.

LANGUAGE AND "WORLD VIEW"

The most famous anthropological approach to the relationship between language and culture is found in the writings of Benjamin L. Whorf, and in the later development of his ideas by anthropologists and linguists, as the *Whorf hypothesis*. Whorf began with the assumption that there is a close connection between language and culture, and that the study of a language gives an indication of the categories and relationships—the "world view"—as seen by speakers of the language. This was also the opinion of Franz Boas and other founders of linguistic anthropology, including Edward Sapir, an important figure in the history of both cultural anthropology and linguistics who was Whorf's teacher. However, Whorf went beyond Sapir and most of his contemporaries by assigning a *priority* to language in this relationship.

Let us return to the observation that the categories in language are, and must be, a sort of generalization based on the selection of a few (out of all possible) features. Whorf recognized this, and drew from it a corollary about the effects of this classification of experience on the psychology of the speakers of languages. He concluded that the *obligatory* categories in language, and the features which speakers must notice, condition the way in which they perceive and experience reality. Each language, then, could be said to enforce its own peculiar logic on its speakers.

Whorf was concerned with English and other Western languages, and also with various American Indian languages. He began his interest in language as an amateur while holding a professional position with an insurance firm; he became interested in the apparent connection between the ways language is used and the occurrence of accidents such as fires and explosions. For example, he noted that "empty" gasoline drums are often treated carelessly, apparently because they are considered "empty" (despite the explosive vapor they still contain). Similarly, a highly inflammable material called "spun limestone" was ignored as a fire hazard, apparently because workers assume that "stone" is incombustible. Whorf went on from examples like this to draw large-scale conclusions about linguistic patterning and its influence on behavior.

The non-European language which he studied most methodically was Hopi, an American Indian language of the southwestern United States. It is Hopi which, in Whorf's writings, provided the greatest interest as a contrast to English. He wrote a grammatical sketch of Hopi and published several articles, in both scholarly and popular journals, on the world view which he found expressed in linguistic materials which he had collected (Whorf, 1956). In his writings, Whorf compared Hopi to what he called "SAE" (Standard Average European—English, French, German, and so on). Most of his discussion concerned broad areas of meaning which he felt must be dealt with, in one way or another, by all languages. Whorf asked: "(1) Are our own concepts of "time," "space," and "matter" given in substantially the same form to all men, or are they in part conditioned by the structure of particular languages? (2) Are there traceable affinities between (a) cultural and behavioral norms and (b) large-scale linguistic patterns?"

Plurality and Numeration   SAE languages can form both "real" and "imaginary" plurals—"ten men" and "ten days." "Ten men" can be seen and counted as a group; "ten days" is considered an "imaginary" plural because it cannot be objectively experienced as an aggregate. This last is also an example of what Whorf considered a characteristic tendency of SAE to *objectify* time and treat it as if it were a measurable substance. Thus we often speak of a "length of time," a "point in time," and "saving time."

Hopi does not form "imaginary plurals"; only objective aggregates can be counted. Units of time are treated as cyclic events, and time is not measured.

Temporal Forms of Verbs   "The three-tense system of SAE verbs colors all our thinking about time." With our objectified sense of time, said Whorf, we "stand time units in a row" with boundaries between them, whereas in consciousness there is actually unity. Many non-SAE languages have basically two tenses: "earlier" and "later." Hopi verbs are marked by *validity forms*, which indicate whether the speaker reports, expects, or speaks from previous knowledge about the situation at hand; and *aspects*, which indicate duration and other tendencies of the action; there is reference to time only when there are two clauses and two different actions, when modes indicate the temporal relationships (simultaneous, earlier, later).

For many readers, a discussion in this vein might have its greatest significance in giving some insight into the limitations of English. By seeing that Hopi may, at times, give a more accurate picture of reality than does English or other SAE languages, one becomes aware of the arbitrary and incomplete nature of linguistic patterning, which might otherwise go unquestioned. Whorf argued that the contrasts go beyond the language itself and relate to differences in ways of thinking and perceiving. For an individual, this is the "thought world," the "microcosm that each man carries about within himself, by which he measures and understands what he can of the macrocosm."

The SAE microcosm, according to Whorf, sees the world in terms of "things," and imposes spatial forms on nonspatial aspects of existence. The Hopi microcosm, by contrast, "seems to have analyzed reality largely in terms of events (or better,

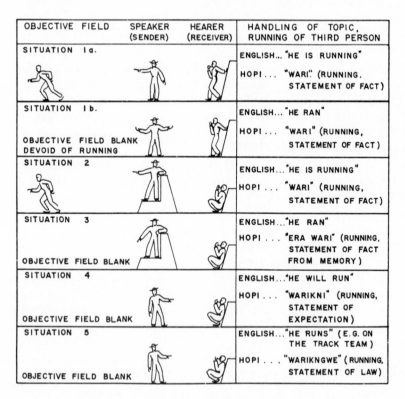

Fig. 18. Contrast between a "temporal" language (English) and a "timeless" language (Hopi). What are to English differences of time are to Hopi differences in the kind of validity. Reprinted from Language, Thought and Reality *by Benjamin Lee Whorf by permission of The MIT Press, Cambridge, Massachusetts. Copyright © 1956 by the Massachusetts Institute of Technology.*

'eventing'). . . ." Perceptible physical events are seen as outlines, colors, movements; perceptible and nonperceptible events are described in terms of intensity, duration, cyclicity. The characteristics of Hopi culture which Whorf saw as related to these linguistic features is *an emphasis on preparation,* especially in relation to religious ceremonials (which include a period of inner preparation in prayer and meditation, public announcement, and an emphasis on correct performance of a number of prescribed steps leading up to the public stage of the ceremonials; Whorf, 1941).

Whorf was not alone in hypothesizing a formative role for language in relation to thinking and cultural behavior. For example, his contemporary, Dorothy Lee, discussed language as the means through which experience is codified in different cultures, including Greek, Wintu of California, and the Trobriand Islands of Melanesia. Her views are quite similar to those of Whorf and Sapir (Lee, 1959). Whorf's writings achieved their greatest popularity in the 1950s several years after his death. More recently, there have been efforts to test and restate the "Whorf hypothesis" of the influence of language on behavior, in a more systematic and controlled way than did its originator.

LANGUAGE AND CULTURAL EMPHASIS

Whorf's goal was to identify parallels between the grammatical categories of language and the "logic" of culture. Assertions of such a relationship can be very persuasive, but they are difficult to prove. There is, however, a much more straight-forward relationship between language and culture to be found by studying vocabulary. Here we can find semantic structures which relate closely to areas of cultural emphasis.

Lexicon   A time-honored example was seen in the number of specialized terms referring to snow and ice, and to seals, in the Eskimo language as described by Franz Boas, discussed above (p. 108). Eskimo life included a great economic emphasis on these features of environment, and they have a correspondingly high value in Eskimo culture. Another example reported by a famous anthropologist relates specialized vocabulary to the economic and cultural importance of cattle and other animals in a pastoral society. The British anthropologist E. E. Evans-Pritchard wrote a classic ethnography of such a people, the Nuer of East Africa, revealing not only the many ways in which cattle are a focus of interest in the lives of these people, but also some of the linguistic reflexes of this interest.

In the following résumé, economic importance is reflected in the highly technical terminology with which the Nuer describe and identify their cattle. Appreciation and concern for the cattle are reflected in the individual names and words of praise which are applied to them, but the predominance of cattle herding over other interests also comes across—perhaps most strongly—in the transfer of cattle terminology into other areas of reference, such as personal names. Evans-Pritchard studied the Nuer in the 1930s. At that time, they lived by a combination of millet farming and cattle herding. In earlier times they kept more cattle and did less farming, and their outlook on life was strikingly dominated by their pastoral concerns. They had, one might say, a pastoral ideology. Evans-Pritchard's work gives many examples of ways in which this constant preoccupation with cattle is reflected in the use of language (though he does not discuss language per se).

First, the Nuer have a rich and varied vocabulary for the identification and description of cattle and the natural features and cultural traits which have to do with cattle (the equipment and processes of dairy work, for example). There is a great profusion of words which identify cattle, especially in regard to color and markings. There are ten "principal colour terms" which describe solid-colored animals (resembling white, black, chestnut, bay, and so forth), about 27 terms for various combinations of white and another color, and special terms for rare combinations of more than two colors.

The descriptive vocabulary becomes more complicated, as there are many special words which name patterns of marking and various combinations of colors. For example, the term *rol* indicates a white shoulder and foreleg, *kwe* a white face; thus, *kwe rol* is a cow with a combination of markings, *rol kwac* indicates a white foreleg combined with black spots, and *kwe looka* is a mouse-gray cow with a white face. There are several hundred combinations of this sort.

But beyond these terms which have primary reference to color and markings on the cattle, there are many others which metaphorically associate cattle with other animals, natural features, or objects. Again, the use of the words is based on the color and general appearance of the cattle. For example, spotted cattle can be called "leopard," "python" or "guinea-fowl," depending on the color or pattern of the spots; a black ox can be called "dark cloud" or "charcoal burning." Evans-Pritchard calls metaphoric terms of this sort the "fancy names" for cattle.

Further, there are six different terms for various configurations of horns; these are used in combination with any of the foregoing terms. And a long list of prefixed elements indicate the sex and age of the cattle, such as *tut*, "bull"; *yang*, "cow"; *nac*, "heifer"; *ruath*, "male calf"; or *kel*, "calf which has not begun to graze"; thus, *tut ma kar looka* specifies a "mouse-gray bull with a white back." There are potentially thousands of such terms, probably more than the total number of cattle owned by the Nuer at any given time!

This elaborate system of terminology is a rough indication of the economic importance of cattle for the Nuer. Cultural emphasis is a harder thing to measure, but it is the pervasive cultural importance of cattle to which Evans-Pritchard's discussion returns again and again. It would seem that every activity and every conversation has some reference, direct or indirect, to cattle: "He who lives among the Nuer and wishes to understand their social life must first master a vocabulary referring to cattle and the life of the herds" (Evans-Pritchard, 1940). Only a few selected examples will be noted here:

(1) *Social relationships are defined in terms of cattle.* Like many pastoral peoples, the Nuer formalize marriage by the payment of cattle. Cattle are owned by families, and each son has a right to animals from the family herd. At the time of marriage, a set number of cattle is given to the family of the bride and distributed among her relatives in a prescribed way. Patrilineal kinsmen—fathers, sons, and brothers—live close together and cooperate in caring for the herd. They know the history of each animal (its former owners, when it was obtained, and its parentage), and they are

concerned with the future distribution of cattle (when they will be given away, and to whom). Ties of marriage, past, present, and future, are directly equated with the payment of cattle from one family to another. That is why Evans-Pritchard remarks, "I used sometimes to despair that the subject of girls led inevitably to that of cattle."

(2) *The social use of cattle extends beyond the living.* Cattle are sacrificed to the ghosts of the dead, and there are also ceremonies for contacting the dead, which might, for example, involve rubbing ashes on the back of a cow. Thus, cattle are the link between the living and the dead. Talk about ancestors as well as about living necessitates constant reference to cattle.

(3) *The herds provide the Nuer "calendar" and "clock."* The whole course of a year's activities, the moving from villages to cattle camps, and other changes through the year, depend partly on the needs of cattle. The round of daily activities is also set by the cattle. Time reckoning is expressed in terms of these annual and daily cycles. Other activities are planned and coordinated by referring to such predictable events as the return from cattle camps, the birth of calves, or, during the day, milking time. There is no expression equivalent to "time" in the Nuer vocabulary; there is, rather, a sequence of activities focusing around cattle which makes up an annual and a daily cycle.

(4) *Cattle terminology is extensively used in names and titles of address.* This is perhaps the most striking reflection in language of the high cultural value attached to cattle. The Nuer make use of a variety of names and titles of address. A child is given a personal name soon after birth, a name which may be handed down from an ancestor or may refer to circumstances at the time of his birth (like "Heavy Rain" or "Cattle Camp"). Each child also inherits a "praise-name" which identifies him with his father's clan, and at times may be called by the praise name of his mother's clan as well.

Besides these, several names are acquired later in life. One of the most important is the "ox-name": at the time of his initiation into manhood, a boy is given a special ox, which becomes his favorite in the herd. His ox-name is a description of this ox, its markings or other attributes—for example, *Luthrial*, from *luth* (a bell worn by the ox) and *rial* (a part of an ox's name, indicating a distribution of colors) or *Duhorrial*, from *duhor* (a tassel worn by cattle) and *rial*. Little boys often call their playmates by names of a similar sort, taken from the calves which they care for, in anticipation of the ox-name which is received at initiation. And older men may take new ox-names when they acquire oxen of which they are especially fond; thus, an individual may have several ox-names, though the one given at initiation remains the one most often used. Ox-names are the ones most used among friends, and they are called out, with embellishments, in dancing and other public events; men shout their ox-names when attacking an enemy in battle or an animal in hunting.

Girls also may have ox-names, using them among themselves; and married women take cow-names. Both ox-names and cow-names are used in combination with other fancy "dance-names" on festive public occasions.

It can be seen that a Nuer is likely to accumulate a number of names in the course of his life. There is a definite etiquette in the use of names, as well as the kinship terms by which a person may also be addressed. Children are apt to be called by patronymics (the father's name), and elderly people by their children's names (teknonymics); generally, relatives try to avoid the use of personal names. Among persons of the same age, ox-names are most commonly used—one of many ways in which terms of address reflect social status (Evans-Pritchard, 1948).

Metaphor and Extension of Meaning   Certain linguists, whose main interest is in semantics (the study of meaning in language), have pointed out a special way in which vocabulary is related to its cultural context. This is in the use of figures of speech including *metaphors*, words or phrases which have their primary reference to one semantic area but are used, secondarily, in other ways. The secondary or transferred meanings are usually, though not always, more general or abstract than the primary meanings. A type of metaphor which seems almost universal is the use of words with primary reference to the human body for talking about inanimate objects or natural features. Thus, in English, we speak of the "eye" of a needle, the "mouth" of a cave or a river, the "foot" of a hill, the "arm" of a chair or of an organization, and the "heart" of a problem. Expressions of this sort are found in many languages, all over the world—so widely distributed that it seems to suggest a natural inclination in human language.

Some of these usages may be explained by what psychologists have called "physiognomic perception"; this is a tendency to perceive environmental features as essentially undifferentiated from the viewer. This type of reaction is especially characteristic of the drawings and descriptions of children, who may often draw a house, train, or mountain with a face, or attribute human motives to a tree, stone, or plaything. Adults also tend to describe abstract shapes by comparing them to human forms or movements. The suggestion that this is a "primitive" (and therefore perhaps universal) type of perception seems to be consistent with the widespread use of metaphors which seem to be based on such a view of the world.

A study by K. Basso is of interest in showing how a metaphoric extension of meaning can serve, in a changing culture, to provide the lexicon for a technological innovation. Rather than borrowing English vocabulary, or forming new Apache words, the speakers of Western Apache extended the range of meaning of existing vocabulary. It is of interest that cars and trucks are treated linguistically as if they were animate beings rather than inanimate things.[1]

Basso's study documents an instance in which "a body of native words was extended en masse" to cover an introduced type of material culture, namely, motorized vehicles. The anthropologist first elicited the Apache terms in reference to human anatomy, with meanings as in the first column below; they apply equally to animals, birds, and other animate beings; he then found that, by extension, they apply to cars and trucks, as shown in the second column.

It is important to note that the anatomical terms are an organized set, and are

---

[1] This sort of extension is not unusual in European languages. When they were younger, the Hickerson children conceived of the headlights of the family car as "eyes," the gas tank at the back as its "rump," and finally designated their mother as its "brain." But unlike the Apache example, these are nonstandardized figures of speech, playful alternatives to the standard lexicon.

WESTERN APACHE ANATOMICAL TERMS WITH EXTENDED MEANINGS

	re: man	re: auto, truck
łikə	fat	grease
dɔ	chin and jaw	front bumper
wos	shoulder	front fender
gən	hand and arm	front wheel
kai	thigh and buttock	rear fender
zɛ'	mouth	gas pipe opening
ke'	foot	rear wheel
yən	back	bed of truck
inda'	eye	headlight
ni	face	area from top of windshield to bumper
či	nose	hood
ta	forehead	top, front of cab
ɛbiyɨ'	entrails	machinery under hood
tsɜs	vein	electrical wiring
zɨk	liver	battery
pɨt	stomach	gas tank
či	intestine	radiator hose
jɨ	heart	distributor
jisolɛ	lung	radiator

extended as a set to apply to motor vehicles. This can be seen in the fact that the more inclusive terms (*ni* and *ɛbiyi'*) name areas for which there is no single term in English.

Basso offers two explanations—one cultural, the other linguistic—for the extension of anatomical terms to motorized vehicles. The first is the fact that cars, and especially pickup trucks, have functionally replaced horses. 'Since anatomical terms were customarily used to describe the horse, they were extended to its mechanized successor." The second explanation (which Basso favors) indicates that motorized vehicles fall into a broader classification grouping, *hinda*, which typically includes animate beings (humans, animals, fish, insects, and so on) and which contrasts with the category *desta,* inanimates such as topographical features and material objects. The basis for the classification appears to be the fact that the vehicles are "capable of generating and sustaining locomotive movement by themselves" (Basso, 1967).

There is another kind of metaphor which may also be universal in its general type, though it differs in specifics from one language (and culture) to another. This is a type which is of great interest because of its connection with cultural emphasis on values. A German linguist, Hans Sperber, asserted that "intense interest" in a subject leads to its use in describing other areas of experience; anthropologically, this would suggest that areas of cultural emphasis might provide vocabulary which is used, metaphorically, for other contexts. This seems a very likely hypothesis; unfortunately, Sperber and later linguists who have discussed his suggestion drew illustrations almost entirely from European history, and we have very little general information about the use of metaphors in other cultures (Ullman, 1966). We got a hint, perhaps, in reading about the Nuer's extended use of cattle terminology, as terms of address; here, words which have primary reference to cattle are used in other ways, in the more general context of human relationships. To this, we might compare information given us by Franz Boas on the use of metaphor in Kwakiutl, an American Indian language of the northwest coast of North America.

There are, in Kwakiutl (as in English), many euphemistic expressions for unhappy events; for example, "to grow weak," "to lie down," "to disappear from the world" are euphemisms in reference to death. There are also a wealth of formal expressions and actions which are used on ceremonial occasions. Many of these have to do with potlatch activities—invitations, speeches, feasting, and distribution of wealth. Marriage, with the formal exchange of property which accompanied marriages between noble families, was similarly rich in metaphoric formulae. Several cultural themes are prominent in the metaphoric expressions which Boas lists:

Salmon: "The guests of a person as well as wealth that he acquires are called his 'salmon.' . . . A great many guests are 'a school of salmon' . . . , and the house or village of the host his 'salmon weir' . . . into which he hauls . . . his guests. The valuable copper plates . . . the symbols of wealth, particularly are called 'salmon,' and the host expecting a copper plate . . . says in regard to it, 'Heavy is this salmon caught in my weir here.' Potlatch rivals are ridiculed by saying that 'they are losing their tails (like old salmon).' . . ."

Warfare: "The invitation to a potlatch in which hosts and guests rival in prodigality may be likened to war. The messengers who carry the invitation are called warriors . . . and the arriving guests sing war songs. . . . The copper plate is also called the 'citadel' of the chief. The orator says: 'Behold, now we stand on War (name of a copper plate), the citadel of our chief.' . . . 'When a copper is broken, by cutting it with a knife, it is 'killed.' A marriage formalized by exchange of property can be called 'to make war on the princesses'; another form is 'to try to get a slave.' "

Hunting and animals: Warriors refer to themselves as serpents, thunderbirds, killer whales: "We are the great thunderbirds and we avenge our late ancestors"; "we shall soar and grasp with our talons the Bella Colla"; rivals are demeaned by calling them "little sparrows," "horseflies," "mosquitoes," "old dogs."

Marriage can be ritualized in terms of whaling: a man "appears carrying a whaling harpoon which he throws into the house, thus harpooning the bride, whom he calls "a whale."

Houses, property: "To offer a copper plate 'which groans in the house for sale' is called to let it 'lie dead by the fire.' . . . The purchaser must 'take it up from the floor'. . . . The term for marrying 'means that the property given to the bride's father walks into his house.' In the course of marriage transactions, a number of chiefs make the first proposal to the bride's father; then they go back 'to shake (the bride) from the floor of the house.' After successive negotiations, she is induced to 'move on the floor,' to 'come right off the floor,' to 'approach the door,' and so on. She is 'dressed' by carrying a copper plate; successive gifts of blankets are called 'tump line,' 'belts,' 'boxes,' and 'canoes' (values measured in terms of blankets)" (Boas, 1929).

Although Boas's article gave no indication of the relative frequency of the various metaphoric expressions, it would appear such expressions were often used as a characteristic formal or ceremonial style. Salmon fishing, hunting (especially of sea mammals), warfare, and the emphasis on property are all prominent in descriptions of Kwakiutl culture.

Boas's article is of great interest since it is one of the few available studies of metaphor in a non-Western culture. We can, perhaps, get some sense of the cultural variability of metaphoric expressions by comparing epithets, or "praise-names," given to chiefs and other individuals of high status in very distinctive, and contrastive, cultural areas:

Kwakiutl: Honorifics given to Kwakiutl chiefs included: Post of our World, Great Mountains Standing on Edge, Overhanging Cliff, Loaded Canoe, and the Cedar that Cannot be Spanned (Boas, 1929).

Iroquois: The Iroquois tribes called themselves, collectively, "House-builders"; individual tribes and villages were named for their geographical location; clans are named for animals. An interesting and completely different set of terms was connected with the political League of the Iroquois. This was called "the Tree of Peace"; members of the League, "the great long roots," and "the great black leaves." A chief was "the main root" (Chafe, 1963).

Swazi: The Swazi of South Africa called their king by the title "Lion," and praised and flattered him with epithets such as "The Sun," "The Milky Way," and "Obstacle to the Enemy." The queen (mother of the king) had the title "Lady Elephant," and was called "The Earth," "The Beautiful," or "Mother of the Country" (Kuper, 1963).

Jukun: This horticultural people of the Nigerian plateau called their king by titles which identified him as the Moon, and in ceremonial contexts used the epithets "Our Guinea-corn," "Our Beans," "Our Ground-nuts," "Our Rain," and "Our Wealth." (One of the king's chief duties was control of the weather: through this, he controlled the crops; Meek, 1931).

Our Own Metaphors Metaphors are extremely common in everyday American English, and are drawn from a variety of semantic areas. Metaphoric reference to food is quite frequent; for example:

1. She's a cupcake.
2. She's a tart.
3. He's just a creampuff.
4. I'm in a pickle.
5. I'm in a stew.
6. That's a fine kettle of fish.
7. That's a tough nut to crack.
8. It's a piece of cake.[2]

[2] 1. She's an attractive girl. 2. She's flirtatious and easily seduced. 3. He has no strength or stamina. 4. I'm in trouble. 5. I don't know what to do. 6. That's a perplexing situation. 7. That's a difficult problem. 8. It's easy and rewarding.

Further, Americans are fond of such expressions as "Eating up the miles," "Eating his words," "A glutton for punishment," "Starved for affection," and "Hungry for success" (which has a "sweet taste"). We do not have enough cross-cultural information about metaphors to know whether food and eating are universally a source of metaphoric expressions, or whether this is a particular emphasis of American culture. Similar expressions, certainly, are fairly widespread.

There does not appear to be any single area of cultural emphasis, and there is no one profession or type of activity which predominates in our metaphoric expressions. This perhaps is expected, as there is a great diversity of social categories in American society, and there is no single occupation which carries high prestige (like cattle herding for the Nuer or salmon fishing for the Kwakiutl). One impressive fact, however, is the great frequency of metaphoric references to sports. It has been suggested that sports are a rather neutral area, a common ground in which Americans of all ages, occupations, and social status can meet and share a mutual interest and enthusiasm. This may help us understand why sports are frequently the bases of figures of speech which are extended in a general way to refer to social and interpersonal relationships. The most fertile source of all would appear to have been baseball, the "national pastime," which is the longest established and most closely identified with American culture. Some of the many such expressions which may be noted are:

1. He made a grandstand play.
2. She threw me a curve.
3. She fielded my questions well.
4. You're way off base.
5. You're batting 1000 (500, zero) so far.
6. What are the ground rules?
7. I want to touch all the bases.
8. He went to bat for me.
9. He has two strikes against him.
10. That's way out in left field.
11. He drives me up the wall.
12. He's a team player (a clutch player).
13. She's an oddball (screwball, foul ball).
14. It's just a ballpark estimate.[3]

Readers can doubtless think of other examples, since expressions of this sort are frequent in idiomatic American English. It would appear that speakers are at times aware, but often unaware, that they are comparing life to a ball game. (It might be of interest to compare American use of baseball metaphors to British or Australian use of expressions derived from the game of cricket.)

The metaphoric use of language is potentially one of the most fascinating links in the interrelationship of language and culture. However, it is a topic on which

[3] He did something spectacular in order to get approval. 2. She did or asked something unexpected, hard to respond to. 3. She answered my questions well. 4. You're not behaving properly. 5. All/half/none of your answers have been correct. 6. What are the arbitrary or conventional limitations? 7. I want to do everything that's expected of me. 8. He defended me, argued on my behalf. 9. He is at a great disadvantage. 10. That's very unusual. 11. It is hard for me to cope with him. 12. He cooperates well with others/does well under difficult conditions. 13. She behaves peculiarly/erratically/badly. 14. It's a rough estimate, probably exaggerated.

there is little detailed information. We do not even know, for example, whether metaphors are rare in some languages and especially plentiful in others (although this seems to be the case), nor do we understand the conditions which give rise to the use of metaphors. Collecting data of this sort demands a very sensitive control of a language, preferably that of a native speaker. Grammars and dictionaries seldom contain information on metaphors and it may be that metaphors, being largely stylistic, are often omitted when communication is difficult (when an anthropologist is asking questions of an informant, for example).

Taxonomy   It has been a concern of anthropologists in recent years to develop field methods for eliciting and comparing systems of classification, or taxonomies. The name *ethnoscience*, which is a special subfield of cultural anthropology, is most often used for this approach. It is also an obvious concern of linguistics, and an area in which linguistic and cultural study should be coordinated, since we often discover close parallels between linguistic and cultural categories. Some researchers have collected exhaustive botanical and zoological vocabularies, with an interest both in the rationale and functional basis for each system and in discovering universal features of taxonomic systems. It is of interest to discover, for example, how and under what circumstances general and specific terms develop, and to learn whether fine terminological distinctions are made (as they often are) in the classification of useful plants, while differences in other plant species may not be recognized (as in our English vernacular term *weed*).

A taxonomic study by J. A. Frisch examines a related topic, the internal structuring of the Maricopa category of food. Maricopa is an American Indian language native to desert areas of the southwestern United States. Frisch collected his data at the Salt River reservation in Scottsdale, Arizona.

The Maricopa word *čamač* ("food") includes anything edible; it is the most general term in the hierarchy. The domain of *čamač* includes three categories of

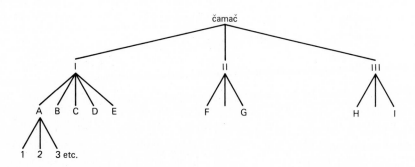

Fig. 19. The domain of čamač. *Reprinted from J. A. Frisch, "Maricopa Foods,"* International Journal of American Linguistics *(1968). Copyright © 1968 by* The University of Chicago Press.

edible things which can be easily distinguished since each occurs with a different verb. These categories are: Class I, foods which take the verb *maum*, "to eat"; Class II, foods which take the verb *cakaum*, "to consume something containing water"; Class III, liquids which take the verb *si:m*, "to drink."

As Frisch notes, a functional consideration in the classification of foods is the amount of water which they contain; this is the apparent semantic distinction between Categories I and II. "A possible explanation for the importance of the water/non-water distinction . . . is that the physical environment of the Maricopa Indians is that of a semi-arid desert with seasonal shortages of water. In aboriginal times such a distinction may have been of prime importance to survival" (Frisch, p. 20).

The lower levels of the hierarchy include the general and specific terms for various foods. Frisch lists only a limited selection of these. For example, Class I includes A. meat (1. beef, 2. pork, 3. deer, and so on); B. vegetables (6. beans, 7. greens, and the like); C. breads; D. canned food; and E. cooked food. Class II consists of F. fruits (10. oranges, 11. grapefruit, 12. watermelon, 13. melons, 14. cactus); G. vegetables (15. lettuce, 16. tomatoes). Class III includes H. juice; I. milk; and so on.

We might note that this Maricopa taxonomy shows both a similarity to and a difference from English. In English, the general class of "food" can be subdivided into solid foods which select the verb *eat* (bread, canteloupe, a ham sandwich, soup, ice cream), and beverages or drinks which take the verb *drink* (soft drinks, beer, clam juice, milkshakes). The striking difference lies in the three-way (rather than two-way) categorization in Maricopa, and in the apparent functional basis of the categorization. With this lack of "fit" between the Maricopa and English categories, a completely accurate translation would be impossible since English must translate both *maum* and *čakaum* as "to eat" (Frisch, 1968).

Frisch's study of Maricopa foods, as we have seen, is primarily a statement about categories in the language, but also suggests a practical basis for the categories in the subsistence culture of the Maricopa. His conclusions seem especially valuable because he uses a dual methodology; that is, he bolsters the ethnographic approach of asking for categories ("What kind of foods are there?" and so on) with strictly linguistic criteria (the fact that the categories select different verbs in the Maricopa language.

SOME TOPICS IN ETHNOLINGUISTICS

Color   (a) *The variety of human experience.* It has often been noted that there are marked differences among languages in the ways in which colors and similar visual phenomena are named and defined. An English-speaking child learns to name the colors of the rainbow as red, orange, yellow, green, blue, and violet (or purple), and he finds the same colors in his set of building blocks, modeling clay, water paints, or Crayolas. In many such contexts, one learns that these are the primary, standard colors. Other shades are considered to be modifications away from the focal values (lighter or darker) or are mixtures of the primary colors (blue green, purplish red, and so forth).

It may be difficult to conceive of the color spectrum as actually continuous; it is, however. Each shade grades into the next, and there are no natural boundaries between color areas. The basic color vocabularies of other languages (the counterparts of our *red, blue,* and so on), often stand for very different ways of dividing up this continuum. Even when there is close similarity between languages in color terms, the categories are seldom identical. A study of American Indian color vocabularies done in 1953 by an anthropologist, Verne F. Ray, demonstrates these points very clearly.

Ray collected the vocabulary used in identifying colors in a total of 60 different American Indian languages. Nine of these, along with English, are used as the basis of discussion in this study. All, including the English, were collected in the northwestern part of North America; it is of interest that there is such variety in color terminology of people living in the same general geographical and cultural areas.

Ray collected color terminology from individual informants who were shown cards of carefully controlled pigmentation under uniform conditions of lighting. The color samples were selected to give an even sampling of the spectrum and were, therefore, not biased in favor of any particular color system. (It might be noted that black, white, and shades of gray were not included.)

In the accompanying chart (Fig. 20), the divisions of the spectrum can be specified in terms of wavelength, shown in the left-hand side (along with approximate descriptive labels in English). Ray notes that the number of terms ranges from three to eight (this is also characteristic of the larger sample of languages); English, with six, is close to the average. The number of terms in a color system does not appear to relate to the technological complexity of the culture, to color in the environment, or to the artistic use of color. Ray was impressed by the fact that four languages spoken by people whose territories are very close to one another (Songish, Chetco, Rogue River, and Santiam—all in Oregon) have color terminologies that "vary as widely as any received" (Ray, 1953).

It should be emphasized that the number of "basic" terms of this sort does not limit the ability of speakers to talk about specific colors. Just as an English speaker can specify a shade as pumpkin color or pale bluish green (which are more specific than orange or green), each language can form similar expressions which Ray calls *descriptors.* But the need for them varies from one language to another: " . . . the person who has but three basic color terms at his disposal must more frequently use color descriptors to express his meaning."

One characteristic of many American Indian languages—which some observers have regarded as a defect—is a so-called blue–green confusion, that is, the range of color divided into *blue* and *green* in English (and other European languages) is covered by a single term. From the point of view of an English speaker, this amounts to a failure to distinguish two very different colors; in fact, some early investigators even suggested that non-Western people have a kind of blue–green color blindness.

A look at the chart shows us that the situation is not that simple. In some cases (Tenino and Chilcotin), a part of the range of green is covered by a term which also includes yellow, while the rest falls into blue. In other cases (Wishram,

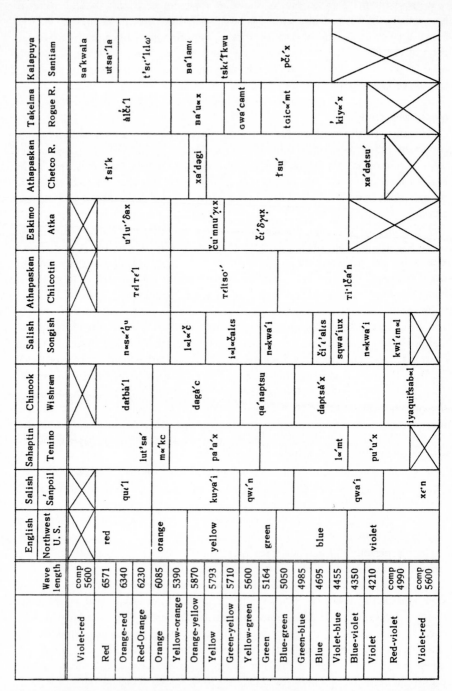

Fig. 20. Color categories in North American languages. Reprinted by permission from V. F. Ray, "Human Color Perception and Behavioral Response," Transactions *of the New York Academy of Sciences.*

Takelma), there are as many terms as in English, but the boundaries are different. In still other cases, there are more distinctions than in English; Ray makes a telling point when he comments that, from the point of view of Santiam, English confuses utsa·'la and t'si·'lílw· (both of which coincide with *red*). Similarly, we might note that for the speakers of Songish, English fails to distinguish či'i'alís and sqwaiux, both of which we lump together as *blue*.

Verne F. Ray's discussion of color terminologies presents a *relativistic* view of the differences between languages and cultures. He attempts to show that despite differences, each system is quite adequate to serve the needs of its speakers. "Color systems serve to bring the world of color sensation into order so that perception may be relatively simple and behavioral response, particularly verbal response and communication, may be meaningful." For color, and all other areas of perception, all languages appear to accomplish the same ends quite adequately (Ray, 1953).

(b) *The "insider's view" of culture.* It is difficult to compare any semantic area across language boundaries since each culture has its own organization, its own way of categorizing things, and of putting the pieces together. For example, in many languages the words which we translate as color terms have their primary reference to vegetation (as do some of our own, like *lilac* or *avocado*); in others, the references are anatomical (*red* often is the same word as *blood*, *yellow* as *bile*, and so on); and in still other cases, terms referring to light and shades of brightness are the source of color vocabulary. All of this is lost in the translation when we simply equate these words with our *red, yellow, blue,* and so forth.

Harold Conklin has made a truly valuable study in which he explores the internal organization of a system of color terminology and looks at its relation to the culture of the Hanunoo, of the Philippines. Conklin was led to collect and analyze color terms while conducting an extensive botanical study. The four main categories into which the Hanunoo group colors are closely tied to their view of the plant world. These are labeled by terms (which include a prefix *ma-*, which means "having" or "exhibiting" ...):

ma-biru	"darkness, blackness"
ma-lagti?	"lightness, whiteness"
ma-rara?	"redness, presence of red"
ma-latuy	"greenness, presence of green"

Thus, these words might be roughly translated into English as *black, white, red,* and *green*; however, they provide the Hanunoo with a four-way division of the spectrum which (like ours) can include any shade or mixture of colors. The four terms divide the spectrum into unequal parts; the largest is mabiru, which includes not only black but many deep shades (dark blue, violet, green, gray, and various mixtures). The range of malagti? includes white and many very lightly pigmented shades. These two terms can be understood as basically an opposition of light and dark.

The other two, malatuy and marara?, derive from an opposition of freshness or succulence, and dryness or desiccation in plants. Of these, malatuy corresponds roughly to light green, light yellow, and light brown; marara? to red, orange, yellow, and mixtures in which these predominate.

Hanunoo native arts feature indigo-dyed textiles and beadwork, with red being the preferred color of beads; native esthetics place an emphasis on the categories mabiru and marara?. By contrast to these, malagti? and malatuy are seen as weak, faded, and colorless. The shades of green which are the most visible features of the natural environment are thus considered unattractive; green is not used decoratively.

The Hanunoo language can designate colors more specifically than this, by words formed from specific terms such as *ashes, turmeric,* or *gold;* both these and the larger categories can be combined or modified. The four basic terms, however, provide the main framework in which color is categorized and discussed (Conklin, 1955).

(c) *The search for universals in language and culture.* In all of the languages of Europe, and in various other languages of industrialized or complex societies, color terms have evolved to an abstract level—that is, color is dissociated from natural objects or materials and other sources of pigment in the environment; divisions of the spectrum are labeled by words which stand for color and nothing else. All of our color terms (except, perhaps, *orange*) are words of this sort, which B. Berlin and P. Kay have called "basic color terms."

Berlin and Kay have argued that abstract or basic terms emerge, in the history of a language, in a predictable order. They administered tests and drew on field data for an initial sample of color terms in 20 languages and supplemented this with printed sources, such as dictionaries, for information on a larger number of languages. They were able to compare color terms cross-culturally by translating them (as they did the Hanunoo terms) with the English glosses: *black, white, red, green, yellow, blue, brown, pink, purple, orange,* and *gray.* According to their interpretation:

1. All languages contain terms for "white" and "black."
2. If a language contains three terms, then it contains a term for "red."
3. If a language contains four terms, then it contains a term for either "green"[4] or "yellow" (but not both).
4. If a language contains five terms, then it contains terms for both "green" and "yellow."
5. If a language contains six terms, then it contains a term for "blue."
6. If a language contains seven terms, then it contains a term for "brown."
7. If a language contains eight or more terms, then it contains a term for "purple," "pink," "orange," "gray," or some combination of these.

Berlin and Kay translate this ranking of languages according to the number of color terms into a developmental series of stages (numbered I–VII). In other words, they suggest that languages go through these stages in order. Their theory thus asserts an evolution of color terminology; they point out that many of the Stage I, II, and III color terms (Hanunoo would be classified as Stage III) are found in languages spoken by technologically simple peoples, while Stage VII is largely (but not entirely) found in modern industrialized societies (Berlin and Kay, 1969).

There are many inconsistencies and problems of interpretation in the data put forward by Berlin and Kay. A close study of certain languages might lead one to insist, for example, that there are *no* color terms of the sort which they define as

---

[4] This was later revised to *grue,* a category including "green" and "blue."

"basic," and that color does not exist as an abstract category. Berlin and Kay have also been criticized for making insufficient allowance for the influence of bilingualism and the borrowing of vocabulary from one language to another, especially under conditions of close cultural contact (Hickerson, 1971). However, some of the ideas on which they base their study do seem to hold true as tendencies, if not as inevitable developments: 1) Basic color terms develop and become more numerous over time; 2) the contrast of *light* and *dark* (or *black* and *white*) is everywhere expressed in vocabulary and seems to take precedence over the development of color terms based on contrasts in pigmentation; 3) words which can be translated as *black*, *white*, and *red* are the most widespread or universal categories. Red is, in physical terms, the most salient area in the spectrum; 4) beyond these three, there is in fact a great deal of variety in color terms, and there are many problems of translation in comparing the vocabularies of different languages.

Berlin and Kay argue that the order in which color terms emerge is determined by human anatomy—sensory receptors and neurological processes—as well as by the physical properties of the spectrum. If this were entirely the case, of course, the color categories of all languages would be exactly the same. Studies such as that of V. F. Ray have indicated that there is much variation; the differences between his findings and the "natural order" suggested by Berlin and Kay are hard to explain.

Nevertheless, Berlin and Kay and numerous students who have followed and been influenced by them have called our attention to the fact that the perception and categorization of color—like any other part of human behavior—is at least partly determined by human biology (the kind of animal we are), as well as by culture and the conditions under which we live. The categories into which languages classify colors do not vary in a random way; there are general, universal tendencies. Yet each system also has its unique, individual characteristics.

(d) *Language as a hierarchical system.* Besides noting the mapping of a field as a series of relations between individual terms and their referents, linguists must also take an interest in the hierarchial relationships among the terms. As we have seen, a semantic field (such as color, kinship, anatomy, or food) is divided into categories by the terms in the lexicon. There also may be levels of categorization, higher- (more inclusive) and lower-order terms. A complete set of such interrelated terms is a taxonomy. The basic color terms of English which we examined above might also be viewed as the middle level of a taxonomy:

This taxonomy is simply the author's classification of the color names printed on a 24-crayon set of Crayolas; on a more abstract level, however, it reflects an English speaker's intuition about the structuring of the field of color. Similar though varied taxonomies might be obtained from almost any native speaker of American English by asking such leading questions, as: Q. What is red? A. It is a color. Q. What other colors are there? A. Blue, green, yellow. . . . Q. Is blue a kind of red? A. No, blue and red are separate colors. Q. Are there different kinds of blue? A. Navy blue, light blue, turquoise blue, powder blue, aqua. . . .

Interrogation of this sort would surely establish that "color" is a higher level of abstraction and a more inclusive category than any individual color name. It would

		color										
I. *Generic term*												
II. *Basic terms*	pink	red	orange	yellow	green	blue	violet	brown	gray	black	white
III. *Specific terms* ("descriptors")	peach carnation pink	violet-red red orange-red	red-orange orange yellow-orange	orange-yellow yellow green-yellow	yellow-green green blue-green	green-blue blue violet-blue	blue-violet violet red-violet	brown	gray	black	white

also reveal that there are a number of units of the same order as red (green, blue, yellow, and so on), and that these are, in turn, more general than the descriptive and compounded terms; they are also more basic in the sense that they vary little from one individual informant to another. At the lowest level, the classification is almost infinitely expandable; millions of shades can actually be distinguished, and English has approximately 50,000 descriptive terms for colors.

It remains an open question whether the domain of color is perceived, categorized, and ordered in other cultures as it is in ours. Some empirical data might suggest that it is not. For one thing, a generic term—comparable to English *color*— is lacking in the vocabulary of many languages. It would seem, too, that the hierarchical contrast between "descriptors" and more inclusive "basic" terms may not be found in every language. This would suggest that there is less need for an abstract concept of color and for generalizing color terms in technologically simple societies where the sources of dyes and pigments are directly related to the material environment.

The Lexicon of Environment   Color term studies deal with the relationships of vocabulary to a continuum, the spectrum. This continuum is an abstraction since it is not ordinarily a part of human experience. After all, elaborate color charts (which show every possible degree of variation in brightness and tint) and precisely controlled samples of pure color are artifacts of industrial civilization; such things are foreign to members of most societies. Testing and eliciting of color terms with the use of such charts and samples are means to obtain data which are uniform and comparable; but it has a negative side in that the data are divorced from their cultural context and are obtained in an unusual situation. In fact, sometimes informants seem to have invented special vocabulary for the test situation which would not be used in everyday life.

Another kind of continuum can be found in the physical environment, the terrain, landforms, vegetation, and hydraulic features with which people do have contact and with which they must deal in order to survive. Environment is always present and is always something which people talk about (though they may not always talk about the colors in the environment).

Every society exists in a complex, reciprocal relationship with its natural environment; the environment provides sustenance and resources and is, in turn, manipulated and reshaped by human exploitation. Perception of the environment— the "environmental image"—derives from this relationship. It is influenced by technology, the means of subsistence and the division of labor, the size and complexity of the community and its ideology, and many other factors. It must be assumed that the environmental lexicon of any language is, in some sense, adaptive, since it is shaped by and facilitates the total interaction between man and nature.

It has been pointed out that even among peoples as culturally similar to one another as are the speakers of modern European languages, there are noticeable differences in the categorization of environmental features. These are sometimes sufficient to cause problems in translation. For example, English *river* must be translated by one of two French words: *fleuve* (roughly, a major river which empties into the sea), or *rivière* (a tributary). English classifies topographic relief features into *mountains* or *hills*; the two words can be roughly matched by German *Berg* and *Hügel*, or by French *montagne* and *colline*. However, in each case the match is inexact. Some large hills, for example, would fall into the *Berg* category; and German has an additional term, *Gebirge,* to use for very large or extensive mountains. English complicates matters by borrowing terms from other languages (such as *butte* and *mesa*) to apply to particular types of terrain.

One writer, architect Kevin Lynch, has commented that "different groups may have widely different images of the same outer reality" (Lynch, 1960). This comment expresses the belief that if different groups utilize the same environment in different ways, they will experience it differently; they will select different features as important and unimportant, and will give names to some and not to others. Each will have, to use Lynch's term, an *environmental image* which is consistent with a particular adaptive strategy.

Such differences have been demonstrated in the man-made environment of cities, which are perceived quite differently by distinctive urban population groups. Commuting office workers, ghetto children, and down-and-out tramps do not perceive or talk about the urban landscape in the same ways. An abandoned building, for example, might be variously perceived as an eyesore, as an exciting play area, or as a "flop" or sleeping place (Spradley, 1970).

A more striking illustration can be drawn from the geographical names given to a natural area which has been utilized by more than one distinctive cultural group. Contrasts in the cultural meaning of the environment, and the imagery which the environment evokes, will be reflected in the geographical terminology and place names which each group applies to the same geographical continuum.

Some information of this sort is available from the southwestern area of the United States, where a number of different peoples (various Indian communities, Spanish-speaking and English-speaking populations, and other immigrant groups) have, for a number of years, occupied adjacent (and sometimes overlapping) areas. Two of these groups are the Hopi and the Navajo (Jett, 1970). A preliminary examination of place names in these two languages reveals both similarities and differences:

1. *Navajo* place names usually have the form of a noun preceded or followed by a qualifying or descriptive term; the most common are those built on the nouns *rock, water mountain,* and *house* (used in reference to prehistoric ruins).

tó tso	Big Spring
tó dich'ii	Bitter Spring/Water
tó naneesdizi	Tangled Water (Farmington, N.M.)
hasbidi bito'	Mourning Dove's Spring
tsé ch'izhi	Rough Rock
tsé łichii'	Red Rock

Most of these place names apply to two types of environmental features—either to sources or bodies of water (springs, rivers, and the like), or to prominent landscape features such as mountains, large rock formations or canyons, and prehistoric ruins which also stand out as important landmarks. These two groups of terms, landmarks and sources of water, have an obvious importance to a nomadic people like the Navajo. Their habitation sites are less permanent, and are named only by reference to landscape features (although in some cases, as can be seen in the list above, the names have been transferred to contemporary communities).

The Navajo are a wandering people. In the recent past, they have migrated and relocated several times, and have been known as raiders and guerrilla warriors. Their subsistence activities involve movement from one pasture area to another with their sheep, seasonal movement from one habitation site to another, and trading expeditions over a very wide area.

Ethnologists who have studied the Navajo speak of their "passion" for geography and for movement. Navajo mythology is filled with references to places and the mythological heroes are constantly in movement, traveling over the mountains and rocks of the Navajo world (Wyman, 1957; Witherspoon, 1977). The telling of myths (which is a part of every ceremonial) is at the same time an assertion of the Navajos' claim to their territory. It is also, for the young, a lesson in the terrain, routes, and landmarks which are recounted in the telling.

2. *Hopi* place names are often marked as such by the final element *-pi* (also sometimes written as *-bi* or *-vi*); it is a suffix which can be translated as "place." Other place names can end in *-pa* (or *-ba*) "spring"; *-ki*, "house"; *-mo*, "mound"; and several others (Voegelin and Voegelin, 1977). These suffixed elements are added to bases which are often the names of animals or insects, body parts, or even manufactured objects:

Awatobi	Bow Place
Boliki	Butterfly House
Chubmo	Antelope Mound
Hochókoba	Juniper Spring
Sikyatki	Yellow House

Superficially, these place names do not seem, in translation, very different from the Navajo names. They are, however, very different in their cultural meaning, since they have a direct connection to the important units in society; each is either named for, or has a traditional association with, a Hopi clan or a clan-related ceremonial group.

The Hopi have a long history as a sedentary farming people. Their residence in the Southwest can be traced, archeologically, for many centuries. Most of the Hopi place names refer to locales within or clustered in the vicinity of their villages; some also refer to the prehistoric ruins which have for the Hopi (as they do not for the Navajo) a historical association as their ancient homes. Each of these named places is linked with a certain clan which may have the responsibility for rituals which are performed at the various springs, peaks, ruins, and other sites which figure in clan history. Many Hopi place names are actually applied to two or more locales; one may be a distant spot, such as a hill which is important in mythology, while another may be a shrine within a village, named for the more distant place. Thus, for example, *chubmobi*, "Antelope Mound," is a hill sacred to the Antelope clan which is the starting place for foot races held during certain ceremonies; it is also the name of a village site used by the ceremonial society associated with the same clan. In effect, most or all named places are apportioned to one or another of the matrilineal clans which are the basic unit in Hopi social organization.

The prominence of the clan in Hopi society is confirmed by an examination of mythology. There is, in fact, no body of Hopi sacred literature; there is simply the mythology of the several clans. Each clan's myths recount the acts of ancestral heroes, the times and routes of their migrations to their present homes, and events which explain or justify their present position; this is especially true for politically power-ful groups like the Bear or Corn clans which hold leadership positions (Eggan, 1950). The stories are localized in specific ancient or modern villages, and action takes place principally at locales within villages, in houses or, most often, in *kivas* (ceremonial houses). There is traveling, but it is usually defined by naming the beginning and ending points, and there is not the same concern with landscape features or the events of travel which is seen in Navajo mythology. While Navajo narrative gives the impression of preoccupation with movement, the Hopi seems to concentrate on locale or situation (Hickerson, 1978).

The form and meaning of place names, then, appears to be consistent with the view of environment and spatial orientation of each cultural group (Stewart, 1975). The Navajo names apply, above all, to prominent landmarks and springs which are widely spaced along travel routes. The places named by the Hopi are most densely clustered within, and in the vicinity of, their villages. The Navajo terms are characteristically descriptive, while most Hopi place names derive from their as-sociation with the clan divisions of society. It is of interest to note that while both the Hopi and Navajo are organized in matrilineal clans, the Navajo clan names are principally derived from geographical locale, while the reverse is the case in Hopi.

Personal Names   All languages provide their speakers with ways to categorize, identify, and talk about themselves and others. One type of vocabulary which is in use in all human societies is *kinship terminology*, words (such as *father, mother, cousin, grandmother, uncle,* and so on) which classify individuals according to their common descent or relationships by marriage. Anthropologists have a long-standing interest in this vocabulary since kinship systems vary in ways which have proved to be significant in the study of such features of society as marriage and descent. There is a rich anthropological literature on kinship, some of it con-cerned with the analysis of the terminology itself, as well as the social relationships in which kin terms are used.

Another universal part of language, which has less often been discussed by either anthropologists or linguists and which forms part of our resources for identifying and categorizing individuals, is the lexicon of *personal names*. Let us consider how names are acquired, and used, in our own contemporary society.

In English-speaking countries, every individual ordinarily has a surname, and one or more given names (a first name and usually a second or "middle" name; in some European countries the second name is a patronymic, but in others, including the United States, it is chosen as arbitrarily as the first). The *surname* is one of the principal indicators of a patrilateral bias in our society since it is passed on from father to children, and because a wife usually assumes her husband's surname at marriage (there have always been some exceptions to this rule, and some women reject it at the present time). English surnames may be analyzable words—com-pound or derivative forms, like Johnson or Armstrong, are common; sometimes they are even identical to words in the regular lexicon of English (as Baker or

Cook). Some are directly imported from other languages (Müller); or they may be modified (Muller) or translated (Miller). But whether or not a surname can be analyzed into meaningful elements, we are accustomed to disregarding its apparent meaning; names are a special category of vocabulary. It is true that a peculiar name (such as Boozer or Hogg) can be the basis for jokes, but this is considered rude, or at best, childish.

Given names are simultaneously arbitrary and personal; that is, names are chosen without any restrictions, usually on the basis of personal taste, and they become an inseparable part of an individual's sense of identity. Most Americans have names which are drawn from a very limited set. There are about a dozen men's names and 20 women's names, each of which is borne by a million or more members of the American population. The number of "Johns" is approximately 6 million, and there are almost as many "Williams," while "Marys" (the most common women's name) number about 4 million (Smith, 1970). The selection is a matter of individual choice, and is usually a decision made by parents, before or immediately after the birth of a child; the basis for the decision varies from one case to another. We are all aware that there are fads in naming; political figures, movie or television stars, athletes, and other public figures play a part in bringing certain names into vogue. But once chosen, a name usually remains unchanged for a person's entire life and is considered a very personal possession; there are times when one must prove his identity or defend his right to use a particular name. We like to assume that our own name is unique—or at least not too common; it is unusual, certainly, if one's own combination of first, middle, and last names is duplicated in the same community or circle of acquaintances.

Our given names are, typically, unanalyzable and are regarded as meaningless; whatever their origin, they are *names* and nothing else. Most of them are sex-specific; in fact, an indication of sex is the one bit of information that we can almost always get from hearing a person's name. Names do have connotations; some are considered especially strong or masculine; some sound dainty or feminine, and they may be selected because of these or other connotations. Some names, also, have associations with class or region or ethnic group. However, all of these associations or connotations are fairly fluid, and change over time. Everyone, certainly, can claim an inalienable right to freedom of choice in naming the baby. Whatever choice is made, the recipient is stuck with it for life; he or she may not like it, but probably will not change it.

It is very likely the workings of this English, and generally European, system of naming which have led to some of the general statements which European writers have made about the nature of names. For example, the philosopher John Stuart Mill called names (both personal names and the names of places) "meaningless marks" which are given to things and people to distinguish them from one another. It appears, in such a definition, that the form or literal meaning of a name is unimportant; the association between persons and their names is arbitrary, and the main function of a name is simply to identify, or distinguish individuals (Gardiner, 1957).

But if we examine the forms and uses of personal names in other societies, it would appear that there is a wide range of variation in both. Names are seldom strictly personal, they are not usually meaningless or arbitrary, they are not often obtained by free choice, and they are rarely individual "possessions" in the way in which we are accustomed to regard them (Hickerson, 1977). In many cases, the names given to individuals are drawn from ordinary vocabulary, and may be identical with words or phrases which are in everyday use. Further, even though an individual is given such a name, it may be that it is not used freely—a person's "real" name may be kept secret, with kinship terms or supernumerary names (what we would call "nicknames") used as terms of address or reference.

Sanuma Naming An account by A. R. Ramos illustrates the kind of cultural and social meaning which names have for the Sanuma (a division of the Yąnomamö) in northern Brazil:

The Sanuma are a horticultural people who also rely heavily on hunting and gathering; they live in small villages of 30 to 50 people. They are patrilineal, and each person has a patronym which is passed from father to children (both male and female) and which indicates membership in a patrilineage. Besides this, each person has a "real name" which is individual and which is bestowed soon after birth. There are several possible sources for these, but the one which is preferred is the name of an animal species; it is obtained through a ritual hunt which is undertaken by the father.

After the birth of a child, both parents are subject to certain restrictions on their activities, and to taboos on the eating of certain foods, which protect the child from supernatural harm. Hunting is one of the activities which is forbidden during this time, except for the ritual hunt which the father undertakes alone in order to find an animal which will provide both a name and a guardian spirit for the child. When killed, the animal (which must be one which is not taboo, as a food, to the father's lineage) is treated with great respect, and must not be touched directly. It is tied in a bundle and carried home, where its spirit eventually comes to live in the child's coccyx; this "coccyx spirit" will provide protection against malevolent spirits. The *humabi* name thus acquired, like all personal names, is never used in direct address during the bearer's lifetime.

Once the animal has been brought home, and the name bestowed, the meat is cooked and sampled by someone in another household, who is not a lineage kinsman of the father. This is an oracle of the child's fate: if the meat is good, the child will live—if not, he will die.

Typical of the names acquired in this way are: Obo (Armadillo), Wisa (Wooly Monkey), Paso (Spider Monkey), Pakola (Grouse). The only restriction is the avoidance of animals which are forbidden as food to the father's lineage. The main determinants, then, are chance and the father's skill as a hunter; a certain percentage of hunts end in failure, and the name is obtained in another way.

It is especially desirable for a first child to obtain a *humabi* name, apparently because mortality is somewhat greater for a firstborn and spirit protection is therefore more desirable. But there are other names; the most common are based on physical or behavioral characteristics, such as Short, Feverish, or Brown Eyes. These can also take the form of animal names: Kazu (Capivara) for a child with eyes as big as those of that rodent, or Kutadaima (Tree Frog), for one who is very small. Another common source of names is found in events or places: place of birth, such as Waikia (a child born during a visit to the Waika), or events at the time of birth, such as Õka (one born at the time of a raid). Such names are fairly common, and provide a sort of chronology of important events, since the occurrences can be correlated with the age of individuals who bear these names.

Names in the last two categories can be given with fewer restrictions than the *humabi* names, and they also can be taken to replace a *humabi* name which is judged to be "bad" (if, for example, the child becomes sickly, or if the father dies). We might note, incidentally, that whatever Sanuma names are based on, they are not based on sex. With few exceptions, there seems to be no basis for associating certain names exclusively with boys or with girls.

Ramos emphasizes the *humabi* naming ritual as the Sanuma norm, even though he found that more names were actually obtained in other ways; it is considered to be the *best* way to name a child. He finds particular interest in the parts of this ritual which dramatize the mutual dependence between the patrilineal kin group (to which both father and child belong) and outsiders—between the father, who kills the animal and obtains the name, and those nonrelatives who sample the meat and thus determine the child's fate.

On another level, we might note the prevalence of names drawn from animal species, the same species which are hunted and used for food. It is intriguing that, even though the Sanuma derive their main subsistence from their gardens and also make use of wild plants, they do not include plant species in their roster of names (Ramos, 1974).

The influential French anthropologist, Claude Lévi-Strauss, has paid particular attention to another widespread type of naming system. This involves a fixed relationship between a group of people—such as a clan, whose members have a strong sense of common identity and unity—and a set of names which are used exclusively by members of that group. To cite an example used by Lévi-Strauss, the Osage (Plains Indians of North America) had clans with animal names, such as Turkey, Fox, Deer, and so on; clan membership was indicated by the way in which children's hair was cut, and was also symbolized by the names they were given. Each clan's names make some reference to "habits, attributes, or characteristic qualities" of the clan animal. Thus, for the Black Bear clan, some of the names are: Flashing Eyes, Tracks on the Prairies, Ground Cleared of Grass, and Fat on the Skin. Each such name, then, would serve both to identify an individual and to give an indication to others of his clan affiliation; the supply of names is finite, and they are reused in successive generations (Lévi-Strauss, 1966).

This sort of naming system was widespread in traditional American Indian societies. It is also typical of Australian natives where names are usually associated with ancestral spirits which are reincarnated, again and again, in the members of a clan or similar group which trace their descent from these ancestors. And they can usually give the anthropologist some clues to cultural beliefs about the nature of man and man's place in the universe. They often seem to reflect beliefs of the sort which have been termed *animistic*—ideas about souls or spirits.

As Lévi-Strauss puts it, names have the linked functions of particularizing and universalizing; that is, they relate the individual to the larger world and the social contexts in which he has a place. Naming systems—the number of names, the way they are selected and bestowed—also appear to be at least partly determined by the size and cohesiveness of social groups. In small-scale societies, there may be an assumption that names should be unique, either invented anew for each individual, or reused only after a previous bearer of the name has died. The bestowal of the same name in successive generations serves to emphasize continuity in descent, and is often associated with a belief in reincarnation. In larger communities, and especially in societies like our own, the same reservoir of names is used and reused; we have learned to dissociate them from other contexts. After all, the group of people who are named "Bill" or "Mary" probably do not have anything in common besides their names (Hickerson, 1977).

Finally, we can see in the history of English names some indication of the changes which can occur in this limited segment of language, as social and cultural conditions change. A historian, C. M. Matthews, has traced a series of stages and transformations in the evolution of English names.

In the centuries before 1100 A.D., Anglo-Saxon names were short words, either simple or compounded. They were easily analyzable, usually drawn from ordinary vocabulary: Aelf (elf), Frith (peace), Wine (friend), Snelgar (bold warrior), Aethelgar (noble warrior), Aethelstan (noble stone), Bealdgyth (bold battle), and the like. There were, Matthews comments, an enormous number of these compounds, because the names were prevailingly individual. They were not to be repeated, at least not within the same community. They were not passed on from one generation to the next; the same name might be coined again, but not intentionally. The Anglo-Saxons, according to Matthews, "honored their ancestors by leaving their names severely alone."

After 1066, the date of the Norman conquest, the naming system changed rapidly. Norman names and naming practices were introduced, and Anglo-Saxon names fell into disuse. The total inventory of names became smaller, since the Normans used names to show loyalty or respect; a child might be named after his father or a deceased ancestor, or after a lord or patron. A little later, saints' names came to be used in the same way: a peasant's child might be named Dennis in honor of the lord of the manor while, at the same time, both peasant and lord showed their respect for St. Dennis. The great popularity of saints' names caused many older names to be abandoned.

With the increasing repetition of a relatively small stock of names, the use of *by-names* was quickly established. This resulted in a double name, consisting of a first named followed by the by-name, which might be a patronymic, a designation of occupation or locality, or a personal description. Thus, "Richard, the son of Gilbert" could be distinguished from "Richard the Barber," "Richard the Stout," "Richard the Faint-hearted," and so on.

The transformation of by-names into inherited *surnames* took place in a brief period, between the late thirteenth and early fourteenth centuries. It coincided with changes in laws affecting the registration, tenure, and inheritance of property. Like most property, surnames came to be patrilineally inherited.

There have been few changes in English surnames between the fourteenth century and the present. The second, or middle, name became popular in the eighteenth century. The double surname was adopted by a number of British families in the nineteenth century, giving us hyphenated names such as Radcliffe-Brown and Pitt-Rivers. Both of these developments seem to be adaptations to the increasing difficulty of maintaining unambiguous individual identification in an ever-expanding society. (We can see our increasing reliance on numerical codes—social security numbers, licenses, credit card numbers, and so on—as a further adaptation to the same dilemma; Matthews, 1966.)

TOPICS FOR STUDY AND DISCUSSION

1. Discuss B. L. Whorf's view of the influence of language on experience. Examine your own way of thinking and talking about time and number; can you find examples which confirm or add to Whorf's findings?
2. In what ways does the Nuers' use of language reflect the importance of cattle in their culture? Think of words and phrases in American English which refer to horses or cattle, ranching, and so forth. How do the two examples compare? How is Nuer distinctive?
3. Go through a dictionary of a non-Western language. Set up one or more categories of vocabulary (such as kinship terms, occupations, environmental features, plants, animals, spatial orientation, and so on) and collect a list of terms along with the translations which are given. How do the words compare with their English equivalents? Are there marked similarities or differences? Can you make any hypotheses based on cultural emphasis?
4. Summarize the different approaches to the study of color categorization and terminology. Do these studies suggest other areas (of sensory perception, visual phenomena, etc.) which might be productive for research? Think of the kinds of materials and testing methods which might be used.
5. Listen for the use of metaphors; write them down, and collect all that you hear in the course of several days. Do you find a number of different types? Besides those noted above, what areas of experience are represented?
6. Use a geographical atlas of place names from your or another state or county (this should be available in your college or public library). What geographical features (hills, canyons, rivers, etc.) are represented? What are common sources of names? Are names borrowed from American Indian languages? Other languages?
7. How do members of your own family select names for children? Are there some boys'/girls' names which are passed on from generation to generation? Would some names be disapproved? Compare, as class discussion.
8. Collect vocabulary for a restricted cultural area—furniture, cars, clothing (men's/women's), food (kinds of sandwiches, desserts, beverages), and so on. Try to distinguish general and specific levels of taxonomy. Use more than one informant, in order to discover areas of agreement and disagreement.

Language Maps and Classifications

No one knows exactly how many languages there are in the world. There are thousands, certainly, but until all are recorded and mapped, and until experts have decided on the boundaries which define their limits, we will not be able to count them. Estimates of the number of the world's languages, therefore, are usually given in round numbers, and range from a low estimate of 2000 to a high of 5000 or more. It seems likely that 3000 is a realistic estimate, if we exclude those which have ceased to be spoken within the present century; the higher figure might be more accurate if these dead or dying languages are included in the count. Another reason for indeterminacy in counting languages is that linguists are still ignorant of the speech of many communities. For some areas, like New Guinea, where there is not yet adequate information, we may not know whether, for example, neighboring communities differ in speech to the extent that they ought to be mapped as separate languages, or whether they are so similar as to be considered local dialects of the same language. Secondly—and this is perhaps a more basic problem—linguists are not certain how to establish and apply criteria for making this decision: where should language boundaries be drawn?

LANGUAGES AND LANGUAGE FAMILIES

Most of the languages of the world have never been the subject of dictionaries or grammars, and many have never even been recorded or written down. However, our general knowledge about peoples and languages continues to grow. It seems unlikely that the scholarly world will ever, in the future, be amazed by the discovery of "lost tribes" which speak languages completely different from those recorded. On the other hand, there are still many gaps in the detailed study, description, and comparison of the languages already discovered. At present, much of the excitement of linguistic study lies not in the discovery of new languages but in detection and proof of the relationships and contacts among languages. These relationships and contacts, all of which contribute to an eventual unraveling of the course of human history, are detected by (1) the recording and analysis of data from individual languages, and (2) comparisons of these data—of vocabulary and grammatical structures—in order to determine the points of resemblance and the differences. By this means, the several thousand languages of the world can be grouped into a much smaller number of language families. The groupings are proposed, in the first place, on the basis of recognizable similarities among the languages. They become established, as families of proven relationship, after comparative study has revealed regular patterns in the resemblances (as discussed in Chapter 2).

A survey of an area may be undertaken in order to make a preliminary classification of languages. A major survey of this kind was undertaken during the 1880s when the Bureau of American Ethnology, a federal agency dealing with native peoples, was first established. As one of its first tasks, Major John Wesley Powell, the director of the Bureau, undertook a definitive survey of the native languages of the United States. For some parts of the country, Powell's study could draw on established knowledge of the American Indian tribes, but for other areas, especially in the West and Southwest, the primary data had to be collected. The basic tool used by researchers in identifying and classifying the languages was a word list. With this as a guide, the same types of vocabulary could be collected in one community after another. The parallel vocabularies were then compared to determine the linguistic affiliations and groupings of the Indian communities. Figure 21 shows a selection of vocabularies which were collected in California in the late nineteenth century. Based on the resemblances in vocabulary, the local groups listed here were all assigned to a single language, Yurok, which was given the status of a separate language family because no close resemblances to any other language could be detected.

The Powell classification, which was published in 1891, grouped several hundred tribes into 58 linguistic "stocks" or families (Powell, 1891). Though some of these family groupings rested only on the comparison of vocabularies, they have

English	1. Al-i-kwa	2. Al-i-kwa	3. Klamath	4. Yu'-rok	5. Al-i-kwa
1. man	pe-gur'h	pa'-gek	pay-gurk	pe-gurk	pu-gur-uk
2. woman	win-chuk	wint'-suk	went-surf	wen'-tens	win'-chuk
3. boy	må-werkh	hōkah	meg'-wah	muh'-wah	må-werkh-sur
4. girl	hak-tchur	wai'-in-uksh	weh-ye-nuf	wurh-yen'-neks	ner-u-luks
5. infant	—	tahai'-nūks	tsaa-noaf	mi-was'-suh	ōk-se
6. father	takht	meg-wa'-she	daat	nek-nep'-sets	takht, ōp-shrekh
7. mother	kak-hus	tsi-ma'-mus	gawk	kok-oss	kak-si
*	*	*	*	*	*
18. head	mōtl-kwa	te-kwe'	oō-mohl	malkh-kob	o-mudtl-kwa
19. hair	lep-taltl	lep-taltl	lep-teilkh	lep-tāl'	lep-toikhl
20. face	—	ta'-le	wit-taw-el-aw	me'-lin	we-luu-ni
21. forehead	te'-we	te'-wek	teh-way	wuh'-to-wai	we-te-we
22. ear	wits-pe-gur	spe-gukh	wats-peg-eh	wuts-peg'-ga	speg-gar
*	*	*	*	*	*

Fig. 21. Comparative vocabularies: Yu-rok family

proved to be quite reliable as the basis for further research and comparison. However, further study of the languages and language families in Powell's classification has enabled later scholars to combine some of them into phyla (or "superfamilies"); the families established earlier usually remain as a lower level of classification. For example, Yurok has recently been shown to have a distant connection with the Algonkian family, a group of languages of the eastern part of North America, and both are now included in a larger grouping of related languages, Macro-Algonkian (see below).

GEOGRAPHY AND LANGUAGE BOUNDARIES

As we all know, languages differ a great deal in their social and political importance; some are spoken widely, extending across the boundaries of many different countries, while others have only a handful of speakers. English, French, and Russian, for example, are *world languages*; native speakers of these languages are numbered in the hundreds of millions, and they are also much used as second languages by many persons who have a need to travel or communicate beyond their own national boundaries. Turkish, Estonian, Guarani, and Nepali could be called "middle range" or *national languages*; they are more restricted in their distribution, though each has several million speakers. Hopi (in North America), Arawak (in South America), Breton (in Europe) and Nuer (in Africa) are *local languages*, spoken by isolated or enclave populations, each with a community of speakers which may number in the thousands or even a few million. However, native speakers of such languages cannot travel very far and would be quite limited in their knowledge of the world without the use of a second language. Thus, it is clear that the word *language* has a geographical dimension; languages can be defined and delimited in terms of geographical distribution and numbers of speakers.

But how (by what criteria) do we define and delimit languages geographically? How do we decide where to draw the boundaries between languages? Can we be sure, in a given geographical area, whether people speak the same or different languages? Indeed, how many different languages are present? The phrase, "to speak the same language," implies a definite and recognizable similarity in the speech habits of speakers, and an ease of communication. However, the overall similarity among speakers may be considerably less in the case of a world language, which encompasses a number of national or regional variants, than in the case of the more restricted local languages. In the first case, the people who claim to speak the same language constitute many separate speech communities (see Chapter 6), each with internal variety as well as distinctive shared characteristics. The communicative links which bind them all together into a sort of supercommunity (for example, the English speakers of the United States, Great Britain, Canada, Australia, and many other countries) may today be maintained largely through mass media and a common literary tradition.

At the opposite extreme, there are certain local languages which are so restricted geographically that the entire population of speakers form a single speech community. For example, Zuni, a native American language, has, for as long as its history is known, been spoken by a small population in a restricted geographical area; at present, there are approximately 5000 speakers. In such a geographically and socially compact population, there was little or no local variation in speech (although some variation related to age and status was undoubtedly present, as there is today). Linguists refer to Zuni as a "language isolate"—it is a single language which shows no close similarities which might indicate relationship to any of its neighbors (Apache, Navajo, Hopi, and other southwestern peoples); remote connections with more distant languages are possible, but have not been definitely proven.

A clearly delimited and undifferentiated language like Zuni is, however, an unusual case. More typically, we do find a degree of variation within the geographical boundaries of a language, and we also must deal with its external relationships (its place within a family of languages). Residents of an individual community—a town in Germany, a primitive village in the highlands of New Guinea, a nomadic band in the desert of Australia—are found to speak almost, but not exactly, like their neighbors. They are aware of distinctive differences and peculiarities in the speech of visitors from neighboring regions, and they may understand some, but not all, of the speech of certain other communities which are more distantly located. In such cases, it is difficult to decide just where one language ends and another begins. Speakers are able to make judgments about the linguistic similarities between communities, but their judgments are apt to be colored by political or various other biases. Long-time allies may be judged to speak "just the same" (overlooking differences), while chronic enemies may claim complete ignorance of one another's speech (perhaps ignoring similarities).

The language boundaries found on maps often turn out actually to reflect traditional political alliances and divisions rather than purely linguistic judgments. A classic example of this is found in India and Pakistan, where Hindi is written in a script derived from Sanskrit and has religious and cultural vocabulary stemming from that ancient language, while Urdu is written in Arabic characters and has borrowed vocabulary related to the Moslem religion. Hindi and Urdu are mutually intelligible—linguists class them as a single language, Hindustani. However, speakers of the two express a feeling of linguistic separateness which, in this case as in many others, is as much a reflection of political and religious loyalties as of actual similarity or differences in speech.

Linguists usually express the opinion that the basis for language boundaries should be *intelligibility*, the ability of members of different communities to speak to and understand one another. If they can do so, they have the same language; if they cannot, they speak different languages. However, as was noted above, this criterion is difficult to apply, especially if one relies on the judgments of the speakers. A number of attempts have been made to develop objective ways of measuring intelligibility, and to use this as a practical basis for drawing language and dialect boundaries. This approach is illustrated by a study, done in 1951, of Iroquoian languages and dialects; the method was developed by C. F. Voegelin, one of the most innovative of contemporary linguists (Voegelin and Harris, 1951).

A Study of Dialect Distance   Iroquoian is one of more than 50 language families native to North America. It is, in other words, a grouping of languages which have been shown (by comparison of vocabulary and grammatical structure) to be historically related and ultimately descended from a common "ancestral" language (see Chapter 3). At the time of first European contact, the Iroquoian-speaking peoples were widely distributed in eastern North America from the St. Lawrence and Hudson River valleys in the north, to the southern Appalachians and the coastal areas of the Carolinas in the south and east (see Fig. 22).

Several divisions of Iroquois were decimated and scattered as a result of intertribal wars, political events of the colonial era, and the Revolutionary War; however, seven still maintain their identity. These are: the "Five Nations" of the Iroquois confederacy—Seneca, Cayuga, Onandaga, Oneida, and Mohawk—whose historical homelands lie between the Great Lakes and the Hudson River; the Cherokee, native to the southern Appalachians; and the Tuscarora, whose historical location is in eastern North Carolina. Many of the Cherokees were removed from the Southeast to an Oklahoma reserve early in the nineteenth century, and Cherokees have also migrated, as individuals or small groups, into

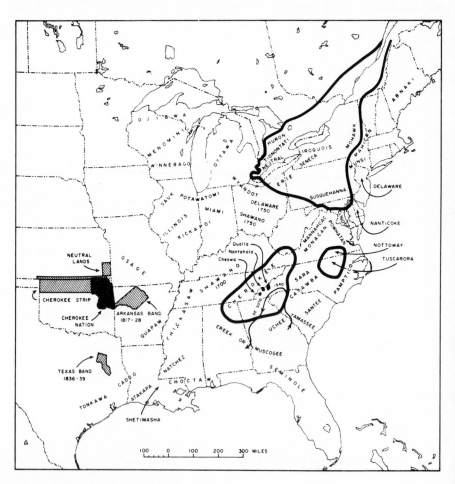

Fig. 22. Geographical distribution of Iroquoian peoples. Reprinted by permission from James Mooney, Historical Sketch of the Cherokee. *Copyright © 1975 by Aldine Publishing Co.*

many other areas. The main body of the Tuscarora voluntarily moved north in 1710, allying themselves with the Iroquois confederacy, and today are mainly to be found in New York State.

The fact that languages are historically related does not necessarily have a direct bearing, pro or con, on the ability of people to communicate with one another. The five tribes of the Iroquois confederacy had, besides a historical relationship, a long tradition of trade and military alliance, social interaction and intermarriage, and a common political identity. These facts have sometimes led outside observers, as well as many of the Iroquois themselves, to underestimate their linguistic differences. One contributing circumstance may be the frequent occurrence of bilingualism (that is, of learned rather than native intelligibility). In the past, political and military alliance meant the presence of interpreters who could understand speeches given in the council house by members of other tribes, carry messages between villages, and assist in other intertribal negotiations. There are still numerous individuals who are fluent in more than one variety of Iroquoian. Intermarriage was common in the past, as it is also in the present, when communities are probably less homogeneous than they formerly were. Furthermore, during the last century, an ever-increasing fluency in English has reduced the practical problems of communication. (English now serves as a *lingua franca* for speakers of many different native American languages.)

Our study of Iroquoian languages and dialects involved two stages of fieldwork, followed by an analysis of the data. In the first stage, a research team visited the eight reservation communities in New York State and Canada and recorded the speech of native speakers of Seneca, Cayuga, Onandaga, Oneida, Mohawk, Tuscarora, and Cherokee. This material included traditional narratives, anecdotes, personal histories, conversations—a variety of materials; all were recorded on tape, and English translations were recorded separately. Two test tapes were prepared, with each one including samples from all seven speech communities. The first tape was made up of two-minute segments, and was used in testing general comprehension; the second included 30-second segments which were played a few words at a time, for closer, word-for-word translation.

In the second stage of fieldwork, the reservations were visited again, and the tests were administered to several representatives of each speech community. The 28 individuals who were tested were screened, eliminating those who claimed to be familiar with varieties of Iroquoian other than their own. Each one was asked to translate all the tapes; the translations were recorded, and were later evaluated for comprehension and general accuracy in translation. In this evaluation, the responses were given a rough percentile score. For the first test, the score was based on a resume of content in the two-minute text; for the second, it was based on the accuracy of translation phrase by phrase. The chart below includes the combined percentile scores for all informants in the second test. (This test, since it is easier to evaluate, reflects intelligibility more objectively than the first.)

Figure 23 was drawn on the basis of these scores, modified slightly by those scores from the first test. It might be noted that informants were inclined to give a high estimate of their own ability to understand, and would sometimes answer the question, "Did you understand that?" in the affirmative, even in cases in which they were able to translate only 25–30 percent of the content. However, 75 percent

	S	C	Ona	One	M	T	Ch
Seneca	97	85	30	12	12	½	0
Cayuga	70	100	13	15	16	0	0
Onandaga	30	40	100	23	23	0	0
Oneida	24	23	10	95	75	0	0
Mohawk	5	25	0	86	96	0	0
Tuscarora	2	2	0	0	0	95	0

was chosen as a figure which correlates well with accurate summaries of content (in Test 1) as well as specific understanding of vocabulary (Test 2). This figure, 75 percent, was designated as *a percentile definition* of intelligibility. By this standard, speech communities with less than 75 percent mutual intelligibility constitute separate languages, while those which score above this figure constitute local varieties, or dialects, of the same language. On this basis, the Iroquoian languages were determined to be: Cherokee, Tuscarora, Mohawk-Oneida, Onandaga, and Seneca-Cayuga. Mohawk and Oneida then, are two dialects of a single language, as are Seneca and Cayuga (Hickerson, Turner, and Hickerson, 1952).

What are the connections among intelligibility, history, and geographical or

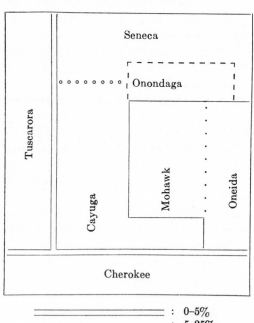

Fig. 23. Chart of Iroquois languages and dialects. Reprinted from H. Hickerson, G. D. Turner, and N. P. Hickerson, "Testing Procedures for Estimating Transfer of Information among Iroquois Dialects and Languages," International Journal of American Linguistics *(1952). Copyright © 1952 by The University of Chicago Press.*

social contact? We can make some interpretations on the basis of our Iroquoian study. The historical separation of the Cherokee, the Tuscarora, and the northern Iroquois peoples is ancient; an Iroquoian specialist, F. Lounsbury, estimates that these three branches of the Iroquoian family separated well over 2000 years ago. There are marked differences in vocabulary, though many similarities can be detected through comparison; grammatical and phonetic differences are also reflected in the complete lack of intelligibility between Cherokee and Tuscarora, and between these two and any of the northern Iroquoian group.

The languages of these five northern tribes—Seneca, Cayuga, Onandaga, Oneida, and Mohawk—have more (but not a great deal more) in common. Lounsbury estimates that ancestors of this group established separate identities between 1200 and 1500 years ago (Lounsbury, 1959). However, geographical contiguity, political alliance, and continuing social contact have fostered the maintenance of linguistic connections as well. There is a sizable body of shared linguistic material in the presence of cultural vocabulary, such as place names and traditions associated with the natural environment, the names of regional animal species, clan names, and the vocabulary relating to the political institutions which these peoples share. This type of cultural vocabulary is very similar throughout the northern division of Iroquoian, and has obviously been borrowed or diffused from community to community along lines of social interaction. Finally, it might be noted that the highest levels of intelligibility, which were interpreted as the division of dialects within a single language, were found between the communities with the closest geographical contiguity: Seneca and Cayuga, Mohawk and Oneida. Continuing social contacts have, in these cases, clearly served to minimize the divergence of speech, despite the historical existence of separate communities.

The study of Iroquoian languages and dialects shows that it is possible, in theory, to establish language boundaries with precision. In practice, this has seldom been done. Political boundaries are often taken as language boundaries, giving an artificial unity to a variety of dialects. In areas of linguistic diversity or complexity, one or another language or dialect often emerges as a *lingua franca*—the language used in international, intertribal or intervillage trade and communication. In the case of complex national states, a particular regional or class dialect sometimes acquires the status of a national standard; used in mass communications, education, and official functions, it may replace other varieties of speech, or become specialized to particular situations. *Diglossia*, the use of two or more language varieties, shows us that communication does not stop at the borders between languages.

LANGUAGE AREAS OF THE WORLD: A.D. 1500

The world today is dominated, linguistically, by languages which have spread as part of the expansion and colonization of large areas by a few European and Asiatic powers. Spanish, English, French, Russian, Portuguese, Arabic, and Mandarin Chinese are among those which have expanded on a global scale in the last few centuries. This linguistic expansion is paralleled by cultural diffusion and movements and mixtures of populations which have taken place during the same historical period.

If we make a mental adjustment and think of the world as it was around 1500, before the full onset of the colonial era, we will find a clearer and simpler linguistic picture. Up to this time, continental areas were fairly self-contained; distinctive racial, cultural, and linguistic groups developed in relative isolation. It is worth noting that each major world area contained a distinctive set of language families within its natural boundaries, and that very few linguistic connections can be traced across these boundaries. Within each world area (Eurasia, Africa, North America, South America, and Oceania), we find one or more large groups of closely related languages with wide distribution, which can be assumed to represent a relatively recent expansion and separation of a formerly united speech community. In each world area, also, there are marginal or isolated languages which appear, in most cases, to be survivors or remnants of language families which must have been more widely distributed at an earlier time, and which have been displaced or pushed aside by the more expansive speech communities.

A primary reason for anthropological interest in the distribution and genetic connections of languages is the insight which they give us into population movements, especially when linguistic classifications can be related to other types of evidence such as culture complexes or identifiable archeological horizons. Language family classifications, and suggestions about possible, more distant relations among language families, are always of interest to historically oriented anthropologists because they are evidence of the historical connections of peoples. It is very difficult to assess cultural similarities as evidence for historical connections, because inventions may spread over great distances simply by borrowing, rather than by direct contact; and similar customs or institutions often develop independently of one another in two or more different locations. Furthermore, cultures which do have a common origin can change so drastically under different environmental or economic conditions that their historical links would be very difficult to discover. The evidence of linguistic affiliations, then, at times may offer the most convincing proof or disproof of the historical origins and movements of peoples. Language family classification is a type of "hard" evidence which can be most valuable to a cultural historian or archeologist.

It must be emphasized, however, that linguistic affiliations are only one type of historical evidence. Populations can adopt—and many have adopted—new languages while retaining a particular cultural identity; and, conversely, culture can change without a change of language. It would be a mistake to assume, for example, that the contemporary people who speak an isolated or marginal language are direct descendants of an ancient population stratum, unless there are other evidences of their special status, such as distinctive cultural retentions, or even unique biological traits, which point to the same conclusion.

On the other hand, dominant languages are often adopted by or imposed on groups of people who subsequently abandon use of their earlier language. In this way, for example, Latin replaced a variety of languages in southern Europe. Certain local populations may tentatively be identified as descended from historic tribes of pre-Roman times, but their earlier linguistic affiliations can seldom be inferred.

Linguists use the term *language family* to refer to a group of languages whose historical relationship and common origin are considered to be proved beyond any doubt by close comparisons and reconstruction of an ancestral language or *proto-*

language (see Chapter 4). Suggestions of broader or more remote relationships may lead to the grouping of language isolates and/or families into a *language phylum.* Such phyla may appear to have a common origin, but this cannot yet be demonstrated in point-by-point detail because the evidence may be more fragmentary than in the case of an established family. The maps given here (Maps 1–5) display, in some cases, language families; phyla are shown when claims of remote relationship appear to be justified. A third category, *language group,* is used for languages which have been traditionally treated together, even though no strong claim of relationship has been given; these are usually geographically restricted groupings which appear to have great antiquity. In some cases (for example, Paleo-Siberian), a language group may include two or more language isolates. Finally, *language isolates* are single languages (or small language families) which have not been shown to have other affiliations (Voegelin and Voegelin, 1964–1966).

In every case, the largest available groupings have been mapped: phyla, families, language groups, and language isolates.[1] It can usually be assumed that a family of languages has differentiated from a common origin over the last two to five millennia. Languages and language families which are grouped together within a phylum may have historical connections at a depth of three millennia or more. Language isolates are sole survivors of earlier families, or have affiliations which are so remote that they remain undiscovered. Therefore, in most cases, it can be assumed that language isolates represent populations which preceded the invasion or spread of larger groupings, that is, families and phyla.

Eurasia I. The *Ural-Altaic* phylum is made up of (A) *Uralic,* or Finno-Ugric, a well-established family which includes Hungarian, Finnish, and Lapp, several small languages located along the Volga in Russia (such as Cheremis and Mordwin), and Samoyed and other languages of central Siberia.

The *Altaic* division, which some experts give separate status as a phylum, is made up of three families: (B) *Turkic,* consisting of Turkish and closely related languages which are scattered over a wide area, including Tatar and Kirghiz of southern Siberia and central Asia, and Yakut in northern Siberia; (C) *Mongol,* a family of closely related languages in Mongolia; and (D) *Manchu-Tungus,* which covers a very large area in Manchuria and Siberia.

The Ural-Altaic languages have been dispersed over an extremely large area with few natural barriers to the movements and migrations of peoples. The distribution of these languages is complex, with the different divisions intersecting and overlapping. It is likely that this distribution reflects the famous mobility of these peoples, most of whom are or have been pastoral nomads (the Mongols, Tatars, and Lapps, for example).

---

[1] The phyla are not, in every case, groupings of great antiquity; some of them express a proposed relationship—which may be very likely—but which has not yet been *proved.* In such cases the languages included in phyla may actually be historically closer than those included in established families. For this reason, it does not seem important to emphasize the distinction among family, phylum, and (in Map 5) macrophylum, though the distinction will be important if (as Swadesh has suggested) it can eventually be linked to differences in time depth.

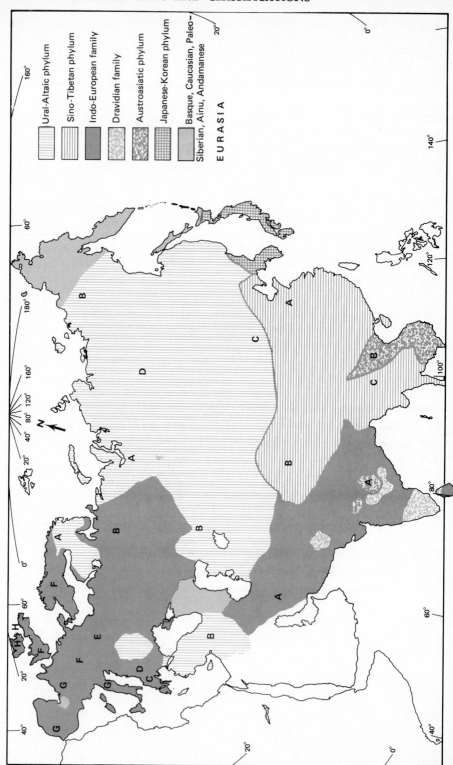

II. The *Sino-Tibetan* phylum includes three families, one of which may be questionable. (A) *Chinese* is a family made up of several regional "dialects," which actually are separate languages (being intelligible to one another). The most prominent languages are Mandarin, or Pekingese, of northern China, and Cantonese in southern China; others include Wu, Hakka, and Min.

(B) *Tibeto-Burman* includes Tibetan and several languages of Burma and the Malayan peninsula (Lolo, Kachin, Garo). (C) The *Tai* languages are of disputed status. Some specialists have classified them as an isolated family but others have suggested a relationship to the Austroasiatic phylum, theorizing that similarities to Chinese are the result of borrowings rather than common origin. Tai includes Thai or Siamese, Lao (of Laos), and other languages spoken in southern China and Indochina (Miao, Yao, Shan, Kadai, and others).

III. *Indo-European* is the largest single family in its geographical expanse and numbers of speakers; it stretches from India to western Europe. There are several extinct languages known only through inscriptions and early written sources; the eight modern branches are essentially regional in distribution: (A) *Indo-Iranian,* with *Indic* and *Iranian* divisions. The Iranian division includes several dialects of modern Persian. Indic includes the classical language, Sanskrit, and modern languages spoken in Pakistan, Indian, and Sri Lanka—such as Hindustani, Bengali, and Punjabi—as well as Romany, used by Gypsies throughout the world.

(B) *Balto-Slavic.* The *Baltic* languages are Lithuanian, Latvian, and Prussian (which became extinct in the seventeenth century). *Slavic* is a large group, including Russian, Czech, Polish, Bulgarian, and other languages of central and eastern Europe. (C) *Greek,* (D) *Albanian,* and (E) *Armenian* each consist of a single modern language. (F) *Germanic* occupies much of northern and western Europe, including the British Isles (where it coexists with Celtic) the Scandinavian peninsula, and Iceland; some of the languages are High and Low German, Dutch, English, Swedish, Norwegian, and Icelandic.

(G) The *Romanic* languages are descendants of Latin and closely related dialects spoken in Italy at the time of the Roman Empire. The modern languages include Italian, French, Catalan, Spanish, Portuguese, and Romanian. (H) *Celtic* languages were once spoken over much of western Europe and the British Isles, and have been partly replaced by other languages, Romanic and Germanic. Modern representatives include Irish, Scots Gaelic, Welsh, and Breton (in northern France). Romanic and Celtic are sometimes grouped together, as an Italo-Celtic subfamily.

IV. The *Dravidian* family is made up of several languages of southern India (Telegu, Tamil, Kannada, Malayalam), Pakistan (Brahui), and Sri Lanka (Tamil). The territory occupied by Dravidian was larger in prehistoric times, before the Dravidian peoples were conquered and pushed back by invading speakers of Indo-European.

V. The *Caucasian* group includes the several dozen languages of a mountainous area in the Soviet Union, between the Black and Caspian seas. The relationships among these languages have not yet been completely clarified. They are not necessarily all of one language family, though they have a number of characteristics in common. Some of these languages are Georgian, Azerbaijani, Abkhazian, Kabardian, and Ubykh.

VI. The *Japanese-Korean* phylum is made up of two languages which in the past have often been treated as isolates. If authentic, the genetic relationship is an ancient one; some linguists have also suggested a remote connection of both languages with the Ural-Altaic phylum.

VII. The *Austroasiatic* phylum includes three widely dispersed families: (A) *Munda*, made up of languages scattered in several regions of eastern India; (B) the *Mon-Khmer* family, spread through Burma, Cambodia, and Vietnam; and (C) *Nicobarese*, located on islands in the Indian Ocean. It seems likely that these scattered languages are remnants of a very early Southeast Asian population, now marginal to both Dravidian and Indo-European (in India) and to the several divisions of Sino-Tibetan (in Indochina).

VIII. The *Paleo-Siberian* group includes two small families, Yeneseian and Luorawetlan, and two isolates, Yukaghir and Gilyak. All are located in northeastern Siberia and are spoken by scattered populations of hunting, fishing, or reindeer-herding peoples.

IX. *Basque* is an isolate located in western France and northeastern Spain. Some grammatical similarities indicate that Basque may be very remotely related to languages of the Caucasian group; however, these suggestions still seem highly speculative.

X. *Ainu*, a language isolate of northern Japan, is spoken by people who can be identified with an earlier culture than that of the Japanese. No real connections have been established between Ainu and any other language, though some similarities in vocabulary to several American Indian languages have been pointed out.

XI. *Andamanese* is an isolate found on islands in the Bay of Bengal, spoken by a small native population whose simple technology and social organization can be seen as evidence of long cultural isolation. Recently, it has been suggested that Andamanese has language-phylum connections with the Papuan languages of New Guinea (see below).

Africa I. The *Afroasiatic* phylum extends beyond the continental limits of Africa, to the Arabian peninsula and neighboring parts of western Asia. Four of the five families which make up the phylum are restricted to Africa, and it seems likely that the earliest dispersal of the group took place within that continent. The divisions are: (A) *Semitic*, the most widespread family, which includes in its northern division, Hebrew, Aramaic, and extinct languages such as Phoenician and Akkadian; the southern division consists of Arabic (which has spread far in its association with the Moslem religion) and Amharic, the main language of Ethiopia.

(B) *Egyptian* is extinct, surviving only as a liturgical language used by Coptic Christians. (C) *Berber* is spoken by scattered peoples in northern Africa (Tuareg, Kabyle, and others). (D) Cushitic is a fairly large family in eastern Africa; some of the languages are Somali, Galla, and Beja. (E) *Chadic* is a family which centers around Lake Chad in west-central Africa; Hausa is the largest of several languages in this group.

II. The *Congo-Kordofanian* phylum has two divisions; the first is *Kordofanian*, a small group of languages in the Sudan (an enclave in the Nilo-Saharan area). The other, *Niger-Congo*, is an extremely large family dominating most of the

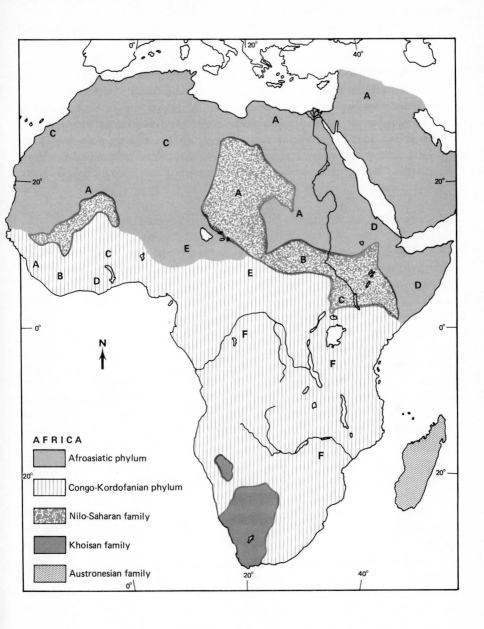

AFRICA

Afroasiatic phylum

Congo-Kordofanian phylum

Nilo-Saharan family

Khoisan family

Austronesian family

African continent south of the Sahara. Niger-Congo includes approximately 300 languages grouped into six subfamilies: (A) *West Atlantic,* including Wolof, Fulani, and other languages of Senegal, Guinea, and Gambia; (B) *Mande,* which includes Mande, Kpelle, Malinke, and other languages of the Ivory Coast. (C) *Gur,* of Nigeria and neighboring countries, with approximately 50 languages including Tallensi and Nupe. (D) *Kwa,* centering in Liberia and Nigeria, contains a number of large language groups such as Akan, Kru, Ewe, Yoruba, and Ibo. (E) *Adamawe-Eastern* is a scattered group of languages east of Lake Chad; Fulani is the largest and most well-known representative. (F) *Benue-Congo* takes in several languages of Nigeria (including Efik and Tiv) as well as the very widespread *Bantu* languages. As we have seen, Bantu languages are spread throughout the Congo and eastern and southeastern portions of Africa. They are, in general, so undifferentiated that they appear to have spread at a fairly recent time. Ganda, Kongo, Kikuyu, Rauanda, Swazi, and Zulu are among the dozens of Bantu languages, as is Swahili, which has long served as a trade language throughout East Africa.

III. The *Nilo-Saharan* family has a marginal distribution between the Niger-Congo family and the southernmost extension of divisions of Afro-Asiatic. The branches are: (A) Songhai, located along the Niger River in Mali; (B) *Saharan,* a large group of languages east of Lake Chad; and (C) *Sudanic,* located north of Lake Victoria and in scattered enclaves elsewhere. The best-known representatives are the Nubian and Nilotic languages (including Nuer and Masai).

IV. Languages of the *Khoisan* family are remnants of a group which was probably quite widespread in Africa before the dispersal of the Bantu. The main concentration at present is in arid regions of South Africa where the two main divisions are Bushman and Hottentot; both of these include a number of languages and dialects. There are other scattered enclaves further to the north, such as Sandawe and Hadza in Tanzania. With few exceptions, speakers of the Khoisan languages are hunting people who appear to be culturally marginal to dominant pastoral and agricultural groups.

V. The languages of Madagascar fall within the Austronesian family; see below.

Oceania I. The *Austronesian* family is one of the most widespread in the world, reaching from Hawaii and Easter Island in the mid-Pacific, to Southeast Asia, and to Madagascar near the east coast of Africa. It contains roughly 500 languages. (A) The greatest diversity is in the *western* division, which includes Malay, Indonesian, Javanese, and languages of various islands of Indonesia, Tagalog, Ilocano, and a number of other languages in the Philippines; the non-Chinese aboriginal languages of Taiwan; languages of the hill tribes in Vietnam and Cambodia; Malagasy and other languages of Madagascar; and the languages of several of the island groups of western Micronesia and New Guinea. It seems likely that the Indonesian area is the earlier center of development and diffusion of the language family, from which the languages spread outward to more distant regions and island groups.

(B) The *eastern* division takes in a Melanesian branch which extends to Fiji and includes such islands as New Caledonia, the New Hebrides, parts of the Solomon

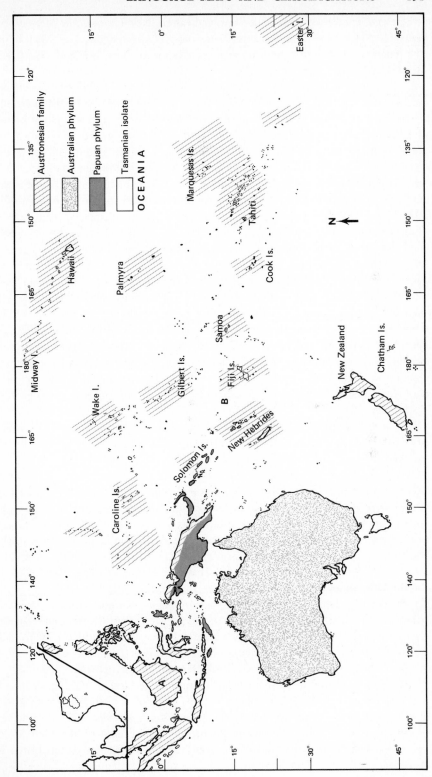

OCEANIA

Austronesian family

Australian phylum

Papuan phylum

Tasmanian isolate

archipelago, and coastal areas of northern and eastern New Guinea. The Micronesian branch includes Gilbertese, Ponapean, and most of the languages of Micronesia. The far-flung Polynesian branch includes Maori in New Zealand, Hawaiian, Marquesan, Tongan, and Samoan.

II. The *Australian* phylum is a comprehensive grouping of all the aboriginal languages of Australia, numbering more than 200. There are several divisions and a great deal of variety in these languages, apparently reflecting a very long period of isolation and diversification. The greatest number of languages is found in the north; northern languages include Tiwi, Murngin, and Yir Yoront. In the south, central, and western desert areas, population density is low, and language differentiation is not as great; Kariera and Arunta are representative of these areas. All of the languages of Australia which have been recorded appear to be genetically related, and may come to be classed in a single family when sufficient comparative research has been accomplished. No definite external relations have been established.

III. The *Papuan* macrophylum also encompasses a large number of languages— now classified in families, phyla, and isolates—all of which may ultimately be genetically related. However, most of the languages now grouped as Papuan have not been adequately described, and the limits, subdivisions, and internal relationships are not yet established. Papuan takes in several hundred languages of interior, southern, and western New Guinea, as well as scattered non-Austronesian languages in eastern Indonesia (the islands of Timor and Alor) and on New Britain, New Ireland, and some of the Solomon Islands in Melanesia. Papuan appears, in these marginal areas, to belong to an older population stratum than does Austronesian. A remote relationship of Papuan to Andamanese has been suggested (see above).

IV. *Tasmanian* apparently constitutes a language isolate; no external relationships have been demonstrated. (The one, two, or more languages of Tasmania are extinct.)

North America   I. The *Macro-Algonkian* phylum unites two large groups of related languages, each of which includes both families and isolates: (A) the largest family included is *Algonkian*, which was spread over much of the northern and eastern portions of the continent. Some of the Algonkian languages are Ojibwa, Naskapi, and Cree (in eastern Canada); Micmac, Penobscot, Delaware, and Powhatan (along the eastern seaboard); Shawnee, Menomini, Fox, and Kickapoo (in the Ohio valley and Great Lakes area); and Arapaho, Blackfoot, and Cheyenne (in the northern Great Plains). The Algonkian languages were early recognized as related because of close similarities in vocabulary; later, more remote resemblances were found between Algonkian and two isolated languages in California, Wiyot and Yurok, which are sometimes clashed together as *Ritwan*. Together, Algonkian and Ritwan make up one of two divisions of the Macro-Algonkian phylum.

(B) The other division also includes a single large family, *Muskogean*, and a number of smaller members. Muskogean covers much of the southeastern quadrant of the continent; some of the included languages are Creek, Koasati, and Choctaw-Chickasaw. Several extinct or nearly extinct small languages of the Gulf Coast (Natchez, Tunica, Atakapa, and Chitimacha) have been shown to be related to

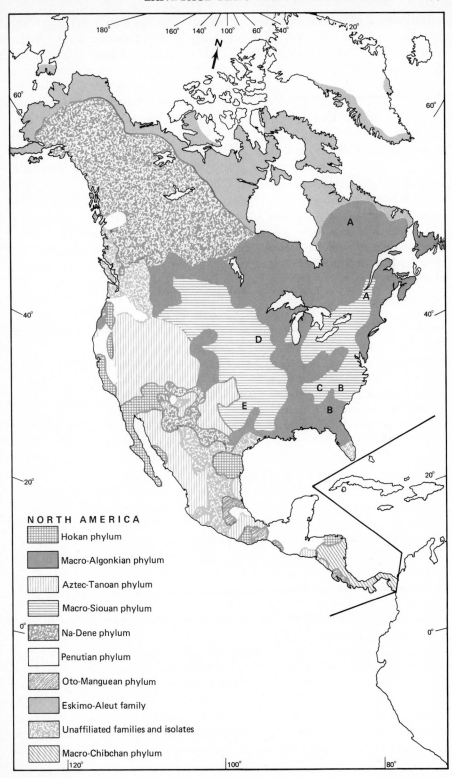

NORTH AMERICA

Hokan phylum

Macro-Algonkian phylum

Aztec-Tanoan phylum

Macro-Siouan phylum

Na-Dene phylum

Penutian phylum

Oto-Manguean phylum

Eskimo-Aleut family

Unaffiliated families and isolates

Macro-Chibchan phylum

Muskogean; together they make up a grouping which has been called *Gulf*. Mary Haas, who demonstrated the validity of this grouping of southeastern languages, also established the existence of more distant connections between Algonkian and Muskogean. Thus, we know that a large part of the North American continent was inhabited by speakers of a single group of related languages, the descendants of a single speech community which has fragmented in the course of several millennia. The dimensions of this large grouping of languages may be extended still further; an earlier classification of American Indian languages suggested a relationship of Algonkian to Wakashan and several other Western languages (see below). If these relationships are demonstrated, Macro-Algonkian will extend the length and breadth of the continent and emerge as the most important of the several large phyla in North America.

II. The *Aztec-Tanoan* phylum is made up of two families, *Uto-Aztecan* and *Kiowa-Tanoan*. Uto-Aztecan is a large family, distributed from the Great Basin to central Mexico; it has a prominence in this southwestern quadrant of North America comparable to that of Algonkian in the northeast. Some of the Uto-Aztecan languages are: Ute and Paiute (in the Great Basin); Shoshone and Comanche (in the Great Plains); Hopi, Pima, and Papago (in the southwestern United States); Luiseño and Gabrileño (two of several small tribes in California); Cora, Yaqui, and Tarahumara (in northern Mexico); and Nahuatl (the language of the Aztecs, in central Mexico).

Kiowa and Tanoan make up a much smaller family. Kiowa is a Plains language which was once considered an isolate; and Tanoan is a small grouping of eastern Pueblo languages, including such contemporary communities as Jemez, Taos, Isleta, and San Juan.

III. *Macro-Siouan* is a phylum which, like Macro-Algonkian, unites large language families which until recently have been considered independent. The distribution of divisions of Macro-Siouan seems generally to be either intrusive into or marginal to areas occupied by Macro-Algonkian. The interrelationships of the several divisions of these two phyla must play a crucial role in an eventual reconstruction of the prehistory of North America.

The divisions of Macro-Siouan are: (A) The *Iroquoian* family, including Huron, Iroquois, and minor languages in eastern Canada and New York, and Cherokee and Tuscarora in the Carolinas (see above); (B) *Catawba*, and (C) *Yuchi* are two isolates located in the Carolinas. (D) The *Siouan* family has its broadest distribution in the Plains (with such languages as Dakota, Omaha, Osage, Crow, and Mandan); it is also represented in the southeast (by Biloxi, Tutelo, and Ofo). (E) The *Caddoan* family is mainly located in the southern Plains, where Caddo, Wichita, and Pawnee are the largest representatives.

IV. The *Hokan* phylum is extremely diversified; it includes the *Yuman* family and a number of isolates with a distribution from California to Central America. It has been suggested that these are the scattered remnants of a very early population which was displaced by later immigrants (Penutian and/or Aztec-Tanoan). The Yuman family is located in southern California and along the course of the Colorado River; it includes Yuma, Mohave, and Havasupai. Other members of Hokan are Pomo, Karok, Yana, Shasta, and Achumawi-Atsugewi (all small tribes in California); Seri (in Sonora); Coahuiltecan (northeast Mexico); Tlapanecan and Tequistlatecan (southern Mexico); and Jicaque (in Honduras).

V. *Penutian*, like Hokan, is a phylum which establishes a relationship among several diverse families and isolates of western North and Central America; connections with South American languages have also been suggested. Penutian includes Tsimshian, which is located on the coast of British Columbia; Chinookan, Sahaptian, and Nez Percé in the Plateau area (Oregon and northern California); and several languages of central California, such as Wintun, Miwok, and Yokuts. In Mexico, the large *Mayan* family has recently been shown to be affiliated with Penutian, as have Mixe, Zoque, and Totonacan. Uru-Chipaya, in Bolivia, may also be a related group.

VI. The *Na-Dene* phylum includes, as its largest component, the *Athabascan* family. Athabascan covers most of western Canada (with such languages as Chipewayan, Dogrib, Hare, Kutchin, Sarsi, and Chilcotin) and is also found in northern California and Oregon (Hupa and other small groups), and in Arizona, New Mexico, and neighboring areas of the Southwest (Navaho and the Lipan, Mescalero, Chiricahua, and other bands of Apache).

Other divisions of Na-Dene are located along the coast of Alaska and British Columbia. From north to south; they are Eyak, Tlingit, and Haida.

VII. The *Oto-Manguean* phylum is restricted to mountainous area in middle America. It includes several families, which are quite differentiated: *Zapotecan, Mixtecan, Popolocan, Manguean,* and *Chinantecan*. These appear to be remnants of larger groups which were absorbed or displaced, perhaps by the expansion of the Aztec and Maya empires.

VIII. The *Eskimo-Aleut* family has two branches; Aleut, in southern Alaska and the Aleutian islands, was the larger in number of speakers but is now almost extinct. In the Eskimo branch, the greatest diversity is in western Alaska; the vast area between Point Barrow in northern Alaska and eastern Greenland shows very little differentiation, and may be considered a single language. This pattern of distribution would indicate that the western location is the earlier, and that a spread to the east, along the Arctic coast, took place more recently. The small Eskimo population in Siberia includes representatives of both branches of Eskimo.

There is evidence of remote relationships between Eskimo-Aleut and some languages of the Paleo-Siberian group; this has been tentatively designated the *American Arctic-Paleo-Siberian* phylum.

IX. The *Wakashan* family is made up of several languages in northwest North America, including Nootka, Kwakiutl, Bella Bella, and Heiltsuk. *Salish* is another family of the western United States and Canada; it includes Coeur d'Alene and Flathead in the plateau area, and Squamish, Dwamish, Tillamook, and numerous small language communities around Puget Sound and on the Pacific coast of Washington, Oregon, and British Columbia. *Chimakuan* is a small family in this same area, consisting of Quileute and Chemakum. *Kutenai* is a language isolate of the eastern plateau area.

A classification of North American languages by Edward Sapir (1929) linked these three small families and Kutenai to Algonkian, making up a phylum called *Algonkian-Wakasha*; this relationship still remains as an unconfirmed hypothesis.

X. *Tarascan*, of Michoacan in Mexico, is a large language isolate; there are still several thousand speakers. The Tarascans were almost unique in late prehistoric times in their successful resistance to the Aztec empire.

XI. Other unaffiliated families and isolates include *Yuki*, a small family in northern California, consisting of two languages, Yuki and Wappo. *Keresan* is a language isolate distributed in several Pueblo communities, including Acoma and Laguna; some linguists suggest a remote relationship to Aztec-Tanoan. *Karankawa* is a large isolate (or a family) of the Texas coast. It is extinct, as is *Timucua*, an isolate of southern Florida.

South America   The names of more than a thousand small language groups have been listed in classifications of South American languages; large numbers of these are extinct, and the status of many of the living languages is unclear. When all of the families, isolates, and unclassified languages are mapped, the picture is quite confusing. In the tropical forest areas, especially, small population groups have tended to migrate and settle by following rivers and their tributaries; this results in very broken distributions. On the other hand, peoples with highly differentiated languages may be situated in a very small map area. The impact of European conquest and settlement has been quite drastic; many native peoples became extinct or lost their tribal identity, while others took refuge by moving further into the interior, retreating far away from their traditional homelands. There are hundreds of languages known only by name or on the basis of a few recorded words and phrases. Identifying, counting, and classifying them accurately appears impossible, so there are many problems in mapping them.

The map of South America (Map 5) is based on Greenberg's grouping of several previously established phyla and dozens of language families and language isolates into three larger phyla (or *macrophyla*). One of these, Macro-Chibchan, includes languages in both Central and South America. The other two, Andean-Equatorial and Ge-Pano-Carib, are both widely distributed through South America; the larger families and languages are listed here, but many of the smaller groupings are omitted.

I. *Macro-Chibchan* includes, as its main divisions, (A) the *Chibchan* family, which has its center of distribution in Colombia and extends into adjacent areas of Central and South America. Some of the Chibchan languages are Chibcha, Andaqui, Tunebo, Coconuco, and Cueva in Colombia, Cuna in Panama, and Rama in Nicaragua. (B) The *Waican* languages are spoken by the Yąnomamö and other peoples in an isolated area along the Venezuelan-Brazilian border. (C) Several more distantly related languages and small families in South America which have been included in Macro-Chibchan are Warao and Yaruro in Venezuela, Esmerelda in Ecuador, and Yunca (or Chimu) in Peru. The distribution of this grouping, thus, is limited to northern and western portions of the continent.

II. The *Ge-Pano-Carib* macrophylum brings together numerous families and three phyla. One main division is (A) *Macro-Ge*, a phylum which includes *Ge*, a compact family of languages in central Brazil, together with a number of isolates (most of which are no longer spoken). (B) Segments of the *Macro-Panoan* phylum, in which the largest division is the Panoan family, are scattered in separate

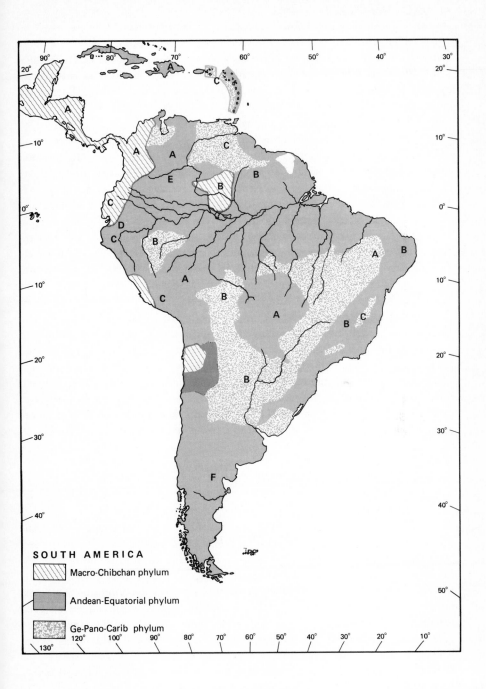

SOUTH AMERICA

Macro-Chibchan phylum

Andean-Equatorial phylum

Ge-Pano-Carib phylum

locations along the border of Brazil and its western neighbors, Paraguay, Bolivia, and Peru. (C) The *Macro-Carib* phylum includes the large *Carib* family and smaller families, the best known of which is *Witoto*. Carib languages are concentrated in northeastern Brazil, Venezuela, and the Guyanas, and have a more scattered distribution elsewhere, including some of the islands of the Lesser Antilles, and isolated areas in southeastern Brazil. Other families included in this macrophylum include *Huarpe* in Argentina, *Nambicuara* in south-central Brazil, and *Bororo* in the Matto Grosso of Brazil and eastern Bolivia.

III. The *Andean-Equatorial* macrophylum includes large language groups which have extensive distribution in both tropical forests and highland areas of South America. It is more widespread, includes more people, and transcends a greater variety of environments than do the other macrophyla. The large divisions are (A) the *Arawakan* family, which is the biggest in the Americas, including over 100 different languages; the greatest concentration of these is in Venezuela, the Guyanas, Brazil, and the West Indies. (B) The *Tupi-Guarani* family has its main distribution along the Amazon basin in central Brazil and in a wide area of southeastern Brazil and Paraguay, where Guarani is the official language. Arawakan, Tupi-Guarani, and several smaller families (Timote, Salivan, Guahibo) and isolates (including Cayuvava and Trumai) make up the Equatorial division of the macrophylum. (C) *Quechumaran* is a phylum which brings together *Quechuan*, the language of the Inca empire, with an estimated 6 to 7 million speakers in Peru, Bolivia, and Argentina; and Aymara, spoken by several hundred thousands of persons, mainly in Bolivia. (D) the *Jivaro* division includes Jivaro, Yaruro, and several language isolates located in northern Peru and Ecuador. (E) The *Tucanoan* division consists of Tucanoan and other small families such as Catuquina and Puinave in northwestern Brazil and Colombia. (F) *Chon* is a highly diversified grouping which includes some of the southernmost languages, most of which were previously classed as isolates: Ona, Yahgan, Alakaluf, Araucanian, and Puelche.

THE LANGUAGE MAP OF THE MODERN WORLD

Before 1500, there were vast areas of the world which Europeans knew nothing about. There had been little travel or established communications among the separate continents, and Oceania and the New World were essentially unexplored. Since that time, there have been tremendous changes in knowledge and technology, in travel and communication, in economic and social and political life—and more. Changes in language have accompanied all of these other developments. The most obvious linguistic effect of the worldwide expansion of Western culture has been the spread of European languages. Other languages have grown and spread on a global scale as well; Arabic, Sanskrit, and Chinese have had wide areas of influence in the past as well as in the present. However, European languages— Spanish, Portuguese, English, French, German, Dutch, and Russian, in particular— have had the greatest impact on the modern world. These are the languages of the European explorers and conquistadors; of the traders who provided the Western market with furs, precious metals and gems, rubber and hardwoods and spices from

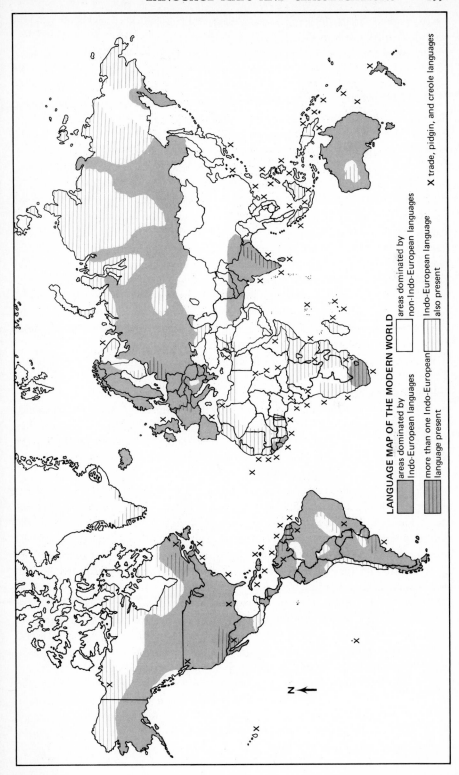

LANGUAGE MAP OF THE MODERN WORLD

areas dominated by
Indo-European languages

more than one Indo-European
language present

areas dominated by
non-Indo-European languages

Indo-European language
also present

X trade, pidgin, and creole languages

exotic foreign lands; of the imperial powers which, by 1800, had laid claim to vast areas of Asia, Africa, Oceania, and the Americas.

The linguistic consequences of the recent expansion of European powers have been, roughly, of three types. (1) Many small languages have ceased to exist; the populations may have died or been absorbed, or their languages may simply have been replaced by the dominant languages. In any case, they are no longer spoken. This has happened most often in areas where large populations of European immigrants have taken over lands formerly occupied by small communities of native peoples (in most of Australia and North America, for example).

(2) Trade or *pidgin* languages usually flourish in areas where speakers of two or more languages are in contact, but where neither group adopts the language of the other. This is especially the case when the contact is either short-term or limited to certain specific activities—the early spice traders in the Orient, explorers in the Pacific, and traders for ivory, gold, and slaves in Africa have all employed pidgin languages in their dealings with native peoples. Pidgins are special hybrid languages, used only in circumscribed situations; they are much simpler than the natural languages of any of the participants. A pidgin language can operate with a rudimentary grammar and a small vocabulary which may be drawn from any of several languages; often, however, most of the vocabulary derives from the language of the dominant social group. For this reason, linguists sometimes speak of "Portuguese-based" or "English-based" pidgins, and so forth.

A pidgin sometimes acquires a life of its own when it replaces the native language or languages of a community of speakers; in this stage it is called a *creole* language or dialect. A creole may, over time, evolve as a new natural language, or may simply develop into a dialect of the dominant language. A variety of examples of creole languages and dialects can be found in the Caribbean area (Haiti, Jamaica, Aruba, Trinidad, the Guyanas, for example), the variety reflecting the differing relationships among West African slaves, other subject peoples, and several European colonial powers.

(3) Large-scale bilingualism has also become a widespread phenomenon in the modern world. In colonial and former colonial areas, it is a common experience that a European language has been imposed on speakers of native languages as the language used in government and education. This was the case throughout colonial areas of Africa, Asia, and the Pacific; it might be compared, as well, to the situation of American Indians in the United States, most of whom have acquired English as a second language. Even after independence, in former colonial areas, such as Africa or India, English, French, or Spanish has sometimes been retained to serve as a *lingua franca* among several native languages. The retention of a European language is also often favored, at least in higher education, because it is useful as a medium of international communication. For reasons of this sort, English remains in use in India and in several new nations of Africa, and French and Portuguese are widely used in their former colonial territories in Africa, even though very few persons of European ancestry remain in some of these nations.

These three developments are shown, in very general terms, in Map 6. The scope of the modern expansion of languages of the Indo-European family can be appreciated by comparing this map and Maps 1–5.

Instances of the development of pidgin and creole languages are indicated by *x*'s; some of these are known historically from a very early time (those in the Mediterranean area, for instance) while others are in use today (Hancock, 1977).

Areas of large-scale bilingualism are indicated by cross-hatching. In most of these areas, Indo-European languages (principally English, French, and Spanish) are in use, officially or by consensus, for purposes of education and interethnic communication. It is worth noting, when these areas are added to those which are solidly Indo-European, that this language family is truly global in its distribution.

TOPICS FOR STUDY AND DISCUSSION

1. Discuss the concept of mutual intelligibility. How can political, cultural, and economic factors help or hinder the ability of people to communicate?
2. What factors account for increase in the number of languages in an area? for decrease? Would you predict that 500 years from now the total in the world will be fewer, more, or about the same?
3. What can you infer about the history of (a) two or more closely related languages; (b) widely separated languages which are members of the same phylum; (c) language isolates? Examine Maps 1–5 and find examples of each.
4. Select an area of the world in which you would be especially interested in traveling, working, or doing research. Now find out what the language situation is in that particular area (use world almanacs, encyclopedias, and other reference books; you might also consult an ethnographic study done in the same general locale). What is the majority language? the minority language(s)? the *lingua franca*? What would be your best strategy for communicating and for getting the information you would need?

Bibliography

Basso, K. H., 1957, "Semantic aspects of linguistic acculturation," *American Anthropologist,* 69: 454–464 (reprinted in Blount, 1974).

Berlin, Brent, and Paul Kay, 1969, *Basic Color Terms: Their Universality and Evolution.* Berkeley: University of California Press.

Bloom, Lois, 1973, "Why not pivot grammar?" In Ferguson and Slobin, 1973.

Bloomfield, Leonard, 1933, *Language.* New York: Holt.

———, 1946, "Algonkian." In Osgood, 1946.

Blount, Ben G., 1974, *Language, Culture and Society.* Cambridge, Mass.: Winthrop

Boas, Franz, 1911, Introduction to *The Handbook of American Indian Languages,* Bureau of American Ethnology, Bulletin 40 (reprinted in part in Blount, 1974).

———, 1929, "Metaphorical expressions in the language of the Kwakiutl Indians." In Boas, 1940.

———, 1940, *Race, Language and Culture.* New York: Free Press.

Brown, Roger, 1958, *Words and Things.* New York: Free Press.

———, 1973, *A First Language.* Cambridge, Mass.: Harvard University Press.

Brown, Roger, and Marguerite Ford, 1961, "Address in American English." *Journal of Abnormal and Social Psychology,* 1949: 454–462 (reprinted in Hymes, 1964).

Buettner-Janusch, J., 1973, *Physical Anthropology: A Perspective.* New York: Wiley.

Campbell, Bernard, 1966, *Human Evolution: An Introduction to Man's Adaptations.* Chicago: Aldine.

Chafe, Wallace, 1963, *Handbook of the Seneca Language.* Albany, N.Y.: New York State Museum and Science Service, Bulletin 388.

———, 1967, *Seneca Morphology and Dictionary,* Smithsonian Contributions to Anthropology, No. 4. Washington, D.C.: Smithsonian Institution Press.

Chomsky, Noam, 1957, *Syntactic Structures.* The Hague: Mouton.

———, 1968, *Language and Mind.* New York: Harcourt.

Claiborn, R., 1977, "Who were the Indo-Europeans?" In Thorndike, 1977.

Conklin, Harold C., 1955, "Hanonóo color categories." *Southwestern Journal of Anthropology,* 11:339–344 (reprinted in Hymes, 1964).

Davis, Flora, and Julia Orange, 1978, "The strange case of the children who invented their own language." *Redbook Magazine,* October 1978.

Diebold, A. Richard, 1961, "Incipient bilingualism." *Language,* 37:97–112 (reprinted in Hymes, 1964).

Dyen, Isidore, and David F. Aberle, 1977, *Lexical Reconstruction: The Case of the Proto-Athapaskan Kinship System.* Cambridge, Eng., and New York: Cambridge University Press.

Eggan, Fred, 1950, *Social Organization of the Western Pueblos*. Chicago: The University of Chicago Press.

Evans-Pritchard, E. E., 1940, *The Nuer*. Oxford: Oxford University Press.

———, 1948, "Nuer modes of address." *The Uganda Journal*, 12: 166–171 (reprinted in Hymes, 1964).

Fenton, W. N., and J. Gulick, eds., 1959, *Symposium on Cherokee and Iroquois Culture*. Washington, D.C.: Bureau of American Ethnology, Bulletin 180.

Ferguson, Charles A., 1959, "Diglossia." *Word*, 15:325–340 (reprinted in Hymes, 1964).

Ferguson, Charles A., and Dan I. Slobin, 1973, *Studies of Child Language Development*. New York: Holt, Rinehart and Winston.

Fischer, John L., 1958, "Social influences in the choice of a linguistic variant." *Word*, 14:47–57 (reprinted in Hymes, 1964).

Frisch, J. A., 1968, "Maricopa foods: A native taxonomic system." *International Journal of American Linguistics*, 34:16–20.

Fry, Dennis, 1977, *Homo Loquens: Man as a Talking Animal*. Cambridge, Eng.: Cambridge University Press.

Gaeng, P., 1971, *Introduction to the Principles of Language*. New York: Harper & Row.

Gardiner, Sir Alan, 1957, *The Theory of Proper Names*. Oxford: Oxford University Press.

Gardner, R. A., and B. T. Gardner, 1969, "Teaching sign language to a chimpanzee." *Science*, 165: 664–672.

Gelb, I. J., 1963, *A Study of Writing*. Chicago: The University of Chicago Press.

Gleason, H. A., Jr., 1961, *An Introduction to Descriptive Linguistics*. New York: Holt, Rinehart and Winston.

———, 1955, *Workbook in Descriptive Linguistics*. New York: Holt, Rinehart and Winston.

Gonzalez, Josué, 1955, "Coming of age in bilingual/bicultural education: A historical perspective." *Inequality in Education*, 19: 5–17.

Goosen, I. W., 1967, *Navajo Made Easier*. Flagstaff, Ariz.: Northland Press.

Greenberg, Joseph, 1966, *The Languages of Africa*. The Hague: Mouton.

———, 1968, *Anthropological Linguistics*. New York: Random House.

———, 1976, *A New Invitation to Linguistics*. Garden City, N.Y.: Doubleday/Anchor Books.

———, ed., 1963, *Universals of Language*. Cambridge, Mass.: The M.I.T. Press.

Gudschinsky, Sarah C., 1956, "The ABC's of lexicostatistics (glottochronology)." *Word*, 12: 175–210 (reprinted in Hymes, 1964).

———, 1967, *How To Learn an Unwritten Language*. New York: Holt, Rinehart and Winston.

Gumperz, J., and D. Hymes, eds., 1972, *Directions in Sociolinguistics*. New York: Holt, Rinehart and Winston.

Guthrie, Malcolm, 1967, *The Classification of the Bantu Languages*. London: International African Institute.

Haas, Mary R., 1944, "Men's and women's speech in Koasati." *Language*, 20:142–149 (reprinted in Hymes, 1964).

Hale, Kenneth, 1974, "Some questions about anthropological linguistics: The role of native knowledge." In Hymes, 1974.

Hall, Geraldine, 1971, *Kee's Home*. Flagstaff, Ariz.: Northland Press.

Hancock, I. F., 1977, "Repertory of pidgin and creole languages." In Valdman, 1977.

Haugen, E., and M. Bloomfield, 1974, *Language as a Human Problem*. New York: Norton.

Hays, C., 1952, *The Ape in Our House*. New York: Harper & Row.

Hickerson, H., G. D. Turner, and N. P. Hickerson, 1952, "Testing procedures for estimating transfer of information among Iroquois dialects and languages." *International Journal of American Linguistics,* 18: 1–8.

Hickerson, Nancy Parrott, 1954, "Two versions of a Lokono (Arawak) tale." *International Journal of American Linguistics,* 20:295–301.

———, 1971, "Review of Berlin and Kay, 1969." *International Journal of American Linguistics,* 37:257–270.

———, 1977, "On the sign functions and socio-cultural context of 'Personal Names,'" *Proceedings of the Semiotic Society of America,* 1:44–150.

———, 1978, "The natural environment as object and sign." *Journal of the Linguistic Society of the Southwest,* 3(1):33–44.

Hockett, Charles F., 1960, "The origin of speech." *Scientific American,* 203(3): 89–96.

Hockett, Charles F., and R. Ascher, 1964, "The human revolution." *Current Anthropology,* 5:135–168.

Hoebel, E. A., 1972, *Anthropology: The Study of Man.* New York: McGraw-Hill.

Hymes, Dell H., 1972, "Models of the interaction of language and social life." In Gumperz and Hymes, 1972.

———, ed., 1964, *Language in Culture and Society.* New York: Harper & Row.

———, 1974, *Reinventing Anthropology.* New York: Vintage Books.

Jett, Steven C., 1970, "An analysis of Navajo place names." *Names,* 18:175–184.

Jolly, Alison, 1972, *The Evolution of Primate Behavior.* New York: Methune.

Jakobson, Roman, and Morris Halle, 1956, *Fundamentals of Language.* The Hague: Mouton.

Kellog, W. N., 1968, "Communication and the home-raised chimp." *Science,* 162:423–427.

Kinkaid, M. D., K. L. Hale, and O. Werner, eds., 1975, *Linguistics and Anthropology: In Honor of C. F. Voegelin.* Lisse: P. de Ridder Press.

Kramer, Cheris, 1974, "Folk-linguistics: Wishy-washy mommy talk." *Psychology Today,* 8(1):82–85.

Kuper, Hilda, 1963, *The Swazi: A South African Kingdom.* New York: Holt, Rinehart and Winston.

Labov, William, 1967, "The effect of social mobility on a linguistic variable." In Lieberson, 1967.

Lancaster, Jane B., 1975, *Primate Behavior and the Emergence of Human Culture.* New York: Holt, Rinehart and Winston.

Lawick-Goodall, Jane van, 1971, *In the Shadow of Man.* New York: Dell.

Lee, Dorothy, 1959, *Freedom and Culture.* Englewood Cliffs, N.J.: Prentice-Hall.

Lenneberg, E. H., 1967, *Biological Foundations of Language.* New York: Wiley.

Lévi-Strauss, Claude, 1966, *The Savage Mind.* Chicago: The University of Chicago Press.

Lewis, M. M., 1959, *How Children Learn to Speak.* New York: Basic Books.

Lieberman, Philip, 1975, *On the Origins of Language.* New York: Macmillan.

Lieberman, Philip, and E. S. Crelin, 1971, "On the speech of Neanderthal man." *Linguistic Inquiry,* 2:203–222.

Lieberson, S., ed., 1967, *Explorations in Sociolinguistics.* Bloomington, Ind.: Indiana University Research Center in Anthropology, Linguistics and Folklore.

Linden, Eugene, 1974, *Apes, Man and Language.* New York: Dutton.

Lounsbury, Floyd, 1959, "Iroquois–Cherokee Linguistic Relations." In Fenton and Gulick, 1959.

Lubbock, Sir John, 1874, *The Origin of Civilization and the Early Condition of Man.* New York: Appleton.

Lynch, Kevin, 1960, *The Image of the City.* Cambridge, Mass.: The M.I.T. Press.

Malinowski, Bronislaw, 1922, *Argonauts of the Western Pacific.* London: Routledge.
———, 1923, "The problem of meaning in primitive languages." In Ogden and Richards, 1923.
Mandelbaum, D. G., ed., 1949, *Selected Writings of Edward Sapir in Language, Culture and Personality.* Los Angeles: University of California Press.
Marshak, A., 1972, *The Roots of Civilization.* New York: McGraw-Hill.
Matthews, C. M., 1966, *English Surnames.* New York: Scribner.
McNeill, David, 1966, "Developmental psycholinguistics." In Smith and Miller, 1966.
Meek, C. K., 1931, *A Sudanese Kingdom.* Westport, Conn.: Negro Universities Press.
Morgan, Lewis H., 1954 (orig. 1901), *League of the Ho-De-No-Sau-Nee or Iroquois.* New Haven, Conn.: Yale University Press.
Moskowitz, A., 1973, "The two-year-old stage in the acquisition of English phonology." In Ferguson and Slobin, 1973.
Ogden, C. K., and I. A. Richards, 1923, *The Meaning of Meaning.* New York: Harcourt.
Osgood, C., ed., 1946, *Linguistic Structures of North America. Viking Fund Publications in Anthropology,* 6.
Patterson, Francine, 1978, "Conversations with a gorilla." *National Geographic,* October 1978.
Pearson, Bruce L., 1977a, *Introduction to Linguistic Concepts.* New York: Knopf.
———, 1977b, *Workbook in Linguistic Concepts.* New York: Knopf.
Phillipson, D. W., 1977, "The spread of the Bantu language." *Scientific American,* 236:106–115.
Postal, Paul, 1964, "Boas and the development of phonology: Comments based on Iroquois." *International Journal of American Linguistics,* 30:269–280.
Powell, John Wesley, 1891, *Indian Families North of Mexico.* Washington, D.C.: Bureau of American Ethnology, Annual Report VII.
Ramos, A. R., 1974, "How the Sanumá acquire their names." *Ethnology,* 13:171–185.
Ray, Vern F., 1953, "Human color perception and behavioral response." *Transactions* of the New York Academy of Sciences, 16(2).
Samarin, W. J., 1967, *Field Linguistics.* New York: Holt, Rinehart and Winston.
Sapir, Edward, 1916, "Time perspective in aboriginal American culture." Ottawa, Canada: Government Printing Bureau, Department of Mines, Memoir 90, Anthropological Series No. 13 (reprinted in Mandelbaum, 1949).
———, 1921, *Language.* New York: Harcourt.
Sapir, Edward, and Morris Swadesh, 1946, "American Indian grammatical categories." *Word,* 2:103–112 (reprinted in Hymes, 1964).
de Saussure, Ferdinand, 1958 (orig. 1916), *Course in General Linguistics.* New York: Philosophical Library.
Saxton, D., and L. Saxton, 1969, *Papago and Pima–English Dictionary.* Tucson: University of Arizona Press.
———, 1973, *Legends and Lore of the Papago and Pima Indians.* Tucson: University of Arizona Press.
Siebert, Frank S., 1967, *The Original Home of the Proto-Algonquian- People.* Canada: National Museum of Canada, Anthropological Series, Bulletin No. 214.
Simpson, George G., 1969, *Biology and Man.* New York: Harcourt.
Slobin, Dan I., 1973, "Cognitive prerequisites for the development of grammar." In Ferguson and Slobin, 1973.
Smith, E. C., 1970, *The Story of Our Names.* Detroit: Gale Research Co.
Smith, Frank, and G. A. Miller, eds., 1966, *The Genesis of Language.* Cambridge, Mass.: The M.I.T. Press.

Spier, Leslie, ed., 1949, *Language, Culture and Personality: Essays in Memory of Edward Sapir*. Menasha, Wis.: Sapir Memorial Fund.

Spradley, James A., 1970, "Adaptive strategies of urban nomads." In Weaver and White, 1970.

————, 1979, *The Ethnographic Interview*. New York: Holt, Rinehart and Winston.

Stewart, George R., 1975, *Names on the Globe*. Oxford: Oxford University Press.

Stoss, Brian, 1976, *The Origin and Evolution of Language*. Dubuque, Iowa: W. C. Brown.

Sturtevant, W. C., 1964, "Studies in Ethnoscience." *American Anthropologist*, 66(1): 99–131 (reprinted in Blount, 1974).

Swadesh, Morris, 1959, "Linguistics as an instrument of prehistory." *Southwestern Journal of Anthropology*, 15:20–35 (reprinted in Hymes, 1964).

————, 1971, *The Origin and Diversification of Languages*. Chicago: Aldine.

Taylor, Douglas M., 1977, *Languages of the West Indies*. Baltimore: Johns Hopkins Press.

Thieme, Paul, 1964, "The comparative method for reconstruction in linguistics." In Hymes, 1964.

Thompson, Stith, 1966, *Tales of the North American Indians*. Bloomington, Ind.: Indiana University Press.

Thorndike, J. L., ed., 1977, *Mysteries of the Past*. New York: Simon & Schuster.

Trager, George, 1972, *Language and Languages*. San Francisco: Chandler.

Ullman, S., 1966, "Semantic universals." In Greenberg, 1966.

Valdman, A., ed., 1977, *Pidgin and Creole Linguistics*. Bloomington, Ind.: Indiana University Press.

Voegelin, C. F., 1956, "Linear phonemes and additive components." *Word*, 12: 429–443.

Voegelin, C. F., and F. M. Voegelin, 1957, *Hopi Domains*. Bloomington, Ind.: Indiana University Publications in Anthropology and Linguistics, Memoir 14.

————, eds., 1964–1966, "Languages of the world." *Anthropological Linguistics*, 6–8.

Voegelin, C. F., F. M. Voegelin, S. Wurm, G. O'Grady, and T. Matsuda, 1963, "Obtaining an index of phonological differentiation from the construction of non-existent minimax systems." *International Journal of American Linguistics*, 29:4–28.

Voegelin, C. F., and Z. S. Harris, 1951, "Methods for determining intelligibility among dialects of natural languages." *Papers of the American Philosophical Society*, 45: 322–329.

Walker, Willard, 1969, "Notes on native writing systems and the design of native literacy programs." *Anthropological Linguistics*, 11(5):148–166.

————, 1975, "The Proto-Algonkians." In Kinkaid et al., 1975.

Washburn, S. L., and I. DeVore, 1961, "The social life of baboons." *Scientific American*, June 1961.

Waterman, John T., 1970, *Perspectives in Linguistics*. Chicago: The University of Chicago Press.

Weaver, T., and D. White, eds., 1970, *Urban Anthropology*. Human Organization Monograph 11.

Werner, Alice, 1919, *Introductory Sketch of the Bantu Languages*. New York: Dutton.

Whorf, Benjamin L., 1940, "Science and linguistics." *The Technology Review*, 42(6) (reprinted in Whorf, 1956).

————, 1941, "The relation of habitual thought and behavior to language." In Spier, 1941 (reprinted in Whorf, 1956, and in Blount, 1974).

————, 1956, *Language, Thought and Reality: The Selected Writings of Benjamin Lee Whorf*. Cambridge, Mass.: The M.I.T. Press.

Witherspoon, Gary, 1977, *Language and Art in the Navajo Universe*. Ann Arbor, Mich.: University of Michigan Press.

Wyman, Leland, 1957, *Beautyway: A Navajo Ceremonial*. New York: Pantheon Books.